T0361666

EMBODIED ECOLOGY

THE OXFORD CENTRE FOR HINDU STUDIES
MANDALA PUBLISHING SERIES

General Editor
Lucian Wong

Editorial Board
John Brockington
Avni Chag
James Madaio
Valters Negribs

The Oxford Centre for Hindu Studies Mandala Publishing Series offers authoritative yet accessible introductions to a wide range of subjects in Hindu Studies. Each book in the series aims to present its subject matter in a form that is engaging and readily comprehensible to persons of all backgrounds – academic or otherwise – without compromising scholarly rigor. The series thus bridges the divide between academic and popular writing by preserving and utilising the best elements of both.

EMBODIED ECOLOGY

Yoga and the Environment

Christopher Key Chapple

MANDALA
San Rafael Los Angeles London

CONTENTS

Introduction

The quality of human life has become imperiled by greed-fueled technology, hard and soft. Our hard technology requires massive extraction of mineral resources from the earth. It has created thousands of artificial chemicals, designed to enhance human comfort. We now can stay warm in the winter, cool in the summer, and move about with abandon. However, we have learned that our heating and cooling and transportation modalities, to the extent they rely upon fossil fuels, are literally choking the very humans who designed them. Our soft technology has flooded the mind and eyes and ears with images that often stray far from reality. Overwhelmed with the terror of detective shows, the allure of salacious images, and the destabilising proliferation of misinformation, many humans have lost their centre, falling into anxiety, stress, and depression. Feelings of fear and insecurity now pervade the life-state of many, particularly the young.

To be aware of these perilous situations is paramount. We must acknowledge the harms caused by our technologies. Henry David Thoreau, Mahatma Gandhi, and J.R.R. Tolkien all called out the dangers of fast transport. Gandhi took the critique further, calling for the overthrow of all colonialism, not only mercantile but also emotional and psychic.

Conscientisation, a term coined by Brazilian educator Paolo Freire, can and must lead to grass roots organising. As we learn the ills of racism, intolerance, hatred, and unbridled consumerism, we must take action. Gandhi critiqued colonial power structures. Rather than remaining subservient to British economic policies, Gandhi called for boycotts and strikes that, over the period of several decades, brought about freedom for India and Pakistan. Though the political and historical details can be instructive and must not be ignored, the singular core tool implemented by Gandhi can inform contemporary needs: a call for *svarāj/swaraj* or self-power. Indian cotton, shipped to India, provided the raw material for the fabrics manufactured in England that were then exported back to India. Salt mined with British technology was sold to the Indian people, heavily taxed. Gandhi organised a daily spinning campaign, so Indians could create their own cloth, and salt marches to the ocean, where they produced their own salt. An excellent translation of the term *svarāj* is 'sovereign', capturing the sound and sense of the original Sanskrit term. More specific than the terms 'freedom' and 'liberation', this word returns power to the people. When it comes to technologies and media, we must free ourselves from their shackles of bondage and harm.

My awareness of environmental difficulty stems from childhood: seeing strip-mining in Ohio, noting the burning of the Cuyahoga River between Akron and Cleveland, realising Love Canal's near proximity to my family, reading about the warming of the earth due to the greenhouse effect, as well as the deleterious presence of lead in the human body along with pesticides and herbicides in the food chain. Simultaneously, my childhood was marked by nature immersion: learning to swim in Lake Ontario (before the detection of dangerous coliform levels), wandering the fields and forests and swimming in the ponds and lakes of western New York, in both the fruit belt of Orleans County and later the Genesee Valley. After-school outdoor reveries were supported throughout my teens with formal daily *zazen* practice and weekly silence with the Religious Society of Friends. Eventually, I trained in Pātañjala Yoga, studying and practicing under the guidance of Gurāṇi Añjali Inti who was originally from Calcutta, India.

This Yoga system integrates ethics and awareness. It promotes an integration between issues of concern and human action. The contemplative practices of Yoga and meditation can serve as base for taking corrective action in the realm of food, consumer choices, and legislative activism.

The Yoga training of Gurāṇi Añjali placed keen attention on environmental issues, calling out the difficulties of pollution, as seen in the refrain of one of her songs: 'The Earth Is Burning!' The practice of Yoga employs the cultivation of opposites (*pratipakṣa-bhāvana*) as corrective action in order to recognise entrenched habits and to exert our will to change course. As students of Yoga we were urged to interrogate our complicity in needless consumer activity and to strategise alternatives. We developed an alternative economy of sorts, including the creation of a restaurant (Santosha Vegetarian Dining), an art gallery, and a bookstore. The training itself included building a new relationship with the elements through the sixth limb of Yoga, concentration (*dhārāṇā*). We directed our attention twenty minutes in the morning and again at night, first to earth for a month, then to water, fire, air, and space in sequence, for a total of five months. Life changing connections and insights emerged, including the knowledge that our bodies cannot be separated from the food and water and heat and breath that nourish and sustain us. We must protect this sacred space, inner and outer.

In many ways, the environmental problems that confront humanity require a return to simple appreciation of the rhythm of life itself. Mental and emotional health are essential for humans to thrive and flourish. Religions throughout history and across cultures have offered advice and guidance for overcoming difficulty and trouble. Religious communities provide a gateway into a sense of meaning, integrating the human narrative with the story of the earth. Religious communities can also influence policy and legislation. The Forum on Religion and Ecology convened a series of conferences at Harvard University's Center for the Study of World Religions in the late 1990s, drawing more than 600 scholars from more than a dozen of the world's faith traditions, exploring avenues through which the various voices of religion could contribute to the ecological conversation. This work remains vital, continuing at all levels and in all traditions around the globe. As seen in the work of the Forum, we can learn a great deal from scriptural texts and religious traditions. A quote attributed to Gandhi perhaps summarised it best: 'Live simply so that others may simply live.'

This book explores how primary sources from the Hindu and Yoga traditions can inform contemporary conversations about the problems of environmental degradation both in India and from a global perspective. It gathers materials that I have published over several decades which have been in some instances updated. The original place of publication is given at the end of each chapter. Most of Chapter 3 on the Upaniṣads is new material and the final chapter has been newly composed for this volume.

The Vedas and early Upaniṣads (*c.* 1500–300 BCE) signal the centrality of Earth-awareness in early India. The ethics of Yoga (*c.* 200 CE) provide guidelines for developing a healthy relationship with the modern ills of over-consumption. Meditation practices as described in the *Yoga-vāsiṣṭha* (*c.* 1050 CE) help develop a sense of intimacy with one's body, with other persons, and with the larger ecosphere. In the modern period, Mahatma Gandhi initiated a thoroughgoing economic critique that helped inspire India's many contemporary eco-activists including Vandana Shiva, M.C. Mehta, the late Anil Agarwal, and Sunderlal Bahuguna. This book seeks to discern how Hindu and Yoga ideals can address the pressing problems of global consumerism, the proliferation of plastic waste, species extinctions, and global climate change.

I
Toward an Indigenous Indian Environmentalism

The rhetoric of environmentalism has a long history of development in the American milieu, which has led to the emergence of various branches and sub-identifications within this movement as found in the United States. As we reflect upon environmentalism in the context of India, it is important to acknowledge that many of the categories developed in the northern hemisphere of the Western world do not necessarily apply within the South Asian context. It is important to define terms and identify presuppositions when discussing environmental issues in each context before attempting a cross-cultural analysis.

In the chapter that follows, I will present an overview of American environmentalism, from the early nature writers to the present. I will then examine the emergence of environmental rhetoric in India. This movement owes a debt to the Union Carbide disaster in Bhopal in 1984, an event that focused world attention on the Dickensian reality of industrial India and prompted a new form of grassroots urban activism. In more rural contexts, such as in the Chipko movement and the debate surrounding the Narmada Dam project, the agricultural working classes have developed their own responses to ecological ravage. From both urban and rural activism, several themes or threads of environmental rhetoric have emerged within India. By surveying some of the literature on Indian environmentalism, and by reflecting on my own experiences in South Asia, I would suggest that India's environmentalism, both in philosophy and practice, will remain distinct from similar movements in different areas of the world.

Some General Considerations

Environmental issues, because they deal with interrelating pieces, require a systems approach. The ecological sciences require an examination of life habitats such as swamps, forests, deserts, mountains, oceans, and so forth. This includes an analysis of the human impact on each of these systems, as well as a consideration of the quality of and acceptable standards for human life. Naïve utilitarians deem all aspects of nature to be at the beck and call of humans. More pragmatic thinkers have seen the consequences of untrammeled human interference with the natural order of things and have come to the conclusion that human health and well-being cannot be divorced from the health of our surrounding ecosystem. However, what might be considered environmentally appropriate by one group or subgroup in a given society might be appalling to another. Hence, anthropology, sociology, and religious studies become important pieces of debate, both in terms of understanding varieties of environmentalism within one cultural context, and the more general features that characterise national attitudes and approaches.

American Environmentalism: A Brief History

The Nature Movement in America traces its origins to a complex array of historical, religious, quasi-religious, and aesthetic factors. European colonists saw America as the New World, a place to escape the confines of European society, to establish more communities of faith without government intervention, to accumulate new capital in a land imagined to be without history, a land into which the European fleeing the past might move freely. The allure of the American wilderness frontier took on Biblical overtones when understood in reference to the Exodus of the Jews from Egypt. Depending upon which account of the return to the promised land one reads, the returning Jews found a paradise of abundant water and fruit trees, or a land long occupied and cultivated by the Canaanites, who resisted Jewish occupancy for many years. Likewise, early accounts of American settlement downplayed the displacement of native peoples and celebrated, rather than critiqued, the pioneer practice of clear-cutting the great forests of the eastern seaboard to establish farms and villages.

With the rise of industrialisation, urban centres grew in importance. In nineteenth-century America, this resulted in huge population increases, westward expansion, the near genocide of the indigenous population, the growth of cities, all assisted by the advent of an intercontinental railroad system. Nature and the wild became more of a memory than a living presence to most Americans, and nostalgia for a simpler life laid the foundation for later environmentalism. Thoreau's essay *Walden* (1854), inspired in part by translations of the Asian literature and philosophy favoured by the Transcendentalists, invited a reconsideration of values that privileged progress and industrialisation over quietude and reflection. John Muir (1838–1914), the great explorer and nature aficionado and contemporary of Emerson and Thoreau, revelled in America's western landscape and lobbied successfully to set aside vast tracts of wilderness, thus initiating America's remarkable network of preserves, parks, and monuments. The National Park Service began in 1872 with the establishment of Yellowstone National Park in Wyoming.

Gifford Pinchot (1865–1946), creator and first head of the U.S. Forest Service (1905), and President Theodore Roosevelt

(1858–1919) helped institutionalise the preservation and conservation movements, ensuring the continued establishment of vast parks and reserves, particularly in the American west. Franklin Delano Roosevelt (1882–1945) supported the National Parks Service and established the Civilian Conservation Corps as part of the New Deal. Stephen Fox notes that: 'At the dedication of Shenandoah National Park in Virginia in 1936, he lovingly invoked a vision of how vacationers would come to the park to find an open fire, the smell of the woods, the wind in the trees.'[1]

Despite the National Parks Service and various other local programmes to ensure open space and bird sanctuaries, industrialisation and development arising from science and technology have burgeoned from the nineteenth century well into the present, encroaching on America's wilderness. The rise of the automobile and the advent of a middle-class consumer economy led to a virtual explosion of new manufacturing techniques involving steel, rubber, innumerable chemical compounds, and eventually plastic. Not only were raw materials being consumed at an unprecedented rate to fuel first two world wars and then the post-Second World War economic boom in America, western Europe, and Japan, but by-products in the form of new toxic pollutants were being spewed forth as never before. Furthermore, not only were the cities of the 'developed' world affected by this significant shift, but the countryside became laced with chemical fertilisers, insecticides, and herbicides, many of which proved to be very harmful to the ecosystem.

By the late 1950s and early 1960s, a new type of environmentalism began to emerge. Although Aldo Leopold had

---

1 Stephen Fox, *The American Conservation Movement: John Muir and His Legacy* (Madison: University of Wisconsin Press, 1985), 199.

spoken of land use policies and the changing landscape in *Sand County Almanac* (1949), it was not until the publication of Rachel Carson's *Silent Spring* in 1962 that the nascent environmental movement found its first voice. Perhaps the most poignant symbol of environmental ravage lay in the decimation of the Bald Eagle population by DDT, which provided a rallying point that made the cleanup of pollution a patriotic cause. With the extensive publicity generated by Earth Day in 1970, the formation of the Environmental Protection Agency in the same year, and the ratification of the Endangered Species Act in 1973 (all during the Nixon Administration), environmental activism and consciousness became an important thread in the American fabric.

The literary world and academia began to find new interest in nature and the environment starting in the 1970s. Annie Dillard's *Teaching a Stone to Talk* (1975) inspired people to pay closer attention to the gifts of the wild. Barry Lopez's *Arctic Dreams* (1986), though dealing with more exotic locale, similarly invited its readers to observe the stark beauty of the landscape and the living beings that inhabit the earth. Meanwhile, the early eco-philosophy that had been built on a rhetoric of individual rights by Peter Singer, Christopher Stone, and others, found its voice augmented with new approaches. Thomas Berry advocated for demythologisation of cosmology and suggested that the scientific story of the flaring forth of the universe and the gradual emergence of diverse life forms, eventually forming our current 'community of subjects', be retold as the New Story, a myth to nurture our consciousness in what he calls the new Ecozoic Era. Biologists, physicists, and ecologists, including Lynn Margulis and James Lovelock, proclaimed the fundamental and essential relationship between life forms and the atmosphere of our planet.

Radical environmentalism, also known as 'deep ecology', first surfaced in the writings of Murray Bookchin, most notably in his 1963 book *Our Synthetic Environment*. Later prominent nature liberation advocates include Edward A. Abbey and Dave Foreman, and today the range of activism spans local single-issue groups to worldwide organisations such as Greenpeace. Groups that advocate radical direct action include Earth First! and the Animal Liberation Front.

American ecological thinking, shaped by science and an emphasis on the principles of inherent worth, natural law, and rights theory, has now been taken up by theologians and biblical scholars, who seek to find threads of environmentalism in the earlier traditions of Judaism and Christianity. This theological trend stems in part from the critique of religion found in Lynn White's watershed article, 'The Historical Roots of Our Ecological Crisis' (1967), an indictment of the dominion attitudes toward nature found in early Western religious texts. Rosemary Ruether and other feminist theologians have stressed the centrality of interconnectedness and cooperation through development of the ecofeminist perspective. Theologian John Cobb advocates a more earth-sensitive economy, while Jay B. McDaniel urges adoption of a more inclusive, panentheistic theology to uphold the integrity of living systems on the planet.

The American mainstream has come to embrace select environmental practices. Recycling programmes in the 1990s proved profitable for cities, municipalities, and corporations. Clothing manufacturers, cosmetic retailers, and fast-food restaurants found that environmental themes helped sell products, particularly following the 1990 twenty-year anniversary celebration of Earth Day. This process is known as 'greenwashing'.

In summary, American environmentalism took shape in the nineteenth century, as Transcendentalists on the East Coast and John Muir on the West Coast rejoiced in the beauties of nature and advocated greater intimacy with one's surroundings. It resulted in the establishment of nature preserves and a sentiment that values experiences of pristine wilderness. Approximately one century after the love of nature emerged as a value and a virtue in America, environmentalism took a new, but not unrelated, course with the lobby against harmful chemical intrusions into the ecosystem. While not losing touch with pastoralism and romanticism, environmentalism took on an urgency previously unknown.

Aesthetically and emotionally, the nature movement of the nineteenth century, inspired in part by the vast landscapes of the American West, stimulated interest in preservation of the wild. Philosophically, environmentalism in the twentieth century called upon the American traditions of rights, liberty, individual pursuit of happiness, individualism, and justice to support not only the preservation of land but also to promote safeguards against pollution. Many Americans now think they have a basic right to live free from fear of harm due to pollutants. Furthermore, the Endangered Species Act extends the concept of inherent worth beyond the human realm, and advocates safety and protection for beings that in years past had no protection under European or American systems of justice. A typology of American environmentalism would include a romantic, reverential awe for the natural order, concern for species and land preservation, and emphasis on the potential hazards caused by industrial toxicity.

Indian Environmentalism

This brings us to our discussion of India. The Indian experience of land differs greatly from that of the North American continent settled by European invaders. Vast segments of the American West have never been densely populated, even by indigenous peoples. In contrast, the Indian subcontinent has been continuously occupied for thousands of years. Mountains and rivers not only have long been considered sacred within India[2] but have been seen as an integral part of the human experience, a source of both spiritual and economic strength.[3]

Consequently, the issues of land preservation and environmentalism differ greatly in the South Asian context. Ramachandra Guha suggests that American environmental approaches may be inappropriate for India. He contrasts the 'vast, beautiful, and sparsely populated [North American] continent'[4] with the densely settled subsistence, village-based economies of India. Whereas it might be possible, even today, to preserve vast tracts of North American forest or desert, it is far more difficult in India to establish more than small nature preserves due to high population density, even in agricultural areas. Furthermore, Guha suggests that for a nation that mostly lives barely above subsistence level, a full-blown programme of preservation might be inappropriate, particularly if suggested by outsiders. It also should be noted that, in general, the Global South, of which India is part, requires far less environment than Global North consumers, who seize the bulk of the world's resources, often at the expense of the global underprivileged.

Given this social and geographic context, the terms of the debate in India, its ecosystems, climate, agricultural uses, cities, economy, and its unique social and religious history require a different environmental strategy. Modern environmentalism in India, as mentioned above, began with

---

2 Anne Feldhaus, *Water and Womanhood: Religious Meanings of Rivers in Maharashtra* (New York: Oxford University Press, 1995).

3 Ann Spanel, 'Interview with Vandana Shiva', *Woman of Power* 9 (1988): 27–31.

4 Ramachandra Guha, 'Radical American Environmentalism: A Third World Critique', *Environmental Ethics* 11, no. 1 (1989): 79.

the disaster in Bhopal in 1984. This event, which killed thousands and permanently injured millions of people, signaled that India's Green Revolution had come full circle. The magic chemicals that increased agricultural production and filled India' granaries beyond capacity, staving off the possibility of famine even during an extended drought, exploded into weapons of unimaginable destruction. India, which prior to this time had only a vague awareness of the environmental movement in the United States, suddenly became a lightning rod for grassroots environmental activity. Although M.K. Gandhi had set forth clear warnings regarding industrialisation and modernity, government policies supported the chemical industry as vital to increased food production. However, while Americans bemoaned the loss of the symbolism of the Wild in the decimation of the Bald Eagle population, in 1984 India faced a more direct threat to human life resulting from environmental irresponsibility.

In an earlier study, I surveyed several environmental organisations and movements that arose in India since the Bhopal crisis. One such organisation is the Centre for Science and Environment in New Delhi, which serves as a clearinghouse for issues of environmental concern. The Centre for Environment Education in Ahmedabad conducts an array of programmes for both urban and rural peoples to help reduce smoke pollution and forest degradation throughout India. In cooperation with the Gandhi Peace Foundation, the Centre for Rural Development and Appropriate Technology of the Indian Institute of Technology in New Delhi has been experimenting with organic farming techniques. Babe Amte, winner of the 1990 Templeton Prize for Progress in Religion, has directed his activism toward environmental issues since the Bhopal disaster, with particular focus on the Narmada River Dam project. Also, on a grassroots level, the Chipko movement, headed by rural women, struggled to preserve the forestlands of Northern India.[5]

In recent years, several new studies have appeared that demonstrate the complexity of the environmental rhetoric now emerging from within India. This discourse interweaves an upholding of traditional Indian culture and civilisation with a resounding critique of the negative influence of modernisation. Beginning with the premise set forth by Ramachandra Guha above, I would like to explore some of the contours of this new debate. Whereas in the American context, the early rallying cry for environmental action came from scientists and social activists, with theologians only taking interest in this issue as of late, in India from the outset there has been an appeal to traditional religious sensibilities.

Brahminical Models

This group of thinkers, activists, and writers seeks to re-examine the texts of earlier phases in Indian religious history to see if they contain insights regarding nature and land use that might be usefully translated into an environmental rhetoric. One of the early works of this genre, O.P. Dwivedi and B.N. Tiwari's *Environmental Crisis and Hindu Religion* (1987) painstakingly quotes numerous texts from the Vedic, Dharma-śāstra, and epic traditions that uphold nature as central to life processes in India. *Ecological Readings in the Veda* (1994), written by Marta Vanucci, a biological oceanographer who lives in India, takes a similar approach, citing passages from the *Ṛg Veda* and *Atharva Veda* that evoke environmental themes. The abundance of nature-based deities makes

5 Christopher Key Chapple, *Nonviolence to Animals, Earth, and Self in Asian Traditions* (Albany, NY: State University of New York Press, 1993).

this task relatively easy; Vanucci particularly emphasises the power of Agni as key to environmental understanding: 'Agni the undeceivable, who spread out all the worlds, keeper is he and guard of immortality.'[6]

Numerous Vedic hymns celebrate the Earth and water, asking for protection and glorifying the root constituents of the natural world. The *Puruṣa Sūkta*, one of the best known hymns of the *Ṛg Veda*, proclaims a continuity between humans and the cosmos, stating that the gods, the heavens, and the Earth itself arose from the primal body (*puruṣa*). This assertion of relationship carries an innate message of interconnectedness that could be used to advocate respect for nature and the elements. Many of the later legal books of the Brahminical tradition stipulate that trees are to be protected and that water must not be defiled.

In the past few years, several articles and books have been published that advance this naturalist, religion-based indigenous approach as a way for addressing India's ecological problems. These include chapters entitled 'Ecology and Indian Myth' by Kapila Vatsyayan and 'Nature as Feminine: Ancient Vision of Geopiety and Goddess Ecology' by Madhu Khanna in a five-volume set called *Prakṛti: The Integral Vision* edited by Kapila Vatsyayan (1995) and published by the Indira Gandhi National Centre for the Arts. Ranchor Prime, an English devotee of the Hare Krishna movement, worked with the World Wildlife Fund to publish *Hinduism and Ecology: Seeds of Truth* in 1992. In this book, he examines largely Vaiṣṇavite resources for environmental protection. He reinterprets the ten incarnations of Viṣṇu in an ecological vein and suggests that Kṛṣṇa provides several examples of environmental wisdom through his care

6 *Ṛg Veda* 6.7.7: Marta Vanucci, *Ecological Readings in the Veda* (New Delhi: D.K. Print World, 1994), 43.

for the Vrindavan forest and purification of the Yamuna River. He cities modern and contemporary figures who have worked to reestablish the pre-British lifestyle in India. These leaders include Mahatma Gandhi, who will be discussed extensively in this book. Sri Sewak Saran, a Kṛṣṇa devotee living in Vrindavan, has sought to simplify the eco-systems there. Satish Kumar, an expatriate Indian, founded Schumacher College in Britain, which specialises in teaching a spiritual approach to the environment. Balbir Mathur left India to seek his fortune in America, but then returned to develop and promote Trees for Life, which has planted thousands of trees throughout India. Prime also writes about Sunderlal Bahuguna, a driving force 'behind Chipko Andolan, the now world-famous tree-hugging movement which started among the Himalayan villages of Uttarkhand in 1973'.[7] The work of Sunderlal Bahuguna has been described in detail by George Alfred James in *Ecology Is Permanent Economy*.[8]

A comprehensive work in this genre is *Pañcavaṭī*, written by Banwari, editor of *Jansata* which is a Hindi newspaper published in Delhi. This book[9] examines the forest culture of India as providing the appropriate ecological model for life upon the subcontinent. He opens with a chapter entitled 'Prakṛti: Approach to Nature', a summary overview of the significance of nature in India's philosophical and religious traditions, especially the Sāṃkhya school. He then shows how key indigenous values and concepts support an ecological worldview.

7 Ranchor Prime, *Hinduism and Ecology: Seeds of Truth* (London: Cassell, 1992), 90.

8 George Alfred James, *Ecology Is Permanent Economy: The Activism and Environmental Philosophy of Sunderlal Bahuguna* (SUNY Press, 2013).

9 Banwari, *Pañcavaṭī: Indian Approach to Environment*, trans. Asha Vohra (Delhi: Shri Vinayaka Publications, 1992).

Banwari suggests that worship of Gaṇeśa, the god of auspiciousness (*māṅgalya*), can lead people to emphasise the spiritual over the material, and perhaps help reduce the greed that leads to overconsumption in India. He writes of mythical trees (*kalpa-vṛkṣa*) and magical forests (*vanaśrī*) and groves (*pañcavaṭī*) to which he attributes India's abundance and traditional economic strength. He writes of the care for forests and trees in India's ancient cities and towns, and celebrates the remote forests as 'the land of no war', the abode of renouncers and meditators. He explains Hindu holy days in relationship to the cycles of nature and concludes the book with discussion of the healing and medicinal powers of trees, as well as advocacy for the planting of trees. The remarkable contribution of this book lies in its careful research of the importance of the tree in Indian history and the implied sense of continuity between antiquity and the contemporary world.

Tribal Models

In addition to citing classical Hindu materials in support of a South Asian environmental ethic, Geeti Sen's *Indigenous Vision: Peoples of India, Attitudes to the Environment* includes several essays that bring forth tribal traditions within India as potent ecological resources. Citing the *ādivāsīs* of Gujarat as true peoples of the earth, Maurice F. Strong suggests that the modern world can learn much from indigenous wisdom and ways. Similarly, Sitakant Mahapatra quotes from Santal and Kondh literature in celebration of the earth, albeit with an additional theme seeking human welfare:

> Let the earth be green with our crops.
> Let there be no hindrance to our movements.

> Let there prevail among us
> the spirit of mutual love and goodwill.[10]

K.S. Singh examines the Munda creation epic, the Sosbonga. In this story, the Munda tribe develops iron technology to the detriment of their environment and then corrects this excess, restoring their land to its natural beauty and bounty. Other essays within this fascinating collection examine the traditional ways of the Oraons, the Bhils, the Gonds, the Warlis, and others, through the prism of environmentalism. The book concludes with an interview with grassroots organiser Medha Patkar regarding her work with tribal activists seeking to resist such projects as the huge Narmada dam and other projects. This discussion, and many of the essays, highlight the trenchant tension between the drive toward modernisation in India and the desire of traditionalists to preserve ancient ways of life.

Post-Gandhian Models

Vandana Shiva, whose work *Staying Alive: Women, Ecology, and Development* (1988) opened a new chapter in world environmental theory, acknowledges the indigenous environmentalist resources available deep within the Indian psyche, but prefers a more political and pragmatic approach to the many problems that India faces. She criticises the Western model of 'maldevelopment', and in the process conjoins a modern feminist perspective with traditional Indian views regarding feminine power (*śakti*).[11] She states that the modern consumerist model

---

10 Geeti Sen, ed., *Indigenous Vision: Peoples of India, Attitudes to the Environment* (New Delhi: Sage Publication, 1992), 71.

11 Rosa Braidotti, Ewa Charkiewicz, Sabine Hausler, and Sakia Wiernga, *Women, the Environment and Sustainable Development: Towards a Theoretical Synthesis* (London: Zed Books, 1994), 92–96.

enhanced by technology disrupts traditional agricultural practices and 'ruptures the co-operative unity of masculine and feminine... Nature and women are turned into passive objects, to be used and exploited for the uncontrolled and uncontrollable desires of alienated man.'[12] She also criticises the manipulation of seed technology and the widespread use of inorganic fertilisers as disruptive to India's ecosystem. She further develops this argument in her essay 'The Seed and the Earth', where she states: 'The crisis of health and ecology suggests that the assumption of man's ability to totally engineer the world, including seeds and women's bodies, is in question.... The main contribution of the ecology movement has been the awareness that there is no separation between mind and body, human and nature.'[13] Drawing from traditional Indian cultural values and a post-modern critique of the prevailing development model, Shiva advocates the adoption of an integrated, holistic view of both humans and their environment.

Similarly, D.L. Sheth of the Centre for the Study of Developing Societies in New Delhi states that the grassroots ecology movements of India 'do not view ecology as merely a cost factor in development... [but] as a basic principle of human existence'.[14] This interpretation of environmentalism in India values the human person within local contexts and surrounding environs.

---

12 Vandana Shiva, *Staying Alive: Women, Ecology, and Development* (London: Zed Books, 1988), 6.

13 Vandana Shiva, ed., *Close to Home: Women Reconnect Ecology, Health and Development Worldwide* (Philadelphia: New Society Publishers, 1994), 141–142.

14 D.L. Sheth, 'Politics of Social Transformation: Grassroots Movements in India', in *The Constitutional Foundations of World Peace*, ed. Richard A. Falk, Robert C. Johansen, and Samuel S. Kim, 275–287 (Albany, NY: State University of New York Press, 1993), 284.

The various authors and activists cited above seek to find models from earlier times that hold forth the possibility of an environment-friendly economy and culture. Dwivedi, Tiwari, Vannucci, Prime, and Banwari hearken back to sacred Hindu texts and stories. Geeti Sen holds forth tribal models for consideration. Both Shiva and Sheth advance a holistic, post-Gandhian approach to environmentalism. All these authors state their cases positively, advocating the study of early traditions, the planting of trees, and development of technology and agriculture that enhances life within India. With the exception of Vandana Shiva, who provides a critique of contemporary 'development' schemes, these authors as a whole do not reject the underlying life-affirming premises of the Vedic traditions, which celebrate and support the pursuit of human pleasure and happiness.

Renouncer Models

From the earliest phases of Indian civilisation, an alternative ascetic religious philosophy has existed in parallel to the Vedic, deity-affirming Brahminical tradition. Possible traces of yogic practice can be found in the ruins of Mohenjodaro and Harappa, with documentation of organised Yoga appearing in the early Upaniṣads, the Buddhist Suttas, and the early texts of Jainism. By probably the second century of the common era, Patañjali summarised and systematised various styles of yogic renunciation in his *Yoga Sūtras*. This brief text builds on Sāṃkhya philosophy to advance modes of gaining control over one's compulsive behavior (*saṃskāra*) through mastery of the body (*kāya*), mind (*manas*), and spirit (*ātman*) continuum.

By the time of Alexander, the renouncer communities and meditative schools of India were collectively referred to as the *śramaṇa* traditions. This vector within the continuum of India's religions emphasised renunciation of worldly involvement and the adoption of a strict ethical and ascetic code. At the heart of this code for all three forms of *Śramaṇism* (Jainism, Buddhism, and Yoga) lay the practice and discipline of non-violence (*ahiṃsā*). Stemming from a concern to avoid injury to all creatures, this vow of non-violence became normative for all three *Śramaṇical* traditions. Its advocates also lobbied for the cessation of animal sacrifices within Brahminical Hinduism, and most likely pressured high-caste Hindus to adopt vegetarianism.[15] Related to the vow of non-violence, both Jainism and Yoga espouse four additional restraints: abstention from falsehood, positively stated as truthfulness (*satya*); abstention from theft (*asteya*); abstention from inappropriate sexual activity (*brahmacarya*); and abstention as much as possible from the accumulation of possessions (*aparigraha*).

The Buddhist tradition adapted a code of ethic nearly identical to that followed by the Jainas and *yogīs*. Both Jainism and the Buddhist monastic code (*vinaya*) developed scores of additional vows, while Patañjali's Yoga system added a list of five positive ethical practices to be observed: purity (*śauca*), contentment (*saṃtoṣa*), austerity (*tapas*), study (*svādhyāya*), and devotion (*īśvara-praṇidhāna*). These vows and observances have been at the core of India's ethical fabric for over two millennia, helping shape both monastic and lay life upon the subcontinent.

Within this ethical landscape, India has responded to historical circumstances in its own unique fashion. Perhaps the most notable application of the non-violent ethic in Indian history can be found in the life and work of Mahatma Gandhi, whose peaceful revolution ousted colonial rule from the subcontinent. Furthermore, his initiative served as a catalyst for decolonisation movements in the rest of Asia and Africa.

---

15 Christopher Key Chapple, *Nonviolence to Animals, Earth, and Self in Asian Traditions* (Albany, NY: State University of New York Press, 1993).

Gandhi combined techniques of passive resistance learned from Quakers and New England Transcendentalists with yogic applications of austerity (*tapas*), such as fasting and weekly silence. Through his personal discipline, he helped forge a new, post-colonial world order. Gandhian ideals continue to fuel a quest for social justice within India, particularly within the uplift of lower castes and marginalised tribes.

Environmental degradation in India raises interesting new challenges for the ethical renouncer traditions. On the one hand, the respect for life emphasised in Jainism, Buddhism, and Yoga accords well with the discourse of environmental ethics. Jainism in particular, with its doctrine of countless life forms (*jīva*) – taking form even as particles of earth, water, fire, and air – presents an operative cosmology that is perhaps the most sympathetic to an ecological worldview.[16] However, the underlying teleology of the *Śramaṇical* traditions lies not in the realm of worldly affirmation, but in self-transcendence.

The goal of Yoga is to achieve *kaivalya*, a state described as disinterested spectatorship. The goal of Buddhism is to escape the suffering snares of *saṃsāra* and enter into a state of desirelessness or *nirvāṇa*. The ultimate goal of Jainism is to ascend through the fourteen stages of spirituality (*guṇa-sthāna*) and enter into a state of eternal, blessed solitude (*kevala*). Without exception, each of these traditions focuses primarily on interior processes and advocates detachment from worldly concerns, seeming detrimental to environmentalism. So also, it might be argued that the *Śramaṇical* religions of India have little to of-

16 See Michael Tobias and Georgianne Cowan, eds., *The Soul of Nature: Visions of a Living Earth* (New York: Continuum, 1994) and Christopher Key Chapple, ed., *Jainism and Ecology: Nonviolence in the Web of Life* (Cambridge, MA: Center for the Study of World Religions, Harvard University Press, 2002).

fer due to their inwardness. However, just as Christianity and Judaism are rediscovering nature metaphors in the Bible as resources for the development of an ecological ethic, *Śramaṇical* texts and practices are being re-examined as rich resources in celebration of the Earth.

Yogic Environmentalism

The Yoga tradition, a pan-India system of spirituality utilised by nearly all the religious traditions of India, includes within its disciplines several resources that can, at minimum, increase environmental awareness. It affirms the reality of the natural world,[17] whereas Advaita Vedānta and other schools of Indian thought assert that the world is mere illusion. It lists several forms of concentration (*saṃyama*) that enhance one's awareness of the body and orientation within the cosmos:

> From concentration on the sun arises knowledge of the world.
> One the moon, knowledge of the ordering of the stars.
> On the polar star, knowledge of their movement.
> On the central energy wheel (*cakra*),
> knowledge of the ordering of the body.[18]

These abilities arise from the mastery of physical postures (*āsana*) and the breath (*prāṇa*) as explained briefly in the *Yoga Sūtra* and in greater detail in later Yoga texts such as the *Haṭha-yoga-pradīpikā.* Through mastery of the physical body comes enhanced awareness of its relationship with the natural world. The senses become rarified and receptive to experiences of how the body relates to the elements (earth, water,

---

17 *Yoga Sūtra* 4.16.

18 *Yoga Sūtra* 3.26–29.

fire, air, and space) and to the movement of heavenly bodies mentioned above. Additionally, Yoga sets forth ethical principles that accord well with environmental precepts: through non-violence (*ahiṃsā*) harm is minimised to animals; through non-possession (*aparigraha*) one consumes only bare necessities; through purity (*śauca*) one becomes mindful of pollution and will seek to avoid it in any form. The ultimate goal of Yoga, as mentioned above, involves the cultivation of higher awareness, which, from an environmental perspective might be seen as an ability to rise above the sorts of consumptive material concerns that can be harmful to the ecosystem. This would be in contrast to the consumerist Yoga that proliferated globally in the 1990s, when Yoga became associated with style, clothing, and various accoutrements such as blocks and mats. Furthermore, as noted by Farah Godrej,[19] contemporary Yoga presents two pathways: overconcern for personal responsibility and cultivating discernment skills that look at wider systems of oppression. This latter path seems more in keeping with the overall intent of Mahatma Gandhi.

Yoga is perhaps India's largest cultural export, in part because it does not require adherence to the many constraints of caste system or to a specific theological position. Its techniques have been employed by Hindus, Jainas, Buddhists, Sufis, and Sikhs, both in India and elsewhere; it has also become common at YMCAs and health clubs worldwide. To the extent that the development of environmental conscience requires awareness of one's mind/body in relation to the physical world, Yoga provides a potent, non-ideological tool.

---

19 Farah Godrej, *Freedom Inside: Yoga and Meditation in the Carceral State* (Oxford: Oxford University Press, 2023).

From within the *Śramaṇical* or renouncer traditions, resources are emerging for the enhancement of environmental theory and action. Though Buddhism does not have a significant presence in contemporary India, Buddhists, primarily in America and Thailand, have used Buddhist principles to develop a new *dharma* for the earth. The Jainas within India and abroad have thoughtfully applied the *ahiṃsā* doctrine to environmental issues through publication and dissemination of materials, as well as hands-on projects such as tree plantings and vegan advocacy. Yoga, perhaps the most amorphous yet most widely known of the *Śramaṇical* traditions, does not have a central theological spokesperson or organisation through which to interpret environmental issues. However, the basic precepts of a yogic lifestyle involve an emphasis on health, exercise, vegetarianism, and non-violence that accord well with core environmental principles.

Religion and the Environment in India

In the material discussed above, the Vedas, the Dharmaśāstras, the Upaniṣads, and even the *Bhagavad Gītā* have been invoked in the name of heightening environmental consciousness. Likewise, nostalgia for a pre-Hindu tribal relationship with nature has been put forth in current literature as a possible model for environmentalism. I have also suggested that the renouncer values that advocate minimal consumption of resources might also be newly interpreted for an environmentally friendly ethic.

Although the integrated reality of village economy, which served as the economic context for both the Brahminical and renouncer traditions of India, certainly sustained agrarian India for millennia, and although many tribal people today continue to eke out a subsistence living, neither model bears direct relevance for the burgeoning urban life that hundreds of millions of people in India have embraced in the past few decades. Although both classical traditions contain nature imagery and promote abstemiousness, and tribal societies generally operate in harmony and reliance on a tribe's immediate ecosystem, these are not likely to capture the imagination of precisely the sorts of people who stand to commit the greatest infractions against the ecological order, the people throughout South Asia who are feverishly buying cars, building condominiums, and filling their flats with prepared foods and plastics at the prompting of global corporations that urge people to pursue the consumerist dream. India's emerging middle class, rather than critiquing its movement toward Western-style development, in fact finds consumerism and its attendant human comforts quite attractive. There is little incentive for the upwardly mobile urban Indian to heed the nascent environmentalist's plea to follow and respect traditional ways. Environmentalism monitored and promoted in the form of legislation and non-governmental agency activism is a construct which originated in the developed world. As Guha and others have protested, why should India buy into a movement that stems from the Global North, the greatest polluters and exporters of technology? From another angle, why should peoples of the Global South deny themselves the sorts of luxuries that have characterised the developed Global North?

To answer these questions, it is crucial that the peoples of South Asia continue to develop their Gandhian suspicion of the benefits of technological consumerism. If, as Vandana Shiva suggests, Indians can reflect on the interconnectedness of the human beings with their environment, then some process of questioning the onslaught of modernisation and its consequent pollution can begin. In fact, as will see in the final chapter of this volume, this awakening has begun in earnest in India. Solar power is overtaking the burning of coal to generate electricity. Strict laws have been passed banning single-use plastics. Highly polluting kerosene engines have been switched over to compressed natural gas and electricity, particular for auto-rickshaws. In fact, India is leading the way for adopting eco-friendly technologies in some sectors

The Brahminical models, stemming from the Upaniṣads and Dharma-śāstras, present both beautiful and bucolic images in support of environmentalism, as indicated in much literature cited above. However, these texts and traditions are also problematic. As Lance Nelson has argued, if the world is seen to be unreal, then perhaps it is not important to respect or maintain.[20] Additionally, attitudes may prevail that such dirty tasks should be left to persons of lower caste status, so one's purity will not be violated, as suggested by Frank Korom.[21] The extolling of wealth, as evidenced in the Artha-śāstra and in the popular worldwide worship of the goddess Lakṣmī among Hindus, does not bode well for a minimalist economic theory. According to the *Ṛg Veda*, human nature is fraught with desire; through desire the many worlds of human endeavour take shape, assisted and abetted by ritual sacrifice and purposeful activity. The mainstream householder culture of India, not unlike the consumerist culture emerging worldwide, places great value on human comfort. Pragmatically speaking, the effectiveness of the environmental movement in India, as elsewhere, will depend upon the extent to which ecological ravage impinges on human pleasure, as demonstrated in the years following the Bhopal disaster.

---

20 Lance Nelson, ed., *Purifying the Earthly Body of God: Religion and Ecology in Hindu India* (Albany, NY: State University of New York Press, 1998).

21 Frank Korom, 'On the Ethics and Aesthetics of Recycling in India', in *Purifying the Earthly Body of God: Religion and Ecology in Hindu India* ed. Lance Nelson (Albany, NY: State University of New York Press, 1998), 197–224.

Conclusion

In my earlier statements regarding the typology of American environmentalism, I identified three areas: awe for the natural order, concern for species and land preservation, and avoidance of harm occurring due to industrial toxicity. India has long revered the natural order, as indicated in the sampling of tribal, Vedic, and post-Vedic materials that were cited earlier. Additional literary materials celebrating nature can be found in the writings of Bāṇa, Daṇḍin, Kālidāsa, Bhavabhūti, Tagore, and many others. Of particular note, however, is that these materials are specific to India, and if nature writing finds resurgence in light of India's environmental issues, then these and other authors might gain recognition.

The second area that I identified involved species and land preservation. India certainly contains an abundance of biological diversity, from tigers and monkeys to colourful tropical flora. Various game preserves have been set aside for land and animal protection, most notably the Bharatpur Bird Sanctuary near Delhi and the Periyar Nature Reserve in Kerala. There are a total of 19 national parks and 205 sanctuaries within India,[22] though none are as large as those founded in the United States. India's identity has long been intertwined with its peoples' relationship with the land and its non-human denizens, as indicated in the many animal

22 M. Krishnan, *The Handbook of India's Wildlife* (Madras: Travelaid, 1982).

stories of Hinduism, Jainism, and Buddhism.[23] However, unlike the North American continent, where the decimation of a relatively small indigenous population paved the way for both massive immigration and preservation of huge tracts of land, India does not have the luxury of defining and setting aside vast wilderness areas as nature preserves. Even in remote areas that have been designated as development zones and may soon be flooded as damming projects proceed, thousands of people suffer possible displacement, sparking great protest and social activism.[24] It is unthinkable that a National Parks programme that requires the removal of human habitats from within their borders could work in a country so densely populated. It must be noted, however, that the many pilgrimage places within India, from the Himalayas in the north to Kanya Kumari at the very southern tip of the subcontinent, form a patchwork of sacralised spaces that could be newly interpreted through the prism of environmental conservation.

The third area I identified as characteristic of American environmentalism is concern about toxic substances. The hierarchical structures of Indian society present obstacles to marshalling a pan-Indian environmental movement to counter the harmful presence of toxins in India. A high rate of illiteracy makes it difficult to communicate even the most basic

---

23 See Padmanabh S. Jaini, 'Indian Perspectives on the Spirituality of Animals', in *Collected Papers on Jaina Studies* (Delhi: Motilal Banarsidass, 2000), 253–266, and Rafe Martin, *Endless Path: Awakening with the Buddhist Imagination: Jataka Tales, Zen Practice, and Daily Life* (Berkeley, CA: North Atlantic Books, 2010), as well as Christopher Key Chapple, *Nonviolence to Animals, Earth, and Self in Asian Traditions* (Albany, NY: SUNY Press, 1993) and *Living Landscapes: Meditations on the Elements in Hindu, Buddhist, and Jain Yogas* (Albany, NY: SUNY Press, 2020).

24 William F. Fisher, ed., *Toward Sustainable Development: Struggling over India's Narmada River* (Arninke, NY: M.E. Sharpe, 1995).

environmental message to the masses. Environmental clean-up requires getting dirty. People in power in India have traditionally avoided filth, leaving it to be handled by less educated members of lower castes. As a result, sanitation projects do not seem to receive high priority. Air pollution initiatives are virtually non-existent, despite the proliferation of highways and overpasses that encourage the growth of largely unregulated and highly polluting vehicle traffic in New Delhi, which now rivals Mexico City in its level of airborne particle pollutants.

Indian environmentalism has traditionally emphasised general education through the news media, direct action such as in the Chipko movement, and each individual's choice of lifestyle.[25] Until very recently, India has not promoted legislation or punitive measures in an effort to cleanse its air and waters to the extent found in the United States. So many aspects of the American environmental programme, from vast forest preserves to the Endangered Species Act to the Environmental Protection Agency, do not readily transfer to the South Asian context. However, India has pressing environmental needs that demand attention. In order for India to avoid mistakes of the past and any future Bhopals, it needs to continue to build its environmental programmes. Even beyond the literacy-based programmes mentioned above, it needs to lift up indigenous sensibilities, Brahminical rationale, *Śramaṇical* orthopraxy, as well as having education reach greater numbers of citizens. Through these emerging indigenous resources and innovativeness, India will devise its own methods and rationalities in defense of the ecosystem.

Adapted with permission from Christopher Key Chapple. 'Toward an Indigenous Indian Environmentalism'. *In Purifying the Earthly Body of God: Religion and Ecology in Hindu India*, edited by Lance E. Nelson, 13–38. State University of New York Press, 1998.

---

25 Chapple, *Nonviolence to Animals, Earth, and Self in Asian Traditions*, 62.

Discussion Topic: Indian Environmentalism

- In what ways do the environmental histories of North America and India diverge?
- How might religious sensibilities inherent in Indian traditions help inform the development and implementation of policies that support ecological restoration?
- How might the principles and practices of Yoga encourage an environmental worldview?

Further Reading

Christopher Key Chapple and Mary Evelyn Tucker, editors. *Hinduism and Ecology: The Intersection of Earth, Sky, and Water*. Cambridge, Massachusetts: Harvard Divinity School Center for the Study of World Religions, 2000.

II
Earth Verses: The *Pṛthivī Sūkta* of the *Atharva Veda*

The *Pṛthivī Sūkta* portion of the *Atharva Veda* praises the Earth and invites sustained reflection on the importance of a healthy ecosystem. India's Vedas are the ancient bedrock for her moral, spiritual, philosophical, and artistic self-understanding. The earliest of these was the *Ṛg Veda,* which was initially composed around 1500 BCE. Its verses (*sūkta*), filled with praise of various gods, goddesses, and cosmic forces, are repeated and quoted throughout the subsequent texts which include the *Yajur Veda* (ritual instructions), the *Sāma Veda* (most efficacious chants), and the *Atharva Veda* (proto-science and medicine). These texts have been transmitted orally for thousands of years through a rigorous memorisation process that begins in a priest's early childhood. To hear a section of one of the Vedas chanted today is to hear the link between lifetimes.

The Earth Verses (*Pṛthivī Sūkta*) comprise a section of the youngest of these text collections, the *Atharva Veda.* This is the first Indic text to mention iron, leading some scholars to date its inception no later than the twelfth to tenth century BCE to correspond with India's Iron Age, although it could be a more recent text. As with all the Vedas, it was transmitted orally for many generations, committed to memory by young Brahmin priests. The written tradition was considered inferior to its precisely memorised oral recitation, a practice that continues into the present. It was also held in secret until the rise of the Brahmo Samaj, a nineteenth-century Bengali movement that cooperated with Sanskrit scholars to make the Vedas more accessible. The Vedas were first translated by Jesuits into Latin, by Goethe into German, and by Max Müller and others into English. These translations helped inspire the New England Transcendentalist movement and the early Theosophists, who in turn inspired Mahatma Gandhi.

The *Atharva Veda* was translated into English several times at the end of the nineteenth century by the premier scholars of the day, beginning with William Dwight Whitney in 1855–1856, Ralph T. Griffith in 1895–1896, and Maurice Bloomfield in 1897. The Orientalist biases of the period classified the text as inferior to the other Vedas. It was described as filled with magical formulas. It was deemed simplistic and superstitious, catering to the 'common' people. Its contents were contrasted with the more lofty philosophical ideas found in the *Ṛg Veda*. In 1965, Abinash Chandra Bose published *Hymns from the Vedas*, in part to reintroduce these texts to Western readers as something more than historical poetry, as part of India's theologically and ethically alive tradition. His book includes translations of various hymns from all four texts and ends with a full translation of the Earth Verses, the *Pṛthivī Sūkta.*[1]

The *Pṛthivī Sūkta* is poetic, mystical, but also practical. It contains hymns devoted to medicinal plants, to inter-human relationships, and to Mother Earth. It celebrates the *dharma* of nature. *Dharma* connotes a range of meanings, including law, righteousness, ethics – in short, all human activities that seek to hold the world together. By developing a deep connection

1 Abinash Chandra Bose, *Hymns from the Vedas: Original Text and English Translation* (Bombay: Asia Publishing House, 1966).

with nature, one finds an emotional foundation for taking correct action to protect the Earth.

Though this text was composed more than 2000 years ago, it carries relevance to the entire planet and its peoples. The intent is to help develop an intimacy with nature that will engender the benevolence necessary to protect and heal global ecosystems. By reinvigorating and reorienting our views about nature from a Hindu perspective, some strength may emerge that will help humans deal with the impending global and ecological catastrophes facing our planet today.

India's ancient wisdom as depicted in the Vedas constitutes what might be viewed as akin to an environmental ethic that encourages us to see the divine in nature. This ethic in turn generates the respect that motivates us to care for nature in all her incarnations. Hindu scriptures contend that it is the responsibility of humankind to protect and maintain the natural unity of God and nature. In the Hindu way of thinking, nature does not exist for humankind to exploit or to dominate, but rather to live in harmony.

Stewardship is a primary virtue in the active life of Eastern cultural and religious traditions. The stewardship of the environment depends on the idea that we imagine life in a particular way known in Hindu thinking as *Vasudhaiva Kuṭumbakam*. Dr. Karan Singh defines this concept as an appreciation of the holistic, symbiotic, and interrelated relationship of all life on earth: '... that the planet we inhabit and of which we are all citizens – Planet Earth – is a single, living, pulsating entity; that the human race, in the final analysis is an interlocking, extended family – [or] *Vasudhaiva Kuṭumbakam*....'[2] The micro-

2 Karan Singh, 'Foreword', in *In Praise of Mother Earth: The Pṛthivī Sūkta of the Atharva Veda,* O.P. Dwivedi and Christopher Key Chapple (Los Angeles: Marymount Institute Press, 2011), p. i.

cosm and the macrocosm integral to the natural world thus creates and sustains the harmonic balance between plants, non-human animals, and human beings. Stewardship for the earth will depend upon how we perceive a common future for our society and how we act, both individually and as a group, to secure that future.

Those who see divinity in nature and who worship nature can increase our sense of the beauty, along with the largeness and expansiveness of life. While Christianity has given us the vision of divine love and charity; Buddhism has shown us a noble way to be kinder and purer; Judaism and Islam have shown us how to be devoted to God and how to be faithful in following his command, Hinduism gives us a profound spiritual vision of Earth's sacred nature. The environmental crisis facing the Earth gives all of us the opportunity to come together and work for the protection and sustenance of the entire cosmos. Meditation on this text can stimulate an understanding of the interlocking, healing, and resplendent essence of the divinity of nature.

Like the philosophy of the Pre-Socratics, the *Pṛthivī Sūkta* venerates various aspects of the elemental world, giving praise not only to the Earth but also to water (*ap*), fire (*agni*), and air (*vāyu*). Alluding to earlier texts of the *Ṛg Veda* and the Upaniṣads, the *Pṛthivī Sūkta* asserts that the Earth arose from the water of the ocean.[3] For a series of verses, it extols the power of fire, claiming that fire energises the Earths's herbs and medicinal plants, as well as the clouds that give rain to the Earth.[4]

The text comprises the first sixty-three verses of the twelfth book of the *Atharva Veda*. Two terms are used to describe the Earth: *pṛthivī* and *bhūmi*. Though the two are used seemingly

---

3 *Pṛthivī Sūkta* 8.

4 *Pṛthivī Sūkta* 19–21.

interchangeably, we have chosen to translate the term *pṛthivī* as Earth and *bhūmi* as Land. These verses give poetic praise to the Earth. They ask for her protection. They also proclaim that humans must protect the Earth, taking care not to foul her soil or waters. These verses describe the Earth, praise her, and acknowledge that she alone is the home of humans and gods. Ultimately, these verses ask for protection from Mother Earth, while promising that humans will do what they must do to protect her and build harmony.

Describing and Praising the Earth

One of the most striking features of this Whitmanesque work can be found in its use of language. The author describes various topographic aspects of the Earth, including 'hills, plains, and slopes' (2) 'snowy mountains, and deep forests' (11) as well as the oceans and rivers that lie upon her. For humankind, she provides agricultural abundance. The author notes that 'On her body food is grown everywhere and on her the farmer toils' (4). In addition to plant life, 'She is the home of cows, horses, and of birds' (5).

Beyond pure description, it acknowledges through praise that human life is contingent upon the existence of the Earth. She is referred to as a wish-fulfilling cow (45, 61) and lauded for her great expanse and generosity: 'You are borderless, you are the world-mother of all things, you are the provider of all things in life' (61). The author states that 'This Land is my mother, I am the son of the Earth' (12). This parental image invoked again in a later verse: 'You are the world for us and we are your children' (16).

Earth as Home of the Gods

The most frequently mentioned Vedic god, Agni, is mentioned in various verses (19, 20, 21, 53). Agni has no shape or form other than his elemental manifestations. Two human-shaped gods find special mention in the *Pṛthivī Sūkta*: Indra and Viṣṇu. In the *Ṛg Veda,* Indra conquers the dragon Vṛtra who symbolises drought. By slaying Vṛtra, India frees the monsoon. The annual return of the rains allows the earth to flourish for another year.[5] Verse 37 echoes this episode, which states that the Earth chose 'Indra as her companion rather than Vṛtra'. The text refers to Indra as the consort of the Earth (6), stating that she is 'protected by the great strength of Indra' (18). It also states that she provides the place where 'Indra is invoked to drink Soma', the substance used for religious inspiration (38). Verse 10 alludes to the famous stanza in the *Ṛg Veda* that describes how Viṣṇu created the Earth in three great strides.[6]

The worship of the gods and goddesses of Vedic India required intricate rituals. The *Pṛthivī Sūkta* reminds the reader that all these sacrificial activities take place on the Earth. The Earth supports religious ritual and sacrifice, and ensures social stability. She yields the medicine used in healing practices (17, 19, 20, 62). She houses the 'sacred universal fire' (6), the 'ever-vigilant and all-caring gods' (7), and serves as the site for sacrifices:

> Events for the welfare of all
> are consecrated by performing sacrifices on this Land.
> Good and virtuous people assemble here to perform
> such functions.
> Strong sacrificial posts are erected on the Earth for making
> offerings.
> Here is where spirituality gets imparted.... (13)
> Oblations and sacrifices are duly performed by the Gods or
> the Land.... (22)

5 *Ṛg Veda* 10.125.

6 *Ṛg Veda* 7.99, 7.100.

> Places for offering oblations can be found on that [Earth].
> Here poles for the sacrifice.
> This is where the sacrificial post is situated.
> This is where Brahmins well-versed in the Vedas recite
> hymns.... (38)
> It is upon that [Earth]
> where the Seven Sages, the creators of worlds,
> performed sacrifices and austerities,
> chanted hymns, and carried out sacred rites. (39)

In an expansive, cosmic sense, the Earth contains all things. She also provides the specific ground upon which human beings may acknowledge their dependence on her through religious devotion.

Protection

In many verses, the author petitions the Earth to render protection for human beings: 'May the world Mother provide us with a wide and limitless domain for our livelihood' (1), 'May She spread prosperity for us all around' (2), 'May the Earth confer on us all riches' (3), 'May that Land replenish us in plenty with cattle and food' (4), 'May that Earth protect us, grant us prosperity, and bestow upon us vigor' (5), 'May you give us wealth and good fortune!' (6), 'May She make our nation on this Land strong, powerful, and brilliant' (8), and so forth. Nearly every verse ends with a request for enhanced well-being.

An extended set of verses also discusses interpersonal relationships. The Ṛṣi asks that the Earth spare one from hatred to prepare one to battle enemies (18, 24, 25, 32, 37, 41). Additionally, several verses ask for protection from the harm and danger to be found in the natural world:

> Keep away from us venomous reptiles
> such as snakes and scorpions which cause thirst when
> they sting;
> keep away those poisonous insects which cause fever,
> and let all those terrible crawling creatures
> which are born in the rainy season keep away from us. (46)
> Although various wild animals such as the lion, the tiger,
> the wolf,
> The jackal, the deer, and others are nurtured in your forests,
> keep all menacing animals away for harming us. (49)

The *Pṛthivī Sūkta* not only extols nature, but sees a need to profit from her, and be wary of her dark side.

The author also asks that the Earth share her sweet fragrance and radiance with the humans who adore her:

> Instill in me with abundance that fragrance which emanates
> from you
> and from you herbs and other vegetation, as well as waters.
> This fragrance is sought by all celestial beings. (23)
> O Mother Earth!
> May that perfume come to us in abundance,
> the perfume that is in the lotus,
> the fragrance worn by gods when the sun marries the dawn. (24)
> The fragrance that you have granted to men and women
> and which is also present in horses, deer, and elephants,
> shines like the radiance in maidens, throughout the Land.
> May that radiance comc to us.... (25)
> Bless us with fragrance.
> Grant us peace, tranquility,
> fragrant air and other worldly riches. (59)

Several other verses also refer to the great elements, particularly fire (*agni*) and water (*ap*).

The *Pṛthivī Sūkta* also proclaims that, despite her magnitude and magnificence, humans need to do their best to not harm or injure the Earth. Along with asking for her blessings, the author of the text puts forth an admonition that the Earth must be guarded from human interference in the following passages: 'May no person oppress her' (2), 'May we never harm your vital parts' (35), 'Please do not become outraged by our destructive tendencies' (45), and 'May I have the strength to subjugate those who poison our Mother Earth' (54). Toward the end of the text, its vehemence increases: 'If anyone tries to harm you, destroy them with the same ease as when a horse shakes off the dust on it' (57) and 'May I have the ability of swiftness and strength so that I am able to vanquish those who exploit you' (58). These verses seem to anticipate a misuse of the Earth, and perhaps even reflect some of the rapid changes inflicted by human interference during the settling of the Gangetic Plains.

Two verses in particular (30 and 47) indicate that human impact was being felt upon the Earth. In verse 30, a specific warning is given in regard to water pollution:

> O Mother Earth!
> May our bodies enjoy only the clean (pure) water.
> May you keep away from us that which is polluted
> and may we do only the good deeds.

Though pollution can arise from many sources, this verse indicates an awareness that unclean water can lead to disease and death. Verse 47 acknowledges that human expansion and road building have altered the face of the Earth. In the following verse, the author states that the Earth has freely given her resources to be used, but asks for protection on the road:

You have given people many roads
where both the chariots move and bullock-carts with
grains ply,
where both the virtuous and wicked people travel.
Protect these networks of transportation from robbers
and thugs.
May we be victorious and may we receive
the auspicious and benevolent things in life.

The first part asks for wholesome resources; the second part acknowledges that trouble can arise where human beings congregate. If we extend the metaphor from this juxtaposition, human beings need clean resources to flourish. If these become endangered, then stability can founder. In an expression of proto-environmentalism, and in a sense responding to the problem articulated above, verse 27 makes an appeal for venerating the Earth, both for her sake, and for the sake of human welfare:

We venerate Mother Earth,
the sustainer and preserver of forests, vegetation,
and all things that are held together firmly.
She is the source of a stable environment.

Without respecting and valuing Mother Earth, forests disappear, water becomes foul, and the air becomes unbreathable. The *Pṛthivī Sūkta* enjoins all human beings to protect, preserve, and care for the environment. This is illustrated in verse 16 which says that it is up to the progeny of Mother Earth to live in such a way that it maintains peace and harmony with all.

O Mother Earth!
You are the world for us and we are your children.
Empower us to speak in one accord,
steer us to live in peace and harmony,

and guide us in our behaviour
so that we have cordial and gracious relationship with all
other people.

These sentiments denote the deep, ideal bond between the Earth and human beings, between the Earth and all other living beings, as well as between humans and other forms of life. The text ultimately provides a guide for human behaviour towards nature that is harmonious.

PṚTHIVĪ SŪKTA

Translation by O.P. Dwivedi and Christopher Key Chapple[7]

1 Truth, strength, artistry, ferocity, dedication, fervor, effulgence, and sacrifice
are the attributes among human beings that sustain the Earth.
Drawing upon Mother Earth's feminine power,
these attributes have been and continue to be all that will be with us.
May the world Mother provide us
with a wide and limitless domain for our livelihood.

2 The Earth is adorned with many hills, plains, and slopes.
She bears plants with medicinal properties.
May no person oppress her
and may she spread prosperity for us all around.

3 Upon her lie the oceans, many rivers, and other bodies of water.
Her agricultural fields produce grain.
All those that live, move, and breathe [depend upon the Earth].
May the Land confer upon us all riches.

4 To the Earth belong all the four directions of space.
On her body, food is grown everywhere and on her the farmer toils.
She sustains all kinds of living-beings.
May the Land replenish us in plenty with cattle and food.

---

7 O.P. Dwivedi and Christopher Key Chapple, *In Praise of Mother Earth: The Pṛthivī Sūkta of the Atharva Veda*. Foreword by Karan Singh. Photographs by Robert Radin, Todd Mansoor, and Shailendra Dwivedi (Los Angeles: Marymount Institute Press, 2011).

5 Our ancestors worked freely on her.
The gods conquered the demons [on the Earth].
She is the home of cows, horses, and of birds.
May that Earth protect us, grant us prosperity, and bestow upon us vigor.

6 O! All sustainer of all!
Bearer of rare treasures and sacred universal fire,
Land of all moving life,
possessor of gold, whose consort is Indra,
may you give us wealth and good fortune!

7 May the Earth, this Land,
protected by ever-vigilant and all-caring gods,
confer upon us many delicious things, and endow us with
splendor.

8 In the beginning, the Earth was inside the water of the ocean.
She was discerned by the sages
whose immortal hearts were enwrapped in Truth.
She resides in space.
May She make our nation on this Land strong, powerful, and brilliant.

9 Just as waters are flowing everywhere,
equally, day or night, without restriction,
the land is multitudinous and bountiful with all kinds of food and milk.
May she endow us with splendor.

10 Her dimensions were measured by the Aśvins [sun gods].
Lord Viṣṇu strode victoriously [on the earth].
The Land was made hospitable by Indra
who also ensured freedom from enemies.
Like a mother to a son, may She nourish us all.

11 O Earth!
Sacred are your hills, snowy mountains, and deep forests.
The [soil] of your Land is brown, black, and red.
Earth, you are protected by Indra.
May I stand on the Earth unconquered, unharmed, uncrushed.
May you be fertile, arable, and sustainer of all.

12 May the Earth bring us closer to her through her middle-portion,
and with the energy which resides throughout her body.
This land is my mother,
I am the son of the Earth.
May she nourish, protect, and maintain us in an appropriate manner.
The Father is the sky who sustains us with rain.

13 Events for the welfare of all
are consecrated by performing sacrifices on this Land.
Good and virtuous people assemble here to perform such functions.
Strong sacrificial posts are erected on the Earth for making offerings.
Here is where spirituality gets imparted.
May the Land bless us with fortune and prosperity.

14 May the Mother Earth grant us strength
to fight those who have hatred against us
and who wish to defeat us.
May you get rid of them for us
if they plan to harm or kill us.

15 O Mother Earth!
Your progeny consists of not only bipeds but also quadrupeds.

Among the bipeds, there are five races of humans
who are sustained by the Sun through its immortal light and rays.

16 O Mother Earth!
You are the world for us and we are your children.
Empower us to speak in one accord,
steer us to live in peace and harmony,
and guide us in our behavior
so that we have cordial and gracious relationships with all other people.

17 May we live longer in order to serve our Land
who is the mother of all the medicinal plants and vegetation.
She is the one who has given us an immense space.
And it is She who grants us the needed firmness.
May our behavior be in accord with Dharma of the Earth
for securing stability and happiness.

18 You are great.
Ruled by your own natural forces,
your movements are swift and astonishing.
You are forever protected by the great strength of Indra.
Dazzling like bright gold, may we get illumined by the Land,
and may no one hate us.

19 Our land is full of *agni* [fire].
It is the same Agni flowing through the herbs and other medicinal plants.
The clouds carry it in the form of thunder and the stones store it.
The same energy, in the form of hunger,
flows through human-beings and cattle and horses.
May that energy sustain us all along

20 The Agni [fire] needed for sacrifice [*yajña*] and worship [*havana*]
comes from the sky where it exits in the form of sunrays
brightening the entire space.
May that energy help us to dissipate diseases.
Let it be available to us all the time.

21 May She, the Earth, who is sustained,
who is scorched by fire and blackened,
enlighten me and make me glorious.

22 Oblation and sacrifices are duly performed by the Gods of the Land.
The human race dwells on the Land,
receiving the life-sustaining nourishment.
May the Land grant us the foundational breath of life.
May the Earth give us longevity.

23 O Mother Earth!
Instill in me with abundance that fragrance which emanates from you
and from your herbs and other vegetation, as well as waters.
This fragrance is sought by all celestial beings.
May there be no hatred against us.

24 O Mother Earth!
May that perfume come to us in abundance,
the perfume that is in the lotus,
the fragrance worn by Gods when the sun marries the dawn.
May there be no hatred against us.

25 The fragrance that you have granted to men and women
and which is also present in horses, deer, and elephants,
shines like radiance in maidens throughout the Land.

May that radiance come to us
and may there be no hatred against us.

26 I pay homage to the Earth.
This Land holds firmly together
goldmines, rocks, stones, and even dust.

27 We venerate Mother Earth,
the sustainer and preserver of forests, vegetation,
and all things that are held together firmly.
She is the source of a stable environment.

28 If we are standing, sitting, or walking,
or whether we run, and even if we start with the right or left foot,
may we never cause pain or misery to others in this Land.

29 I Invoke you O Mother Earth!
You give shelter to all seekers of truth.
You provide us the strength-giving food and ghee.
You give us nutrition.
You are the source of all creative energy.
Render us safe on this Land.

30 O Mother Earth!
May our bodies enjoy only the clean (pure) water.
May you keep away from us that which is polluted
and may we always do only good deeds.

31 May all the directions (East, North, South, West) in the Land,
as well as other various sub-directions (Northeast etc.),
be beneficial to us to tread upon
and in whatever country we live,
may we never falter.

32 May harm not follow us to those regions East, North, inside, below, and so forth.
Be gracious to us on this Land.
May our enemies not locate us in our travels.
May the one who is stalwart among us go to kill our enemies.

33 With the help of the Sun, may my vision survey a vista as wide as yours, O Land.
May my eyesight never get diminished year by year.

34 You provide us all sanctuary, O Land.
May we not be injured while lying down,
whether we turn upon our right side or left,
or whether we lie straight, O Land.

35 May the crop grow faster when we plow and seed the Land.
But, while doing it, may we never harm your vital parts.

36 May each part of the cycle of seasons, O Land,
the summer, the rains, the autumn, the winter, and the spring,
which constitute a year,
pour happiness on us here on Earth.

37 This earth who is a purifier,
who carries the fires within her waters;
who moves like a serpent;
who has chosen Indra as her companion rather than Vṛtra;
and who has driven away the enemies of Gods,
may that one make us strong and mighty.

38 Places for offering oblations can be found on that [Earth].
Here are the poles for the sacrifice.
This is where the sacrificial post is situated.
This is where Brahmins well-versed in the Vedas recite hymns.
This is where Indra is invoked to drink Soma.

39 It is upon that [Earth]
where the Seven Sages, the creators of worlds,
performed sacrifices and austerities,
chanted hymns, and carried out sacred rites.

40 May the Land fulfill our desire for riches.
May Providence assist us!
May Indra lead us!

41 This is the Land where mortals sing and dance,
where war drums sound
and the war cry is raised by specially initiated brave ones.
May our enemies be driven from this Land,
and free us from our foes, O Mother earth.

42 We pay homage to that Land
that is the source of all grains: rice, barley, and wheat.
The five races of human beings live here.
Here the rains make her fertile.

43 May the Lord of Creation [Prajāpati]
grant upon this Earth continued splendor and exquisiteness
unto her in all regions for our enjoyment.
Cities were built here by the gods
and fields were cultivated.
She is the universal mother of them all.

44 May the Goddess Earth,
the bearer of many treasures like gold, gems, and other riches
that are hidden in her secret places,
be generous and bountiful to us,
and bestow upon us her special favors.

45 O Mother Earth!
You care for the people who belong to different races,

practice various religions and spiritual beliefs,
and speak different languages.
Like the wish fullfilling cow,
may you bless us all in a thousand-fold manner.
Please do not become outraged by our destructive tendencies.

46 O Mother Earth!
Keep away from us venomous reptiles
such as snakes and scorpions which cause thirst when they sting.
Keep away those poisonous insects which cause fever,
and let all those terrible crawling creatures which are born in the rainy season
keep away from us.
Be kind to us and grant us that which is beneficial.

47 You have given people many roads
where both the chariots move and bullock-carts with grains ply,
where both the virtuous and wicked people travel.
Protect these networks of transportation from robbers and thugs.
May we be victorious.
May we receive the auspicious and benevolent things in life.

48 The Earth which bears both the good and wicked
permits wild animals such as boar and deers to move about freely.

49 Mother Earth!
Although various wild animals
such as the lion, the tiger, the wolf, the jackal, the deer, and others
are nurtured in your forests,
keep all menacing animals away from harming us.

50 O Land!
Protect us from the evil spirits such as Gandharvas, Apsaras,
the demons, and those who are bent upon stealing our wealth.

51 The two-winged swans, falcons, eagles,
and birds of all kinds fly fearlessly [above the Earth]
where the wind comes rushing,
raising dust storms and uprooting trees,
as well as fanning fires.

52 May the Mother Earth graciously grant us a suitable abode
where the bright light and darkness are recognizable,
where the day and the night can be distinguished in this land,
and where rains make the land richer and fertile.

53 May I be blessed with power and energy
derived from heaven, earth, and space.
May I draw inspiration from the fire, the sun, the waters,
and the Gods
so that I may act with wisdom.

54 People, behold!
I am the accomplisher of great deeds.
I am victorious everywhere, the ruler of all.
May I have the strength to subjugate those who poison
our Land.

55 When requested by gods, O Goddess, you revealed your
grandeur and charm.
Thereafter, the four geographical directions were evidently
established.
May your timeless magnitude continue to be with us.

56 Irrespective of the place and region in this Land,
whether in a rural area, in the woods,
in the battleground, or in a public place,
may we always sing your praises.

57 O Mother Earth!
You are the protector and keeper of the Creation.
You are the sustainer of forests and vegetation.
Since you came into being, you have been the leader of all.
If anyone tries to harm you,
destroy them with the same ease as when a horse shakes off the dust on it.

58 Give us the strength so whatever I speak is pleasant like honey.
Whatever I see, my glances are met with respectful return from others.
May I have the ability of swiftness and strength
so that I am able to vanquish those who exploit you.

59 O Mother Earth!
May you bless us with milk that flows from your full breasts.
Bless us with other nourishments from your Land
including grain, agricultural produce,
as well as with fragrance.
Grant us peace, tranquility,
[clean] fragrant air, and other worldly riches.

60 When you were shrouded in the depths of the ocean,
Viśvakarma [the Cosmic Architect] brought you out by offering oblations.
When you appeared out of the ocean (at sunrise)
you revealed all your hidden hunger-fulfilling items
and other valuable materials
for the enjoyment of those who are devoted to you, Mother.

61 O Primeval Mother!
You are the wish fulfilling cow.
You are borderless.
You are the world-mother of all beings.
You are the provider of all things in life.
Let Brahma [Prajāpati], the first among all born,
replenish any deficiencies you might have.

62 O Mother Earth!
May all those who dwell upon you
be free from diseases, especially, from Yakṣma [tuberculosis]
and may they all flourish.
Be watchful over them, and grant them a long life,
so that they continue to be healthy, and always offer tribute
to you tributes.

63 O Land!
With your gracious kindness and intellect,
bless us with prosperity and fortune
so that we live in harmony with the powers of Heaven.
O All-knowing Mother, establish us in the most appropriate
manner.

Adapted with permission from Om Prakash Dwivedi and Christopher Key Chapple. In *In Praise of Mother Earth: The Pṛthivī Sūkta of the Atharva Veda*. Los Angeles: Marymount Institute Press, 2011.

Discussion Topic: Earth Verses

- In light of looming environmental difficulties such as species extinctions and climate change, how might you invent new earth verses?
- How might the verses in honour of Agni, the god of fire, be interpreted in light of energy consumption and related issues?
- This text asks often for protection. Discuss what protections are needed to protect humans and the earth today.

Further Reading

Abinash Chandra Bose. *Hymns from the Vedas: Original Text and English Translation*. Bombay: Asia Publishing House, 1966.

O.P. Dwivedi and Christopher Key Chapple. *In Praise of Mother Earth: The Pṛthivī Sūkta of the Atharva Veda*. Los Angeles: Marymount Institute Press. 2011.

William Dwight Whitney. *Atharva-Veda Saṃhitā*. Cambridge, Massachusetts: Harvard University. 1905.

इन्द्र शर्मा

III
Upaniṣads: A Sense of Place within India's Sacred Geography

Knowing one's ecosystem, the source of one's water and food, and the rhythm of one's climate can be a starting point for recovering the sacred. This chapter will explore passages from the Upaniṣads that signal a metaphorical approach to the natural world that can help enhance one's sense of connection to their ecosystem. In particular, this chapter examines the horse sacrifice passage at the beginning of the *Bṛhadāraṇyaka Upaniṣad*, the story of Satyakāma Jābāla in the *Chāndogya Upaniṣad*, the veneration of breath in several Upaniṣads, and the early descriptions of Yoga and meditation.

We often look to Aristotle as the father of science in the West, but if we look earlier to the Pre-Socratics, we see an approach to the human relationship with the natural world that bears similarities to systems found worldwide, particularly in the attention given to the elements. In this chapter we will draw from Asian traditional knowledge systems, which in most instances have remained intact for centuries, and have established a working narrative cosmology that emplaces the human within the cosmic order. This will not be an explication of the 'science' of Asia but will be an attempt to examine several different philosophical underpinnings of Asian cultures that have influenced the reception of science and technology from the West. This chapter will conclude with some reflections on the topic of intercultural globalisation, with an eye on some of the ways in which Asian worldviews have now become commonplace worldwide.

Vedic Worldview

The Indo-European cultural and linguistic continuum extends from South Asia, arcing through the northern Middle East into Russia and Europe. With the spread of Buddhism in the first century, its key philosophic terms were transmitted and translated from Sanskrit to the languages of Southeast Asia, China, and eventually Korea, Japan, and Tibet. With European colonial expansion starting in the fifteenth-century, Indo-European languages spread to the Americas, reaching all the way to Hawaii. The oldest surviving Indo-European text is the *Ṛg Veda* (*c.* 1500 BCE). Its content, like that of the later Pre-Socratics, honours the stability of Earth, the fluidity of waters, the power of fire, the strength of the wind, and the vast expanse of sky. Hymns from the *Ṛg Veda* recount the seasonal monsoon cycle that brings life-giving waters to the Indian subcontinent each summer. The clouds, associated with the end of dry season, taking the shape of the dragon Vṛtra, must be rent asunder by the heroic god Indra, who flings his thunderbolts, like his Western cousins Zeus, Jupiter, and Thor, to release the rain and ensure the success of the next year's agricultural cycle. The monsoon allows the cycle of life to continue and, through the process of sacrifice (*yajña*) to various gods and goddesses, human beings accomplish myriad goals: wealth, power, love, harmony, and so forth. In Vedic narrative, the natural world cannot be separated from the human world.

As one of the best-known Vedic hymns, the *Puruṣa Sūkta* holds a model for thinking about the human-cosmos relationship. The hymn correlates the human body with the far-flung regions of the universe:

> The moon was born of his mind; of his eyes, the sun was born;
> From his mouth, Indra and fire; from his breath, wind
> was born;
> From his navel there was the atmosphere;
> From his head, heaven was rolled together;
> From his feet, the earth; from his ears the directions.[1]

By identifying body parts with heavenly bodies, the heavens and the Earth, and the elements of fire and wind, sanctity is given to both self and cosmos. Like the moon, our mind reflects and changes. Without the light of the sun, we cannot see. Our mouth proclaims our intentions and desires, and like the god of war Indra, allows us to stake our claim in the world. Each breath we take generates and relies on the circulation of air. Our head pulls upward; our belly gathers us toward the centre and allows us to expand; our feet anchor us to the Earth. Our ears stabilise us within the space of the four directions. Through this sacrificial vision, each human being finds a place of importance within the cosmos. This sacrifice signals a continuity between human persons and their place in society and within nature.

Additional texts became appended to the Vedas known as forest books (*Āraṇyakas*) and wisdom books (*Upaniṣads*). In these works, the philosophy of correlationism specifies a relationship between the microphase or human aspect of reality and the macrophase of externalities. In the *Bṛhadāraṇyaka Upaniṣad,* the horse comes to symbolise myriad meanings. Its body represents the year. Its head represents the dawn. Its eye represents the sun; its belly, the atmosphere; its flesh, the clouds, and so forth. However, this homology is not merely an abstraction, but laced into the ritual life of the Indo-European landscape

1 *Puruṣa Sūkta* x.190.

even beyond India. A horse sacrifice was conducted every twelve years until as recently as the seventeenth-century. Even during the Islamic and British colonial periods (1000–1947), hundreds of Hindu kingdoms existed on the subcontinent who practiced this sacrifice. To begin the sacrifice, the king would abandon his duties for one year. He would follow his horse as it wandered, eschewing all regal comforts of fine clothes, fine foods, and his harem. At the end of the year, the horse would be ritually slaughtered, with each part correlated to the body of the king, and the kingdom, and the cosmos, establishing order for another twelve years. Any lands traversed during this time became part of the king's domain.

The evocative first segment of the *Bṛhadāraṇyaka Upaniṣad* invites the listener to visualise a magnificent horse, correlating its bodily parts and functions with the passage of time, heavenly bodies, climatic forces, the solidity of earth, and the fluidity of water. The presence of a horse in the company of a human evokes a sense of wonder and awe. Horses hold the capacity to transport people with saddle or chariot. They also can cause great harm to the human due to their size and strength. A tame horse brings comfort and peace, while a horse that runs wild defies all attempts of human control.

The word dawn (*uṣā*) opens this Upaniṣad, signaling the start of the day. The next line opens with the word heaven (*dyauḥ*), introducing a series of images that describe the body of the horse. The third and final line of this opening segment begins with the word for undigested food (*ūvadhyam*) brokering a discussion of inner organs of the horse, followed with a return of the horse intact, active, and loud. The final word of this segment serves as a mirror image of the first word: voice (*vāk*). Hence, this poem proclaims the horse is akin or even identical with the goddess of the dawn at the beginning, and the goddess of speech at the end.

The first line introduces correlations between the light, wind, fire, and time. Dawn is the head of the sacrificial horse. The sun is its eye, the wind its breath, the year its very self. The dawn brings new light to the world each day. The rays of the sun allow all things to take shape, to be perceived by the eye. The wind, when it enters the body, becomes breath, essential for all life. The opened mouth (*vyāttam*) of the horse emits a warmth like that of the sacrificial fire and the heat found within all bodies. In its sheer presence, the horse calls into awareness the fullness of the year. Three great elements: light, wind, and heat, as well as the marking of time open this invocation of the sacrificial horse.

The second line calls out to the heavens above, invoking their meeting point on the back of the horse. Its belly is akin to the atmosphere and sky; it marks the earth with its hooves. The sides of the horse are the four directions; the ribs at the fore and aft of each side mark the intermediate directions. The limbs of the horse carry the world through the seasons, with the joints of the limbs marking the months and half-months. Day and night unfold like the galloping of the horse. Although the text provides no description of horse slaughter, the horse clearly has been killed. The author peers inside, declaring that the stars are like the bones of the horse, the flesh like the clouds.

The third line continues with a description of the now dismembered horse. The food in its stomach is like the sands of the ocean shore. The entrails, veins, and arteries glimmer like rivers. Its liver and lungs are like mountains. The hair of its mane and tail and pelt are like trees and plants. The magnificent animal has been torn asunder, yet the teller of this tale concludes by describing the spirit of the horse as inseparable from the cosmos. The east, the direction of the dawn, is the front part of the horse. The west, the place of the setting sun, is the back part of the horse. Now that the horse is dead, we might be reminded of its yawn whenever a new day dawns. When it thunders, we can think about the pounding of the horse's hooves on the Earth. When it rains, we can contemplate the rain emerging from the cosmic body of the horse. When we speak and when we are listened to, we lift up and recognise the voice of the horse.

How does this particular passage correspond to the topic of the present study, the questions of ecology and environmental protection? First, it establishes a remembrance of the power of ritual. Ritual actions regenerate the world. In a practice similar to the Jewish jubilee or sabbath, the king disengages from the realm of power, takes leave and rest, and then reintegrates into society, renewed and refreshed. So much of modern consumerist-driven lifestyles ignore the call for periods of restoration, abstention from work, or monetise such experiences, robbing them of their power. Stores and delivery services make goods available around the clock, ignoring the glimmers of light that signal a new day. This passage reminds us to remember the year, the months, and days as part of a grand cycle designed not to be controlled but to be venerated. Second, the images in this passage point toward a continuity between microcosm and macrocosm. The body parts of the horse, shared in common with the body parts of the human being, connect with larger forces: earth, water, fire, and air. The whole world breathes as a horse breathes. The whole world awakens with the dawn; the sun empowers every eye to see. Bodily functions depend on food from the earth, on water that flows, on air that energises. Third, this passage teaches us to think metaphorically and symbolically and perhaps emotionally. The king and horse have been companions for years. Now the horse is dead. Although the text does not speak of grief, we can only imagine the emotion and pathos of the king as the horse is killed, dismembered, and eventually even eaten. The horse has been killed for the benefit of the king and the kingdom. The sacrificial process connects the reader to a larger sense of the price paid for life itself.

The symbolic reading of literature requires engagement at many levels simultaneously. One must be familiar with the context and nuance. Understanding the literal meaning of words leads to their symbolic connotations. The philosopher Sri Aurobindo, reflecting on the horse symbol within Indian culture, invites the reader to see a connection between its literary mention and its larger meaning:

> [T]he word *aśva*, usually signifying a horse, is used as a figure of the Prana, the nervous energy, the vital breath, the half-mental, half-material dynamism which links mind and matter. Its root is capable, among other senses, of the ideas of impulsion force, possession, enjoyment, and we find all these meanings united in this figure of the Steed of Life to indicate the essential tendencies of the Pranic energy.[2]

Aurobindo states that we must read sacred literature symbolically, noting 'Speech... contains indeed a constant psychological element and is therefore more free, flexible, constantly self-adaptive... its constituents yield themselves only to more subtle and less trenchant methods of analysis.'[3] The reader and interpreter of texts must engage in slow reading, a process of reading and re-reading that allows deeper meanings to emerge.

By allowing the words and images of this text to sink in, to be felt and understood, one develops a form of analogical

2 Sri Aurobindo, *The Secret of the Veda* (Pondicherry: Sri Aurobindo Ashram, 1971), 46.

3 Ibid., 47

thinking that enhances ethical acuity. It is one thing to follow rules (the first stage of ethical engagement). At a more subtle level, one must be able to extend one's ethical horizon to take appropriate action, informed by both logic and sentiment. In this instance, the frame story is quite dramatic: after a full year of wandering together, the king must kill his steadfast equine companion, eat and share its flesh, and emerge from this period of removal and violence to take up the old life informed by new experiences. As one reflects on this process and the words that describe the nature of the horse itself, an expansion of awareness dawns. The horse is more than a horse. The horse symbolises all aspects of life and of the cosmos itself. The start of the day can be seen in the appearance of a horse. The sky above and the earth below can be seen in the physical presence of the horse. The breath of life and movement itself can be seen in the bodily rhythms of the horse. One's own body can be seen in the body of the horse. By seeing oneself as not fundamentally different from the horse, one can also see other human persons as not different, heightening a sense of fellow-feeling, tenderising the heart, mind, and perhaps even the actions of the hands. Furthermore, in many ways the visualising and thinking about the horse sacrifice eliminates the need to actually slay a horse. Eventually, horse sacrifices became more and more rare until they were no longer practiced.

Other insights and practices of the Upaniṣads celebrate the constructive powers of the senses, the mind, and the breath in each person. This developed into the Sāṃkhya system, known for its description of a reciprocal exchange between the two key principles of materiality (*prakṛti*) and awareness (*puruṣa*). Sāṃkhya describes a network of twenty-five essential human components known as *tattvas* that link the internal world with the external world. This philosophy posits that anything made of the great five elements (earth, water, fire, air, and space) depends upon the human capacity for receptivity to receive data through the five senses and to move in the realm of objects through sensory and motor capacities. The construal of the world depends on conditionings within the mind (*manas*). The mind is connected with a sense of self (*ahaṃkāra*) and an intellect that holds filters created by *karma* that determine each individual's personality and intentions. The continuum of *karma*, emotion, mind, body, and world continually moves and changes through *prakṛti*'s three modalities of rest (*tamas*), action (*rajas*), and clarity (*sattva*), presenting this array of experiences to an inner, unseen awareness unique to each individual awareness (*puruṣa*).

The Education of Satyakāma Jābāla

The story of Satyakāma Jābāla[4] appears in the fourth book of the *Chāndogya Upaniṣad*, one of the two oldest Upaniṣads, dating perhaps from 2800 years ago. During the early period when India was lightly settled, cowherds were sent out into the forests and meadows to tend to flocks in distant quarters. One such young drover, Satyakāma Jābāla, achieved great spiritual insight while in the wild, learning profound truths from the elements of nature and from non-human animals.

The young Satyakāma asked his mother about his father, seeking indirectly to learn of his caste or *varṇa*. She responded that she does not know which man caused her pregnancy, and hence he is known as Satyakāma (desirous of truth), son of Jabālā, his mother's name. He sought out the renowned teacher Hāridrumata Gautama and, when asked about his family origins, shared guilelessly the story told by his mother. Satyakāma's honesty earned him accolades from Hāridrumata

4 *The Thirteen Principal Upanishads*, tr. Robert Ernest Hume (Oxford: Oxford University Press, 1921), 218–224.

Gautama, who proclaimed him to be a Brahmin, a member of the prestigious priestly caste, and agreed to teach him. First, however, service needed to be rendered. The teacher charged the young man with tending a herd of 400 cattle. Rising to the task, Satyakāma vowed not to return until the herd grew to a thousand head. He retreated into a landscape of forests and meadows for a period of years and then encountered four experiences there that transformed him into a sage.

The first encounter began when a bull from the herd notified Satyakāma, 'We have reached a thousand.' Then the bull himself proceeded to tell Satyakāma the first of four teachings about the nature of *brahman*. He alerted Satyakāma to the four directions: east, west, south, and north, resulting in an experience of all the areas and spaces in which light shines (*prakāśa*). The bull indicated that his next teaching would come from the fire. That night, the fire instructed Satyakāma about the worlds to be found in the Earth, the atmosphere, the sky, and the ocean. After another day of driving the cattle back toward the home of Hāridrumata Gautama, a swan came in the evening and told him of the fourfold nature of the luminous, which included fire itself, the sun, the moon, and lightning. A diving bird gave Satyakāma the final teaching, a fourfold analysis of that which supports one's experience: the breath, the eye, the ear, and the mind.

Through these four remarkable encounters, Satyakāma learned the importance of locating oneself within the four directions. He also grasped the vast expanse of the Earth below, the surrounding air, the largeness of space, and the unfathomable ocean as well. He moved on to understand the many manifestations of fire and light and then discovered the inner working of the human being, living in a body through the senses and the mind. His forest teachers were not human. He received instruction from a bull, a fire, a swan, and a diving bird, creatures of the earth, water, fire, and the air. When he returned to his human teacher, Hāridrumata Gautama proclaimed to Satyakāma: 'You shine like a knower of Brahman!' Satyakāma himself became a great teacher, sharing wisdom based on his experience in a living universe.

The Upaniṣads introduce the idea of reincarnation, with the *Kauṣītaki Upaniṣad* stating that '[One] is born again here according to [one's] deeds (*karma*) as worm, or as a moth, or as a fish, or as a bird, or as a lion, or as a wild boar, or as a snake, or as a tiger, or as a person.'[5] In the later Purāṇic period, an abundance of gods and goddesses arise in both literature and in the arts. Non-human animals became elevated to deity status in Hinduism, such as the eagle Garuḍa, the monkey Hanumān, and the elephant-headed Gaṇeṣa. Each anthropomorphic deity has a well known companion animal, including Gaṇeṣa's rat, Durgā's lion, Sarasvatī's peacock, Lakṣmī's elephant, and Śiva's bull.

The Upaniṣads contain speculative discourses and dialogues about the nature and function of the human body and mind. By reflecting on the functions of the body, particularly the breath, and by seeking to still the mind, the Upaniṣads state that one can establish a connection with one's inner self or *ātman*, often translated as soul. Passages from the early Upaniṣads such as the *Chāndogya* and *Bṛhadāraṇyaka Upaniṣads* emphasise the primacy of breath and the relationship between the microphase and the macrophase aspects of reality. By getting to know oneself through focusing on the power of the breath, one feels an intimacy with the larger aspects of the earth and heavens, perhaps most aptly conveyed in the first section of the *Bṛhadāraṇyaka Upaniṣad*, which first correlates the various functions and regions of the universe with the

5 *Kauṣītaki Upaniṣad* 1.2. Hume, *The Thirteen Principal Upanishads*, 303.

cosmic horse, and then makes a similar series of correspondences with the human body. By understanding one's desires and impulses, as well as the structures and functions of one's body and mind, one gains an understanding of the cosmos.

The later Upaniṣads and the *Bhagavad Gītā* speak directly of Yoga as the technique to be utilised in order to feel that intimate connection with the flow of life and one's place within reality. The *Śvetāśvatara* and *Maitrī Upaniṣads* state that by drawing the senses inward and controlling the breath, one can reach a state of equipoise. The *Bhagavad Gītā* comes to describe the yogi as one who comprehends the relationship between the 'field' or nature (*prakṛti*) and the 'knower of the field' or spirit (*puruṣa*). Within the body of Kṛṣṇa, the entire world, in its splendour and terror, can be seen, appreciated, and embraced. The metaphor of the human body becomes extended in the *Gītā* to include all aspects of the universe.

The Power of Breath in the Upaniṣads

Life outside the womb begins with breath. At the end of life, breath departs the body, escaping into and merging with the wind, as indicated in the Cremation Hymn of the *Ṛg Veda* (10.16), the *Īśa Upaniṣad* (17), the *Bṛhadāraṇyaka Upaniṣad* (3.2.13), and the *Śatapatha Brāhmaṇa* (10.3.3.8). In between, the breath (*prāṇa*) moves in myriad ways, infusing the body with the energy of life.

The *Bṛhadāraṇyaka Upaniṣad* states that the breath is the essence of the limbs (*āṅgirasa*) and the lord of speech (*bṛhaspati*) (1.3.19). The breath, because of its inseparability from wind, bests even fire, the sun, and the moon:

As Breath holds the central position among the vital breaths [or functions], so Wind among these divinities (Fire,

Sun, Moon); for they have their decline, but not Wind. The Wind is that divinity which never goes to rest.[6]

The wind continues to blow in darkness. The body continues to breathe while asleep.

The *Chāndogya Upaniṣad* describes a contest wherein speech, the eye, the ear, the mind, and the breath declare themselves to be superior. To establish their claim, they leave the body, one by one. First, speech departs for a year, yet the body survives. The eyes go blind for a year, yet the body continues to function. In a third year, the ears fail, but the body continues to breathe, to speak, to see, and to think. The mind departs during the fourth year, but even without thought, the body continues. Finally, 'when the Breath was about to go off as a fine horse might tear out the pegs of his foot-tethers… [the other four cried out] Sir! Remain! You are the most superior of us. Do not go off!'[7] Each recognises that their very existence relies upon the presence of the breath.

Breath takes five forms: inhalation, exhalation, diffused breath, up-breath, and middle breath (*prāṇa, apāna, vyāna, udāna, samāna*).[8] Reflecting on these breaths places one within a cascade of connections, as seen in Table 3.1.[9]

6 *Chāndogya Upaniṣad* 3.13.1–5.

7 *Chāndogya Upaniṣad* 5.1.12.

8 *Bṛhadāraṇyaka Upaniṣad* 3.9.26.

9 *Chāndogya Upaniṣad* 3.13.1–5.

Table 3.1. Five Forms of Breath and Their Correlations

prāṇa	eastern	eye	sun	radiance	food
apāna	southern	ear	moon	prosperity	splendour
vyāna	western	speech	fire	knowledge	food
udāna	northern	mind	rain	fame	beauty
samāna	upper	wind	space	vigour	greatness

The breath corresponds with the directions, with the senses, the sun, the moon, the elements, rain, food, and the best of human qualities. The breath becomes the gateway through which one relates to both the inner and outer worlds. However, these alignments are somewhat fluid; a latter passage in the *Chāndogya Upaniṣad* aligns the diffused breath (*vyāna*) with the ear and moon, the exhalation (*apāna*) with speech and fire, the middle breath (*samāna*) with mind and rain, and the up-breath (*udāna*) with wind and space (5.19–23). To further confound any notion of fixity, the *Taittirīya Upaniṣad* assigns the first breath to sight, the second to hearing, the third to mind, the fourth to speech, and the fifth to touch (1.7). A consistent theme emerges: breath energises bodily functions and connects us to the cosmic order.

Other passages from the Upaniṣads delineate different numbers of breath. The *Bṛhadāraṇyaka Upaniṣad* describes the fourfold breath, which includes the inbreath (*prāṇa*), the outbreath (*apāna*), diffused breath (*vyāna*), and the up breath (*udāna*), as soul (*ātman*) (3.4.1). The *Muṇḍaka Upaniṣad* lists seven breaths, explained by *Śaṅkara* as correlating to the two eyes, the two ears, the two nostrils, and the mouth and to the seven fires of the Vedic sacrifice:[10]

10 Robert Ernest Hume, *The Thirteen Principal Upanishads* (London: Oxford University Press, 1921), 371, fn.

> From [the imperishable] come forth the seven life-breaths
> (*prāṇa*),
> the seven flames, their fuel, the seven oblations,
> the seven worlds wherein do move
> the life-breaths that dwell in the secret place
> [of the heart] placed seven and seven.[11]

The *Kauṣītaki Upaniṣad* praises the breathing spirit (*prāṇa*) as life, immortality, speech, sight, hearing, thinking, the animator of the body, the source of smells and tastes, and the obtainer of all things (*sarvāpti*) (third chapter), noting more than ten realms accomplished through the facilitation of breath.

What are we to make of the many different ways in which the Upaniṣads describe the breath? On the one hand, the multivalent descriptions speak to a philosophy of unbounded possibilities. Is the breath fivefold or fourfold? Does the in-breath correspond to the mind and rain or to the wind and space? These seeming contradictions point to a comfort with incommensurability that reflects the grammar and speaking forth of the many avenues that could be explored. Every verb in the Sanskrit language may be construed in a mode known as the optative (*liṅ*). William Dwight Whitney, the renowned Sanskrit scholar, described this mode as follows:

> The optative appears to have as its primary office the expression of wish or desire.... But the expression of desire, on the one hand, passes naturally over into that of request or entreaty, so that the optative becomes a softened imperative; and, on the other hand, it comes to signify what is generally desirable or proper, what should or ought to be, and so becomes the mode of prescription; or yet again, it is weakened into

11 *Muṇḍaka Upaniṣad* 2.1.10.

> signifying what may or can be, what is likely or usual, and so becomes at last a softened statement of what it is... a regular means of expression of the conditional and contingent.[12]

Philosophically, the optative mode resists fixity. For the Jain philosophers, it became a way to regard the world as an array of possibilities rather than certainties. In fact, the sevenfold Jain analysis posits that 'in a certain way, a thing exists, does not exist, both exists and does not exist, is unspeakable, exists but is unspeakable, does not exist yet is unspeakable, and both exists and does not exist and is unspeakable.'[13]

Another way to view the seemingly disparate descriptions of breath would be as invitation to imaginative speculation. The process of imagination (*vikalpa*) counts as one of the five great ways that the working of the mind finds expression. Distinct from error or mistake, imagination allows one to conjecture, conjure, invoke, and aspire. The Upaniṣads invite one to engage the connections between the five breaths and the cosmos creatively. The moon can connect both through the outbreath and the diffused breath. One can move into the emotional feel of the rising of the sun as a great inhalation. As the breath in all its forms energises the body, it brings the qualities of radiance, beauty, vigour, and fame. However, it can serve also as a portal into meditative equipoise, as described in the later Upaniṣads.

---

12 William Dwight Whitney, *Sanskrit Grammar*, Second Edition (Cambridge: Harvard University Press, 1889), 215.

13 See summary of this philosophy in Christopher Key Chapple, *Nonviolence to Animals, Earth, and Self in Asian Traditions* (Albany, NY: State University of New York Press, 1993), 87.

Meditation in the Upaniṣads

The term Yoga as spiritual practice makes an early appearance in the *Kaṭha Upaniṣad*, dating from sometime after 500 BCE. Death instructs the young boy Naciketas that one must enter the fearless place hidden in the heart, and through the 'Yoga-study of what pertains to self, the wise one leaves joy and sorrow behind'.[14] Death goes on to define Yoga as follows:

> This they consider as Yoga:
> The firm holding back of the senses.
> Then one becomes undistracted.
> Yoga, truly, is the origin and the end.[15]

By practising Yoga, a connection is made within the heart that purifies oneself and allows one to understand and no longer fear death itself.

The later Upaniṣads give more specific delineations of how to practise Yoga. The sixfold Yoga of the *Maitrī Upaniṣad* begins with restraint of the breath (*prāṇāyāma*) followed with inwardness (*pratyāhāra*), meditation (*dhyāna*), concentration (*dhāraṇā*), contemplation (*tarka*), and absorption (*samādhi*) (6.18). The text describes how the restraint of breath allows one to become 'void of conceptions', entering the fourth condition (*turīya*) (6.19). The *Yoga Sūtra* lauds holding the exhaled breath (I:34) and also refers to this as an experience of the fourth state (*caturtha*, II:51). The *Maitrī* also urges joining the breath with the syllable Oṃ, attaining 'oneness of the breath and mind... the relinquishment of all conditions of experience' proclaiming

14 *Kaṭha Upaniṣad* 2.12.

15 *Kaṭha Upaniṣad* 6.11.

'This is designated as Yoga' (6.26). The *Śvetāśvatara Upaniṣad* describes a fivefold Yoga:

> When the fivefold quality of Yoga has been produced,
> Arising from earth, water, fire, air, and space,
> No sickness, no old age, no death has he [sic]
> Who has obtained a body made out of the fire of Yoga.
> Lightness, healthiness, steadiness,
> Clearness of countenance and pleasantness of voice,
> Sweetness of odor, and scanty excretions –
> These, they say, are the first state in the progress of Yoga.[16]

As we have seen in Chapter 1 and will continue to see in the following chapters, Yoga and meditation took root and wings from the time of the Upaniṣads onward, providing techniques to connect the transactional self of the breath with the transcendent Self of the cosmos.

Conclusion

The Upaniṣads expand upon the celebration of nature found in the *Ṛg Veda* and the *Pṛthivī Sūkta* of the *Atharva Veda*. They interpret the widely practised and highly dramatic horse sacrifice as a way of establishing periodic connection with the cosmic order, integrating the wild into the body of the king and the kingdom. Both the body of the horse and the body of the human are deemed to be continuous with the larger realm of earth, atmosphere, and sky (*bhūḥ, bhuvaḥ, svaḥ*). Microcosm reflects and embodies the macrocosm. The animal and elemental realms communicate with the human realm in a shamanic mode in the Upaniṣads. The future sage Satyakāma receives teachings from a bull, a fire, a swan, and

16 *Śvetāśvatara Upaniṣad* 2.12–13.

a diving bird. Furthermore, animals and humans are seen as kin, with humans having taken birth as animals, a theme later expanded upon in the *Yoga-vāsiṣṭha*. Furthermore, a repeated motif within virtually all Upaniṣads honours the breath as the gateway to all wisdom and knowledge. Without healthy breath, there cannot be a healthy human. As we will see, one of the greatest challenges facing modern India today is how to ensure the ongoing availability of life-giving air.

Portions adapted with permission from Christopher Key Chapple. 'Asian Systems of Knowledge'. In *Science and Religion: One Planet, Many Possibilities,* edited by Lucas F. Johnston and Whitney A. Bauman, 144–158. New York and London: Routledge, 2014.

Discussion Topic: The Upaniṣads

- Discuss the role of animals in the Upaniṣads, including the horse, Satyakāma's cattle, and the wisdom of birds.
- How do the Upaniṣads describe the breath and its relationship to other bodily functions?
- How do the Upaniṣads describe meditation? Does this accord with your own experience and understanding?

Further reading

Robert Ernest Hume. *The Thirteen Principal Upanishads Translated from the Sanskrit*. London: Oxford University Press, 1921. Revised edition 1971.

Patrick Olivelle. *The Early Upaniṣads. Annotated Text and Translation*. New York: Oxford University Press, 1998.

Sarvepalli Radhakrishnan. *The Principal Upanishads*. London: Allen & Unwin, 1953.

IV
Ecology in the *Mahābhārata* and the *Bhagavad Gītā*

This chapter will explore India as a sacred place within the *Mahābhārata* narrative, and also examine the indwelling, panentheistic theology expressed in the *Bhagavad Gītā*.

The *Mahābhārata* has been told and retold many times through many different media. The *Bhagavad Gītā* has been translated hundreds of times into scores of languages. These texts carry stories at the core and kernel of Indian civilisation, coding life paths and psychologies even far beyond India to Southeast Asia, Indonesia, and beyond. The ecological insights of this literature provide roadmaps for understanding the geography of the Indian psyche, explaining what Carl Jung would refer to as the shadow. Its parables regarding land, city, and people can perhaps provide some guidance to our current state of ecological peril, wherein people struggle with finding their place not only in the realm of nature and the cosmos but also within their own bodies.

Inspired by self-styled 'geologian' Thomas Berry, Mary Evelyn Tucker and John Grim have advanced a methodology for doing resource retrieval, revisiting religious texts and traditions in light of current ecological needs and concerns. This chapter will explore two of the five avenues suggested in their series foreword to the ten-volume set titled *Religions of the World and Ecology*.[1] The first is to 'identify and evaluate the distinctive ecological attitudes, values and practices' found in the *Mahābhārata* and the *Bhagavad Gītā*. The second is 'to articulate in clear and moving terms a desirable mode of human presence with the earth; in short to highlight means of respecting and valuing nature, to note what has already been actualized, and to indicate how best to achieve what is desirable beyond these examples'.[2] In the Indian milieu, philosophers have examined ways in which to both connect and to differentiate between body, self, and world. Hence, by examining prime narratives from the *Mahābhārata* that indicate bodily awareness and describe the pervasiveness of divinity within body and world, some tentative move may be made toward revealing depths of connection between the human and the Earth. In turn, this might inspire ongoing action for the protection of both.

Ritual

The *Mahābhārata* begins and ends with ritual. A traveling bard by the name of Ugraśravas came upon a group of Brahmins performing a twelve-year sacrifice in the Naimiṣa forest. He tells them that he had come from a snake sacrifice undertaken by King Janamejaya, the great grandson of Arjuna, to avenge the death of his father, King Parīkṣit, who had been poisoned by a snake. The sacrifice was described as follows:

---

1 Mary Evelyn Tucker and John Grim, eds., *Religions of the World and Ecology*, 10 vols. (Cambridge, MA: Harvard Center for the Study of World Religions, 1997–2003).

2 Christopher Key Chapple and Mary Evelyn Tucker, eds., *Hinduism and Ecology: The Intersection of Earth, Sky, and Water* (Cambridge, MA: Center for the Study of World Religions, Harvard University Press, 2000), xxiii.

First, a huge fire was built. The flames leapt high,
mantras were recited by the Brahmins
as ritual oblations, no cost spared,
were poured into the blaze by black-robed priests.
Then snakes appeared, drawn irresistibly
toward their death. Serpents by the million,
of every color, some as thin as threads,
others thick as trunks of elephants;
snakes from the dark recesses of the earth,
snakes from the forest, snakes from ponds and rivers
fell hissing, terrified, into the furnace.
Wildly they writhed, fruitlessly they screeched
as the flames devoured them. The race of snakes
would have been entirely extinguished
but the fulfillment of a prophecy:
a brahmin will disrupt the sacrifice.[3]

The arrival of the Brahmin *Āstika,* whose mother was a handler of snakes, put a stop to the sacrifice, and during this hiatus, Vyāsa told the story of the *Mahābhārata*. Interrupting the sacrifice for this narration, we find the ritual space expanded beyond the physical act of burning objects within the sacrificial pit, to a space for reflection and sharing.

Toward the very end of the more than 75,000-verse epic, we return to another sacrifice, this time not an occasion for story-telling, but the culmination of a story told. Every twelve years of his reign, a king was expected to renounce his duties, renounce his luxuries, and follow a horse in its meanderings for the length of a year. At the end of that year, the dramatic *aśva-medha* sacrifice would take place, empowering the King

3 Carole Satyamurti, tr., *Mahabharata: A Modern Retelling* (New York: W.W. Norton, 2015), 4–5.

to expand his realm to include the newly visited territories and, through ingestion of the horse by himself and the members of his court, to acquire the strength and cosmic power symbolised by the horse. After a long period of gloominess following the devastating loss of people and property during the great war, Yudhiṣṭhira, eldest of the five Pāṇḍavas, decides, following the birth of Arjuna's grandson, to hold a horse sacrifice to cement and expand his domain. He chooses his brother Arjuna to follow the horse, 'a most beautiful piebald'.[4]

What ensues is no less than a geographic account of the Indian subcontinent. Arjuna follows the horse out of Hastināpura first to the Trigarta kingdom, and then far afield. To the far west, Arjuna and the horse traveled to Sindh, the southern part of modern-day Pakistan. From there they wandered far to the east, to Manipur. As summarised by Satyamurti:

> The sacrificial horse meandered on
> over the earth, between one mighty ocean
> and the other, from the palm-fringed shores
> of the south to the sparking Himalaya.
> It moved among the ebony Dravidians,
> among the green-eyed warriors of the north,
> among the war-like and peaceful peoples
> of the Western Ghats.[5]

He also traveled as far as Gandhāra in what is now Afghanistan before returning to Hastināpura. This extensive travel links the *Mahābhārata* to the entire subcontinent, inculcating a deep sense of place in the reader or hearer of the tale.

---

4 Satyamurti, *Mahabharata*, 783.

5 Satyamurti, *Mahabharata*, 788.

The culmination of the full year sojourn resulted in the ritual sacrifice of the horse whom Arjuna had followed:

> Gold bricks were brought to build a fire altar
> four tiers high, shaped like Garuda.
> Three hundred sacrificial birds and beasts
> were bound to the stakes on the sacred ground.[6]

Sacrificial destruction establishes a connection with larger life cycles. Animals serve as gateways of connection to the gods: 'Birds and animals were killed and cooked, each dedicated to a specific god'.[7] Finally, the sacrifice comes to an end:

> The sacrificial horse was brought, then stifled.
> A chief queen, Draupadi lay beside it.
> Then it was dismembered, and its entrails
> were roasted on the fire. The rising smoke –
> that smoke capable of cleansing sin –
> was eagerly inhaled by the Pandavas,
> to the great joy of Yudhisthira.[8]

The huge number of animals captured, killed, and consumed, as well as the drama of slaying Arjuna's year-long companion underscore the cathartic nature of sacrifice. Furthermore, as presented here, the animals, consumed into the human body, having been sacrificed to the gods, serve to bring the powers of heaven into human flesh.

---

6 Satyamurti, *Mahabharata*, 791.

7 Satyamurti, *Mahabharata*, 792.

8 Satyamurti, *Mahabharata*,792.

Cataclysm

Three cataclysmic events in the *Mahābhārata* carry a sense of poignancy in light of the topic of this chapter. Although they have been commented upon extensively by many scholars, they bear re-examination, particularly through the lens of *pralaya*, the teaching that periodic purgation must occur for the renewal of the cosmos and the person. We will start with the narrative of Arjuna's vision in the eleventh chapter of the *Bhagavad Gītā*, and then turn to the destruction of the Khāṇḍava forest by fire and the submersion of Dvārakā into the ocean.

In the chapters prior to chapter eleven of the *Gītā*, Kṛṣṇa has revealed himself to be the best of all things, the source of all nobility as well as inexplicable occurrences. In chapter eleven, however, Arjuna asks to see Kṛṣṇa's true form, and, when Kṛṣṇa complies, he encounters utter destruction and devastation. Arjuna remarks:

> Without beginning, middle or end, with infinite power,
> with countless arms, with the sun and moon as Your eyes,
> I see Your face shining like a blazing fire,
> burning this universe with your own radiance.[9]

With his hot radiance, Kṛṣṇa devours all the enemies of Arjuna in the conflagration that has become his mouth:

> All the sons of Dhṛtarāṣṭra, along with the hosts of kings
> and Bhīṣma, Droṇa, and Karṇa
> together with the chief warriors on our side,
> are quickly entering into Your fearful mouths with spiky tusks.
> Some are seen with their heads crushed, caught between
> Your teeth.

9 *Bhagavad Gītā*, 11.19.

> As the many torrents or rivers rush to the ocean,
> so do these men of the world enter Your flaming mouths.
> As moths fly swiftly into a burning fire and perish there,
> so also do these men swiftly enter
> into Your mouths to their own destruction.[10]

Kṛṣṇa explains that he is time itself, eventually taking the lives of all beings. As had been stated earlier in the *Gītā,* all things have a beginning, a middle, and an end. Arjuna, by having been given a glimpse of the end, came to understand the ultimate destination of all beings. While Kṛṣṇa had assured Arjuna that all things will take another form, that the soul cannot truly be killed, he reveals to Arjuna that all things in their particular form in any given moment of time will sooner or later meet their demise. The immediate message suggests that Arjuna must overcome his attachment and enter into battle, becoming the instrument for the inevitable. On a more cosmic level, Arjuna has witnessed the *pralaya,* the cessation of existence that leads to purgation and eventually to renewal.

Several years prior, Kṛṣṇa and Arjuna engaged jointly in a different form of *pralaya,* the destruction of the Khāṇḍava forest. Prior to building the fully adorned city of Indraprastha, and prior to the birth of Draupadī's five sons, one each sired by the five Pāṇḍava brothers, Kṛṣṇa and Arjuna encountered what appeared to be a gaunt Brahmin. 'His hair and beard were red, his skin coppery, and he was radiant as the morning sun, blazing with glory.'[11] He identified himself as Agni and asked for the heroes' help in satisfying his appetite:

> 'I am Agni. I am Fire itself.
> This Khandava Forest is the feast I crave,

10 *Bhagavad Gītā,* 11.26–29.

11 Satyamurti, *Mahabharata,* 145.

> but every time I try to gobble it
> with my fiery mouth, Indra sends bank on bank
> of voluminous black thunderclouds,
> dousing the flames with deluges of rain,
> frustrating my voracious appetite.[12]

With great glee, Kṛṣṇa and Arjuna helped the hungry god, who had suffered from too much ghee offered in everyday sacrifices and needed the flesh and fat of forest animals to balance his diet. With great skill at weaponry, and with Arjuna in direct battle with his own father, Indra, god of war, the two men routed the animals and humans from the forest, scorching the earth. They called down birds from the sky and summoned snakes from beneath the earth for the skirmish:

> Indra summoned predatory birds,
> with razor beaks and claws, to strike the warriors;
> and snakes slid all around, their susurration
> filling the air, their scalding venom shooting
> from burning mouths. Arjuna's heaven-made arrows
> diced them up, to shrivel in the flames.[13]

Two important beings survived: the snake Aśvasena, son of Takṣaka (the snake who later killed King Parīkṣit, Arjuna's grandson), and Maya, an *asura* most likely of an indigenous tribe, renowned for his skill in architecture. This refugee of the great fire went on to build the magnificent assembly hall in Indraprastha for which the Pāṇḍava received great acclaim.

Christopher G. Framarin, drawing on earlier studies of the Khāṇḍava fire by Biardeau, van Buitenen, and Hiltebeitel,

12 Satyamurti, *Mahabharata*, 145.

13 Satyamurti, *Mahabharata*, 149.

states that this seemingly anti-environmental story served multiple purposes. First, it underscored that 'all beings exist by sacrifice'. In order for one being to live, the life of another must be surrendered. By involving fire on three levels: the sacrificial fire, the digestive fire, and the literal forest fire, one gets a sense of the inevitability of loss in the processes of life. Second, the fire served the practical function of clearing land so that the great assembly hall could eventually be built and the town flourish. Third, this enabled the elimination of harmful beings who could poison or kill the Pāṇḍavas and their family and citizens of Indraprastha. Framarin bases his argument on the importance of the idea of *pralaya*, the notion that the 'socio-cosmological order can only be regenerated by means of the destruction of the entire universe'.[14] Eco-systems inhabited with humans often require periodic burns. In some ways, the account of the burning of the Khāṇḍava forest simply describes the techniques for clearing land employed in the settling of the American heartland and the current practices employed in the Amazon. Today one can only imagine the vastness of India's forests, 85 per cent of which have been converted to agricultural and urban purposes. In the *Mahābhārata*, the settlement of Indraprastha is celebrated for its

> tranquil parks and gardens, planned and planted
> with arbors, cooling fountains, lily ponds
> and many kinds of tree and flowering shrub –
> kadamba, jasmine, mango and rose apple
> and others too numerous to name – so all
> who strolled there could enjoy bright, scented flowers

14 Christopher G. Framarin, *Hinduism and Environmental Ethics: Law, Literature and Philosophy* (London: Routledge, 2014), 103.

> and luscious fruits at all times of the year.
> Peacocks picked their way beneath the trees
> which were a haven for melodious birds.[15]

Though descriptive of a settled environment, this and other passages in the *Mahābhārata* pay close attention to the realm of nature, celebrating its beauty and bounty.

The closing narratives of the *Mahābhārata* carry a wistful air, particularly in the sad tale of Kṛṣṇa's demise. Gāndhārī, Dhṛtarāṣṭra's wife, had cursed Kṛṣṇa for his role in the great battle and the death of her 100 sons, and her curse came to pass as Kṛṣṇa's city of Dvārakā, on India's west coast, fell into ruin:

> Signs of doom and decay were everywhere.
> Rats and mice infested every house
> and ate men's hair and nails as they were sleeping.
> Freshly cooked food rotted instantly.
> There were unceasing cries of raucous birds.
> People became deranged, wives attacked husbands,
> fathers killed their children. Priests and elders
> were treated with contempt.[16]

A melee broke out and friend killed friend, brother killed brother, father killed son. Kṛṣṇa himself was eventually killed by a hunter, who had mistaken him for a deer. Arjuna arrived in time to lead the survivors to high ground as a combination, presumably, of earthquake and tsunami submerged forever the fabled city of Dvārakā:

> No sooner had the last cart left the city
> than the ocean breached the sea defenses.

15 Satyamurti, *Mahabharata*, 131.

16 Satyamurti, *Mahabharata*, 819.

> The sky grew black and seemed to be torn in two.
> The planet Mercury swung from its usual course
> and a tempest plowed the foaming ocean
> into troughs and mountainous peaks of water.
> The sea retreated from the land, then, rearing,
> seemed to hang, impossibly still, before
> it crashed forward, a voracious beast
> savaging the city with watery claws,
> devouring streets, squares, palaces and gardens,
> indiscriminate in its appetite.
> The houses of the poor dissolved instantly.
> The mansions of the rich took a little longer;
> soon every one of the well-constructed buildings,
> every tower and pinnacle, was drowned.
> It was as if Dvaraka had never been.
> The people stared. Then they turned their backs
> in resignation. The past closed up behind them.[17]

Though this careful description of natural disaster, one gets a sense of the gravity and power of nature, both benign and unforgiving.

The Panentheism of Kṛṣṇa

A recognition of the end of things must be part of a mature, wise worldview. In this regard, the *Mahābhārata* spares no detail in accounting for the inevitable end of things. However, in the middle, there can be great beauty and celebration. This section will explore the panentheism of Kṛṣṇa, the notion that God can be found in all things. The term panentheism, as described by Loriliai Biernacki, 'suggests that God is both in the world, immanent, and also beyond the confines of

17 Satyamurti, *Mahabharata*, 825.

mere matter, also transcendent'.[18] Several passages from various chapters of the *Bhagavad Gītā* attest to a Hindu form of panentheism; Biernacki has noted that 'Hinduism, with its fluid multiplicities, offers one of the easiest, most fluent representatives of a panentheistic worldview anywhere'.[19] Kṛṣṇa declares of himself:

> My material nature is eightfold:
> Earth, water, fire, air, ether, mind, reason and ego.
> This is my lower nature, but learn also of My higher nature,
> O mighty-armed one, which is the indwelling spirit
> by which this world is sustained.[20]

These broad, inclusive, and distinctly metaphysical and physical categories are supplemented with specifics that indicate a deep relationship between the physical human body of Kṛṣṇa and the cosmos:

> In water I am the taste, O son of Kuntī;
> in the sun and moon I am the radiance;
> in all the Vedas I am the sacred syllable Oṃ,
> in ether the sound, and in men their manliness.
> In earth I am the pure fragrance
> and in fire I am the brightness.
> I am the life in all beings
> and the austerity in ascetics.[21]

---

18 Loriliai Biernacki and Philip Clayton, eds., *Panentheism across the World's Religions* (New York: Oxford University Press, 2014), 2.

19 Ibid., 161.

20 *Bhagavad Gītā* vii.4–5.

21 *Bhagavad Gītā* vii.8–9.

Earlier in this chapter, we saw that Arjuna bore witness to the terrifying destructive aspect of Kṛṣṇa. Here Kṛṣṇa describes his benevolent aspect.

In metaphorical language, Kṛṣṇa declares: 'Just as the mighty wind that blows everywhere rests in the ether (*ākāśa*), likewise know that all being rest in me.'[22] He proclaims himself to be the ritual, the father and mother, the guardian, the Vedas, the friend, the origin, the dissolution, the ground, the seed, the creator of heat and rain, both immortality and death. He states if one devotes all actions as offerings to his divine self 'you will be liberated from the bonds of action, which bear good or evil result... you shall become free and come to Me'.[23] In the tenth chapter, Kṛṣṇa claims to be the best in all things, citing himself to be the best among gods, heavenly beings, sacred texts, mountains, priests, trees, seers, sages, elephants, weapons, cows, serpents, fish, titans, beasts, birds, purifiers, warriors, fishes, rivers, letters, hymns, and more. He states 'whatever is glorious, prosperous or powerful, recognize it to have sprung from a spark of My splendor'.[24]

This indwelling theology places the sacred in all aspects of nature and in human behaviour. If a person acts from a place of selfishness and greed, one cannot experience the connections between God and the cosmos. But if one appreciates beauty and practises generosity, then a spiritual connection can be made.

The Ritual Rhythm of Karṇa

One of the most interesting and tragic figures of the *Mahābhārata* is Karṇa, Kuntī's firstborn who had been given up

---

22 *Bhagavad Gītā* ix.6.

23 *Bhagavad Gītā* ix.28.

24 *Bhagavad Gītā,* x.41.

for adoption by his royal mother and taken in by a driver and his wife. Throughout his childhood he displayed magnificent qualities and eventually trained successfully as a warrior and archer. Despite his royal and divine origins (his father was none other than the sun itself), he was condemned by the Pāṇḍavas and by Draupadī for his lowly birth. Rejected by those who were actually his brothers, he accepted hospitality from Duryodhana, the eldest son of Dhṛtarāṣṭra, who crowned him as King of Aṅga, an Eastern kingdom. Stung by ongoing ridicule yet loyal to his adoptive mother and father and to Duryodhana, he lived a life haunted by the question, 'Who am I?' He found solace in only one activity which he undertook daily: his ritual *pūjā* in the Ganges River, into which he waded at dawn, waiting for the warming rays of the sun, his own unknown father, to bless him. This certainty gave him the perseverance to endure the difficulties, many self-inflicted, that endeared him to Duryodhana and stoked scorn from the Pāṇḍavas.

The ritual performed by Karṇa provided daily access to a grounding state of reverie. Building on the descriptions in the original text, Shivaji Sawant has written:

> I (Karna) woke at dawn to bird-song, opened the window, and gazed out. Darkness was slowly lifting from the horizon. The Ganga flowed through a silk-filmy mist. All Hastinapura was slowly stretching awake... Lost in thought, I reached the ghat... I respectfully *namaskared* the spectacle; then dived into the water... After an hour or so, the haze scattered. I swam back to the ghat, changed... I stared ahead. In the distance, the Sun-God was slowly climbing up the sky. His soft rays caressed the waters awake. I offered *arghya* to the Sun-God in sacred *anjali*. How profound he looked! ... Every day a wonderful manifestation, every day a wonderful radiance. Today's compelling glory was never tomorrow's again. ... I felt mysteriously lightened in my body. My hands joined by

> themselves in prayer… For endless miles I saw nothing but dazzling light – an intensely intense radiance… Without any reason I felt that there was a kinship between me and that effulgence, that there were unknown threads that linked me to that single ocean – vast brilliance that scattered the darkness of the universe.[25]

This experience of expanse and self-transcendence echoes the ritual connection with the cosmos expressed in the panentheism of the *Bhagavad Gītā*.

Karṇa also connected with the geography of India in a significant way. While the Pāṇḍavas were away on their thirteen-year exile, Karṇa formed alliances through diplomacy and conquest that galvanised the Kaurava military. The places he traveled to included Afghanistan, the Punjab, modern day Orissa, and many locales in between. The text names so many different peoples that he conquered: 'the Kambhojas, Avantyas and Kekayas, Gandharas, Madrakas, Matsyas, Trigartas, Tanganas, Shakas, Panchalas, Videhas, Kulindas, Kashis, Kosalas, Suhmas, Angas, Vangas, Nishadas, Pundras, Kichakas, Vatsas, Kalingas, Taralas, Ashmakas, and Rishikas'.[26] Through these exploits, as with the *aśva-medha* conducted by Arjuna many years later, he connected with the broad swath of the subcontinent. Karṇa cultivated a rich inner life through his daily performance of *pūjā* to the Sun-god in the Ganges and gathered a wealth of experience of the outer world through his travels.

The inclusion of Karṇa here speaks to the grim aspects of environmental ethics. Karṇa represents ambiguity in the

---

25 Shivaji Sawant, *Mrityunjaya the Death Conqueror: The Story of Karna*, trans. P. Lal and Nandini Nopanyi (Calcutta: Writers Workshop, 1989, Fifth edition 2014).

26 Adam Bowles, tr., *Mahābhārata Book Eight: Karṇa Volume One* (New York: New York University Press and JJC Foundation, 2006), 95.

Mahābhārata, the anguish of good intentions resulting in horrific, unanticipated results. The current environmental crisis arose due to good intentions. The scientists and industrialists who forever altered the landscape and atmosphere of planet Earth did so in order to make life more bearable, more comfortable for humans who struggled for thousands of years to stave off hunger, to keep cold at bay, to survive disease. Likewise, in the *Mahābhārata*, the tragedy of Karṇa, and of the great war, arose from a place of not knowing origins and not anticipating outcomes. Just as Karṇa allied himself to the people who showed him generosity and kindness, so also the general population of earth has embraced the many comforts that arise from the ready availability of fossil fuels and antibiotic drugs. However, loyalty to the seemingly obvious easy path can lead to dangerous consequences. Karṇa had no ill intent and perhaps merely responded in a very human way to his circumstances. Yet, he met an ignominious death. Let us hope the same fate does not happen to the human species.

Accepting Loss, Preparing for Loss, and Celebrating Nature through Ritual

We have examined various resources available from the *Mahābhārata* and *Bhagavad Gītā* that might inform how we think about environmental ethics. Above all, the *Mahābhārata* is a great tragedy: family fights family until the bitter end. Not even Kṛṣṇa, the incarnation of Viṣṇu, is spared a sad and lonely death. The *Mahābhārata* narrates a disintegration of civilisation due to selfishness and greed. At the same time, it prepares people for their own demise: Kṛṣṇa gives wise counsel regarding the inevitability of death and shows Arjuna the ultimate fate of all his kin, each of whom perish.

The environmental state of the world, as warned by Bill McKibben in his many books and as acknowledged by Pope

Francis in *Laudato Si'*, relies on the balance of carbon in the atmosphere. If the count exceeds 350 parts per billion, then the course toward global warming cannot be reversed. Glaciers will continue to melt, destructive hurricanes and typhoons will occur with great frequency, drought will plague some areas while others will be stricken by floods and rising tides. Species will continue to dwindle and those humans who survive will do so in a physically and psychically pauperised world.

Yet the *Mahābhārata* and *Bhagavad Gītā* provide some tools that might encourage some of the very changes needed to remedy the situation. First, the *Mahābhārata* celebrates a sense of place. One cannot read the descriptions of the flora and fauna and varied landscapes of India without feeling a sense of fondness for the mountains, the rivers, the forests, and the well-tended agricultural areas of India. These feelings can help generate concern; concern can lead to informed action to clean up the rivers, protect the forested mountains, and ensure high quality, unadulterated food. Second, these texts celebrate a rhythm of ritual grounded in a panentheistic theology that values personal connection with the body and the cosmos. In the Vedas, the Upaniṣads, and the epics, we find glowing descriptions of how the human body reflects the cosmos and that the cosmos can be best understood through self-knowledge. This wisdom, rooted in bodily experience, can likewise inspire persons to do what is necessary: to appreciate the senses rather than the objects of sense, to look to oneself for solutions rather than blaming others, to examine immediate consumer choices as a path toward global rectification.

In the nineteenth and twentieth centuries, Mahatma Gandhi pioneered a lifestyle inspired by the last nineteen verses of the second chapter of the *Bhagavad Gītā*. 'When people brood over the sense objects, attachment to them arises. From attachment arises desire, and desire breeds anger. From anger comes delusion of mind, and from delusion, the loss of memory; from loss of memory, the destruction of discernment; and from the destruction of discernment, the people perish'.[27] By tracing problems to the source of origin, corrective actions may be pursued. Gandhi saw the necessity of delivering India from the shackles of colonialism. He used personal power to effect global change. In the latter half of the twentieth century, Vinoba Bhave used the same methods to campaign effectively for the Bhū Dan Campaign, the redistribution of land in India so that each family may support itself with dignity. In the twenty-first century we face the complex global issues of environmental degradation. Just as self-control, as inspired by the *Bhagavad Gītā*, proved successful for Gandhi and Vinoba, so also, self-control, combined with celebration of a sense of place and a sense of the allure nature's beauty, will be important tools in the quest for ecological stability and justice.

Adapted with permission from Christopher Key Chapple. 'Ecology in the *Mahābhārata* and the *Bhagavad Gītā*'. *Journal of Vaishnava Studies* 24, no. 1 (2015): 125–137.

---

27 *Bhagavad Gītā*, ii.62–63.

Discussion Topic: The *Mahābhārata* and the *Bhagavad Gītā*

- Discuss the role of the snake and horse sacrifices in the *Mahābhārata*. How might the prospect of ritual killing inspire or discourage a sense of nature appreciation?
- Various episodes of the *Mahābhārata* include detailed geographical descriptions. Describe the geography of your immediate environment, noting watersheds, elevations, and variations of vegetation. How might this exercise establish a sense of intimacy with the land?
- Panentheism, or the idea that the divine resides in all aspects of creation, finds poetic expression in the *Bhagavad Gītā*. Reflect upon a moment of spiritual connection in your own experience.

Further Reading

Loriliai Biernacki and Philip Clayton, eds. *Panentheism across the World's Religions*. New York: Oxford University Press, 2014.

Carole Satyamurti, tr. *Mahabharata: A Modern Retelling*. New York: W.W. Norton, 2015.

Shivaji Sawant. *Mrityunjaya the Death Conqueror: The Story of Karna*. Translated by P. Lal and Nandini Nopany. 1989. Fifth edition: Calcutta: Writers Workshop, 2014.

V

Person of Steady Wisdom: The Non-violent Hero in the *Bhagavad Gītā*, Gandhi, and the Quakers

Ecological activists learn to gird themselves to withstand difficult work. To call attention to urgent issues, individuals organise themselves and others. They stage demonstrations that can number from a streetcorner gathering of a handful of people holding signs to hundreds of thousands or even a million protestors. The solitary eco-warrior can also make a major impact. Julia Butterfly, as will be discussed later in this book, lived atop her beloved Luna, a California Redwood, for 738 days. Greta Thunberg has inspired millions with her direct action on behalf of climate change. From where do such leaders find the inner resolve to take on this work? Mahatma Gandhi, perhaps the most documented figure of the twentieth century, drew personally upon the *Bhagavad Gītā*'s teachings to steel himself and to train others who endured tremendous inconvenience and even death for the sake of a greater good. This chapter examines the cultivation of yogic equipoise as an essential tool for those who have taken on the heroic work of effecting systemic change.

The heroic figure in the *Bhagavad Gītā* must exhibit fluency and facility in four Yoga practices: discernment, aplomb, devotion, and meditation. Through discernment or *jñāna-yoga,* one knows that the soul can never be killed. Through aplomb or *karma-yoga,* one is able to hold to one's dignity in the face of humiliation or glory. Through devotion or *bhakti-yoga,* a person devotes heart and soul to a cause higher than oneself. Through mindful meditation one cultivates a place of abiding calm. The simultaneous manifestation of all four Yogas allows a person to dwell in an attitude of non-violence (*ahiṃsā*) at all times, serving as a beacon of safety even in the midst of turmoil.

Mahatma Gandhi was a person in turmoil. While in India, he struggled within his father's home, feeling selfish and lustful as a teenaged newlywed, seeking his own pleasures even when his father was mortally ill. In England, he struggled adapting to a foreign culture. In South Africa, he suffered the indignity of personal insult due to his race. In India, he felt the vast suffering of a nation under the thumb of colonial domination that inflicted famine and misery on millions.

More than two centuries earlier, in the English midlands, George Fox wandered the countryside as a young man, at one point writing 'my body being, as it were, dried up with sorrow, grief and troubles'.[1] As well documented by William James in *Varieties of Religious Experience,* Fox rose from this state of despair into a place of undying purity, eventually establishing the Religious Society of Friends or Quakers. Another Quaker, Benjamin Lay, while in Barbados and Philadelphia, lamented deeply the injustices of slavery and, arising from a similar state of despair, successfully worked against the status quo to effect gradual and lasting change. Both these Quakers were deeply committed to non-violence.

1 George Fox, *The Journal of George Fox,*. ed. Rufus M. Jones (New York: Capricorn Books, 1963), 73.

Gandhi discovered the *Bhagavad Gītā* while in England, which for him became the touchstone, the narrative through which his own story could take on greater meaning. In particular, one portion of the text spoke to him deeply: the last eighteen verses of the second chapter. According to his secretary Narayana Desai, Gandhi recited these verses every day, finding inspiration in their simple meaning: be the best person you can possibly be, at all times and in all circumstances. In these verses Gandhi found a template for the hero. This chapter will examine, in addition to *Bhagavad Gītā* II:59–72, several other passages that similarly describe that exemplary person who is able to maintain dignity and calm in the midst of chaos and difficulty. It will be argued that such a person embodies the non-violence described in the *Yoga Sūtra*, adhering to this core principle regardless of time or circumstance.

> Arjuna asks Kṛṣṇa:
> How can the person of steady wisdom be described,
> that one accomplished in deep meditation?
> How does the person of steady vision speak?
> How does such a one sit and even move?
> The Blessed One responds:
> When a person leaves behind all desires
> that arise in the mind, Arjuna,
> and is contented in the Self with the Self,
> that one is said to be steady in wisdom.
> The person who is not agitated by suffering (*duḥkha*),
> whose yearnings for pleasures has evaporated,
> whose passion, fear, and anger have evaporated,
> that sage, it is said, has become steady in vision.
> One whose passions have been quelled on all sides
> whether encountering anything, whether pleasant or unpleasant,
> who neither rejoices or recoils,
> such a person is established in wisdom.

And when this person can draw away from the objects
 of sense
by recognizing the senses themselves
like a tortoise who draws in all five of its limbs,
such a person is established in wisdom.
For some, the sense objects will recede
but the hunger remains within the body.
Having seen the Supreme, the flavor
and the hunger cease.
Arjuna, even in the case of the resolute person
who has achieved some insight,
the rapacious senses
carry away the mind as if by force.
One who is able to apply restraint on all sides,
who is disciplined, intent on me, should sit
with the senses firmly under control.
Such a person is established in wisdom.
Fixation on objects
generates attachment.
Attachment generates desire.
Desire generates anger.
Anger generates delusion.
From delusion, mindfulness wanders.
From wandering mindfulness arises the loss of one's
 intelligence.
From the loss of intelligence, one perishes.
By giving up desire and hatred
even in the midst of the sense objects
through the control of the self by oneself,
a person attains peace.
This peace generates for that person
the end of all sufferings (*duḥkha*).
The one with a peaceful mind indeed
attains steady intelligence.

There is no intelligence if one is not disciplined.
Without discipline there is no meditation.
Without meditation there can be no tranquility.
Without tranquility, how can there be happiness?
When the mind is governed
by the wandering senses,
all wisdom goes away
like wind drives a ship on the water.
Therefore, O Arjuna of Mighty Arms,
when the senses are gathered inward on all sides
and directed away from objects,
that person is established in wisdom.
When it is night for all other beings,
the adept remains wakeful.
When those beings are wakeful
it is night for the sage who sees.
Just as waters continually enter the ocean
and yet it remains full, unmoving, and still,
so also, all manner of desires can enter but do not disturb
the one who has attained tranquility.
This is not so for those who desire desire.
The person who abandons all desires
moves about free from lust,
free from possessiveness, free from ego.
That person attains tranquility.
This is the godly state, Arjuna.
Having attained this, one is not deluded.
Staying in this even up until the time of death,
one reaches *brahma-nirvāṇa*.[2]

---

2 *Bhagavad Gītā* II:59–72. Translation by author.

This poem-within-a-poem can be parsed into four basic messages, starting with the initial volley of Arjuna's question. Arjuna has been utterly paralysed by his situation. He feels miserable, defeated, confused, and impotent. His world has been so radically shaken by treachery committed by his own cousin-brothers that he cannot move forward. Likewise, Gandhi grapples in his autobiography with his own lust, his feelings of 'less-than', his rage at his own mistreatment and the mistreatment of others, and the seeming enormity of the intransigence of British imperialism. Like Arjuna, he seeks a hero, a template, an exemplar. The words spoken by Kṛṣṇa to Arjuna speak also to Gandhi's condition. So, the first message lies in the opening question: we must look for a way of being in the world that will provide peace and tranquility.

The second message of this *Gītā* portion asks for a reconsideration of the fixity of the external world. The external world 'arrives' because we say it is so, because of agreed-upon conventions about right and wrong, tasty and disgusting, worthy and unworthy. Kṛṣṇa provides a measured critique and analysis of this habitual way of engaging the world. He calls into question the relationship between the senses and the objects of the senses. Kṛṣṇa urges one to 'dial it back', to recognise that a sense object does not exist before the sensory organ (*indriya*) 'lands' upon it, seizes it, and makes it real. Careful direction of the senses can help shape one's emotional relationship with the world. By learning to step back into a place of consideration before, in Nietzsche's words, 'going under', in this case under the thrall of the senses, one can gain a measure of mastery that ultimately leads to self-understanding and self-control.

Third, Kṛṣṇa articulates a cascade of unfortunate consequences that can result if one does not gain self-control. Attachment leads to desire. Thwarted desire leads to anger.

Anger confuses the mind. A confused mind knows no tranquility. The emotional fallout from uncontrolled desire not only can ruin one's day, but can take down entire families, villages, and nations.

Fourth, Kṛṣṇa emphatically declares the possibility of freedom. If one can reverse the outflows of the senses through managing one's emotions, one can become like a still ocean. One can be wakeful in the midst of ignorance. Echoing the description of freedom found in both Buddhism and Sāṃkhya, one can move away from ego fixity and obsession into a state of no ego, no possessions, no lust for the things that bring bondage. In short, the *sthita-prajña*, the person established in wisdom, becomes godlike, attaining *brāhmī-sthiti*, and enters the divine abode of *brahma-nirvāṇa*, a term that describes ascent to a heaven-like transcendent realm, a place where the winds of desire no longer blow.

After the Enlightenment: What to Do, How to Act

In the sixth chapter of the *Gītā*, Kṛṣṇa reiterates the central role of Yoga in bringing about this way of freedom. In Chapters 7 through 10, Kṛṣṇa suggests that Arjuna pursue a devotional route, a theology of incarnationalism, wherein he suggests that Arjuna view the world as an extension of Kṛṣṇa's own body. This method culminates in Chapter 11, where Arjuna witnesses the vast expanse of Kṛṣṇa's cosmic and eternal form, into which all manifestations eventually are drawn, like moths to a flame, to their death. Whereas in Chapter 2, Kṛṣṇa teaches that all souls can never be destroyed, in Chapter 11 he shows Arjuna that all bodies can and will be devoured in the jaws of time. The first ten chapters of the *Gītā* attempt to dislodge Arjuna from his depression through a gospel of positivity. The eleventh chapter performs a very different move. Kṛṣṇa thrusts

Arjuna into a Bosch-like vision of Hell's unavoidability, creating a temporary psychosis that leaves Arjuna stammering, begging to see once more Kṛṣṇa's two armed form.

Though often overlooked, the latter chapters of the *Gītā* provide a sustained examination of how one can learn to live a life of freedom. The following passages, which are much shorter, from Chapters 12, 14, 16, 17, and 18, provide concrete instances of how one can cultivate the life of the *sthita-prajña*, the person of steady wisdom.

Chapter 12 describes the qualities of a *yogī* who is able to abide in tranquility in the midst of all situations, freed from obsession over possessive identitarianism.

> 13 The one beyond hate who shows loving kindness
> and compassion for all beings,
> free From 'mine! mine!' and free from ego,
> unruffled in suffering or happiness, patient:
>
> 14 That *yogī*, who is content at all time,
> whose self is controlled, whose resolve is firm,
> that person, whose mind and intelligence are fixed on me,
> that person who is devoted to me is dear to me.
>
> 16 The one who is of even eye, pure, capable,
> neutral, free from wanting things to be a certain way,
> who has given up all baggage,
> devoted to me, is dear to me.
>
> 17 The one who neither elates nor hates,
> neither mourns nor hankers,
> giving up obsession over purity or impurity,
> full of devotion: that one is dear to me.
>
> 18 The same whether with an enemy or a friend,
> the same in honor and disgrace,

in heat or old, happiness or suffering,
free from attachment,

19 maintaining equipoise when blamed or praised,
content with whatever happens,
without fixed abode yet steady minded,
full of devotion: that one is dear to me.[3]

Kṛṣṇa encourages Arjuna to adapt a stance of neutrality in the midst of life's vicissitudes. To remain unruffled in the midst of difficulty communicates a stance of ease and peace that can calm the anxious. Similarly, to accept without undue elation life's happy moments can help prevent an exuberance that can lead to an inevitable let-down. Trudy Goodman, a teacher of Buddhist meditation, tells the story of going to her Korean Zen master with the good news of her abiding sense of joy and peace and happiness. His reply: 'Don't worry. It won't last!'

The Three *Guṇas*

The three *guṇas*, introduced in the second chapter of the *Gītā* II.45, describe the changes and fluctuations of states of being, cycling through heaviness and lethargy (*tamas*), action (*rajas*), and buoyant illumination (*sattva*). Kṛṣṇa advises Arjuna to recognise these qualities and to simply observe that whatever happens, it is 'merely the *guṇas* working on the *guṇas*' (III:28). In the fourteenth chapter, Arjuna asks for details, wanting to know the 'qualities of the one who has gone beyond the three *guṇas*'. Just as he had asked for Kṛṣṇa to describe the qualities of the enlightened sage in Chapter 2, he now asks for a description of the conduct (*ācāra*) of the one who goes beyond the three *guṇas* (*trīn guṇān ativartate* XIV:21). In language

3 *Bhagavad Gītā* XII:13–14, 16–19.

that echoes the earlier descriptions, Kṛṣṇa states that such a person not only goes beyond the dualities of the positive and the negative, but transcends the tripartite qualities of 'illumination, activity, and delusion (*prakāśa, pravṛtti, moha* XIV:22)' neither hating (*dveṣṭi*) nor desiring (*kāṅkṣati*) their appearance. Knowing that it is 'only the *guṇas* working' (*guṇā vartanta ity eva* XIV:23) that person 'stands firm, not wavering' (*avatiṣṭhati na iṅgate* XIV:23). Kṛṣṇa then returns to the negation of all dualisms, proclaiming that this person remains the same in the midst of suffering and happiness, love and disdain, blame and praise. However, Kṛṣṇa also includes an allusion to a threefold distinction that might correlate to the *guṇas* here as well: a lump of earth, which may refer to *tamas*, a stone, which might refer to *rajas*, and gold, which might correlate to *sattva*. Similarly, Kṛṣṇa offers one more threefold description of how the person who has transcended the *guṇas* operates: equanimous in honour and dishonour (*tamas*), equanimous whether with friends or enemies (*rajas*), and renouncing all attachment to all undertakings (*sattva*) (XIV:25).

Chapter 16 gives specific qualities that characterise one with 'divine endowment' (*saṃpadam daivīm*).

1 No fear, purity of *sattva*,
standing persistently in the Yoga of knowledge,
practicing giving, self-control, and sacrifice,
study of Self, austerity, appropriate behavior,

2 non-violence, truth, no fear,
giving up attachment, manifesting tranquility,
without ill words,
compassion for beings, without craving,
kind, modest, and steady,

3 vigorous, patient, firm, pure,
without malice, without excessive pride,

this, Arjuna, is your birthright,
this divine endowment.[4]

At the centre we find the quality of non-violence, *ahiṃsā*, the epitome of the most refined and dignified way of engaging the world. These qualities in the aggregate define *sattva*, the mode of being in the world that brings one closest to the pure witness, the consciousness that give purpose to all experience. Through careful observance of these behaviours, one moves into the paradigm of the spiritual hero.

Non-violence (*Ahiṃsā*) and the *Sattva-Guṇa*

The practice of non-violence finds mention again in the seventeenth chapter, along with many other salubrious qualities that describe the *sattva-guṇa*. This sequence begins with praise of a reverential attitude (*pūjana*) toward gods and priests and teachers of wisdom, accompanied with purity, appropriate behaviour and comportment, and non-violence. These are called bodily austerity. Next Kṛṣṇa describes austerity of speech as calming words which are truthful, lovely, and beneficial, informed by the study and practice of sacred texts. Kṛṣṇa concludes this triad with a discussion of austerities of the mind, which include cultivation of peace, gentleness, self-restraint, silence, and purity. All these austerities (*tapas*) of body, speech, and mind further emphasise the role of self-development in the practice of moving Arjuna's experience of the world from one of helplessness, despair, and alienation into one of constructive engagement.

Two verses at the end of chapter 17 encapsulate Krishna's message to Arjuna:

4 *Bhagavad Gītā* 16.1–3.

26 The word truth (*sat*) refers to a state of being (*sadbhāva*)
and a state of goodness (*sādhubhāva*).
Thus, Pārtha (Arjuna), the sound of Sat itself
is implied in every praiseworthy action (*praśaste karmaṇi*).

27 Sat is also said to be found
in sacrifice, austerity, and generosity (*yajña, tapas, dāna.*)
Every action directed toward this purpose
can be seen as Sat.

These verses contain an abundance of sage advice to Arjuna: Be true. Manifest goodness. Do not fear sacrifice or austerity. Be generous. To paraphrase the words of Shakespeare, 'to your own (best) self be true'.[5]

These many exhortations urging Arjuna to move toward a place of greater light and lightness are accompanied with various warnings about the results of self-interested action (*rajas*) as well as lethargy and doubt (*tamas*). However, by the eighteenth and final chapter, the teachings have been conveyed and received. Arjuna has been prepared to take the next step of re-entering the field of *dharma*, the realm of activity, in a heroic state of mind. Three qualities predominate: sacrifice, giving, and austerity. Arjuna no longer acts from a place of self interest. Rather than stewing in memories of regret and fear of the future, he is prepared to act and to give freely. Furthermore, he is prepared to give up the fruits of his action, leaving behind all doubt. He has become freed from attachment and ego, steady, resolute, and unconcerned with success or failure (XVIII:26) which allows him to declare: 'I stand here now with my doubts dispelled, my delusion

5 Polonius speaking to Hamlet, *Hamlet*, Act I, Scene III.

destroyed. I have regained my memory and am now ready to do what you command' (XVIII:73).

The enduring question remains: how can Arjuna enter this horrific battle yet remain grounded in the place of non-violence? This chilling contradiction was addressed by Mahatma Gandhi in a very specific way. He came to regard the epic tale as a metaphorical inspiration to place oneself into the state of pure *sattva* to undertake any action. Gandhi advocates emulating the warrior who remains unruffled. He cultivated and taught a profound commitment to do no harm. He forged a new pathway for effecting social change, one that has proven effective in so many social change movements. Since the precedent of Gandhi's example, three major changes have utilised this method to effect lasting improvement: the civil rights in the United States of America, the replacement of the Marcos regime in the Philippines, and the disassembly of apartheid in South Africa. Martin Luther King, Jr. and Nelson Mandela evoked and invoked the journey of the non-violent hero as exemplified by Gandhi.[6]

To be non-violent, one must abide in a place of lightness and luminosity, within the modality of the *sattva-guṇa*. One ascends to this state through abandoning self-interest. Gandhi has written:

> Even in 1888–89, when I first became acquainted with the Gita, I felt that it was not a historical work, but that, under the guise of physical warfare, it described a duel that perpetually went on in the hearts of mankind, and that physical warfare was brought in merely to make the description of the internal duel more alluring. ... The author of the Mahabharata

6 Peter Ackerman, and Jack DuVall, *A Force More Powerful: A Century of Nonviolent Conflict* (New York: Palgrave, 2000), 395.

> has not established the necessity of physical warfare; on the contrary he has proved its futility.[7]

For Gandhi, the primary message of the *Gītā* lies in the renunciation of attachment to outcomes: 'One should work without selfish motives. The state of mind in which such motives will have disappeared most is the *sattvic* state',[8] that 'When there is no desire for fruit, there is no temptation for untruth or *himsa*'.[9] Non-violence can proceed when one dwells in *sattva*.

Gandhi and the Journey of the Non-violent Hero

This chapter began with reflections on the life and dilemma of Mahatma Gandhi and how the *Bhagavad Gītā* inspired him to become a non-violent leader. Arjuna, who took up arms, suffered the loss of his three sons, and eventually fell willfully to his death. Arjuna descended into the depths of hell before being rescued by his eldest brother and restored to the realm of his father Indra. In contrast, Gandhi chose to make the first precept of Yoga, *ahiṃsā*, his primary concern and path. Taking to heart the proclamation that *ahiṃsā* is the highest *dharma*, he designed a campaign for personal and national freedom that required steady enactment over a long period. As set forth in the *Yoga Sūtra*, he recognised that just as it took many years or perhaps many lifetimes to arrive in his current mental and bodily state, which he sought to purify through Yoga and diet, so also he recognised that British colonialism had gained its

7 Mahatma Gandhi, *The Bhagavad Gita according to Gandhi: Text and Commentary. Translated from Gujarati* ed. John Stohmeier (Berkeley: North Atlantic Books, 2009).

8 Ibid., 190.

9 Ibid., xxii.

momentum over the course of many decades. It would take decades for Gandhi to find the fortitude within himself to rise to a position of leadership, and it would take decades of sustained action to undo the injustices wrought by the British.

Operating from the Upaniṣadic adage of *so'ham* or 'I am that', Gandhi sought to style himself after the spiritual hero as defined in the *Bhagavad Gītā*. He regularly engaged in study, chanting, fasting, and reflection. He strengthened his body and mind by performing austerities. He also did this in a very public manner, maintaining correspondence with perhaps hundreds of people, keeping journals, publishing essays, and giving interviews that interwove his own personal quest for freedom with his desires for India's economic and political freedom. He emulated the best qualities as he learned them from the *Bhagavad Gītā* and wished the same for the people of India and beyond. He sought restitution and change in the face of injustice.

George Fox and Non-violence

Mahatma Gandhi (1869–1948) was influenced during his time in England and South Africa by several members of the Christian faith. Thomas Merton suggests: 'It was through his acquaintance with writers like Tolstoy and Thoreau, and his reading of the New Testament, that Gandhi rediscovered his own tradition and his Hindu *dharma* (religion, duty).'[10] Perhaps the one branch of Christianity most closely associated with non-violence in the Christian world is the Religious Society of Friends, popularly known as the Quakers. Established by George Fox in the seventeenth century, the Quaker narrative

10 Thomas Merton, ed., *Gandhi on Non-Violence: A Selection from the Writings of Mahatma Gandhi. Edited and with an Introduction* (New York: New Directions, 1964), 4.

parallels Gandhi's path in several ways. These include a commitment to truth and non-violence, as well as willingness to sacrifice one's freedom for the cause of a greater good. Women played important leadership roles in the Religious Society of Friends. Many women convened silent meetings for worship in their homes clandestinely in the early years of the movement, among them the widow Margaret Fell who eventually took Fox as her husband. Sarah Grimke (1792–1873) converted to Quakerism in 1821 while living in Philadelphia and became an outspoken advocate for both Abolition and Women's Rights. Elizabeth Cady Stanton (1815–1902), another Quaker woman, joined forces with Susan B. Anthony (1820–1906) in Rochester, New York, to campaign for women's suffrage, the next major cause to arise following Abolition. Following World War One, Quakers were instrumental in gaining conscientious objector status for individuals whose conscience forbade participation in warfare. Many Quakers endured imprisonment because of activism to end the Vietnam War. During the U.S. invasion and occupation of Iraq that began in 2003 and lasted until 2011, a team of Quaker citizen ambassadors attempted to negotiate peace. Tom Fox (b. 1951) was held hostage and killed on March 6, 2006, making the ultimate sacrifice.[11]

Two non-violent heroes of the Quaker movement will be profiled here, George Fox (1624–1691) and Benjamin Lay (1682–1759), not as Gandhians or adherents to the teachings of the *Bhagavad Gītā*, but as examples of heroes of non-violence who share affinity with Gandhi and the *Gītā*.

George Fox underwent a prolonged spiritual quest as a young man, wandering from village to village, questioning and challenging the authorities of the day. His disruption of

---

11 Patrick O'Neill, 'Quaker Hostage Killed in Iraq', *Indy Week*, 15 March 2006. https://indyweek.com/news/quaker-hostage-killed-iraq.

Church of England services resulted in years of imprisonment. He described his apotheosis as follows: 'I knew nothing but pureness, and innocence, and righteousness; being renewed into the image of God by Christ Jesus, to the state of Adam, which he was in before he fell. The creation was opened to me; and it was showed to me how all things had their names given them according to their nature and virtue' (97). Due to his convincement that he had risen above a life of sin, he was imprisoned several times for blasphemy. He was accused of being 'taken up in the raptures' while speaking in the town of Derby in 1650, to which he replied when asked if sanctified: 'Yes; for I am in the paradise of God. Then they asked me if I had no sin. I answered, "Christ my Saviour has taken away my sin".' (120–121). He was sentenced to six months in jail and when he refused to admit any sinfulness and continued to speak with others, his jail term was extended for nearly another six months. While in Derby Jail he convinced his jailers to spare the life a woman condemned to death for stealing. He wrote in his journal: 'they could not endure to hear of purity, and of victory over sin and the devil. They said they could not believe any could be free from sin on this side of the grave' (123). At one point they offered to release him so that he could participate in armed rebellion with the forces of Cromwell against King Charles Stuart, to which he replied: 'I lived in the virtue of that life and power that took away the occasion of all wars', that he 'was come into the covenant of peace, which was before wars and strifes were' (128). He refused to fight and remained in jail.

Two years later Fox was imprisoned again, this time in Carlisle with the threat of death because of his blasphemy and heresy. In 1656 he was jailed in Launceston where he endured filth and hunger and cold for refusing to doff his hat. In 1661, several Quakers were killed in Boston. When George asked

Simon Broadstreet, a New England magistrate, why, he was told: 'They were subject to the laws of England, and had put our Friends to death by the same law that the Jesuits were put to death in England' (378). In 1662 Fox was jailed in Leicester for refusing to swear an oath. By 1666, it is estimated that at least 4500 Friends were imprisoned in England and Wales for their beliefs.

Fox also undertook fasting as a spiritual practice, noting in 1653 that 'I was in a fast for about ten days, my spirit being greatly exercised on Truth's behalf' (180). Fox was imprisoned under the rule of Cromwell but argued successfully for his release. Cromwell was favourably impressed that Fox was a teetotaler. After the death of Cromwell, Fox was imprisoned in Lancaster by the order of those serving King Charles II. He eventually spent two years in America (1671–1673). In December 1673 he was imprisoned in Worcester, where he stayed in jail for fourteen months, despite the pleas of his wife directly to King Charles II. After recovering from ill health inflicted by his long incarcerations, he continued to work tirelessly, traveling to Holland and elsewhere to give witness to the Inner Light and to advocate peace. On 16 May 1686, King James II issued an edict ordering the release of the thousands of Quakers who were imprisoned for denying the teachings of original sin, for not swearing oaths, and for not attending the Church of England. Fox died on 13 January 1691. In the words of Friend Rufus Jones (1863–1948): 'Few men in the dying hour could say more truly, "I am clear".' (578).

With the conquests of the New World, enslavement of non-white peoples robbed millions of once-free people of their dignity. Fox witnessed this emergence first hand by visiting the American colonies in 1671 and 1672. He urged that 'after certain years of servitude, they would make them free' (491, footnote). He was hosted by Native Americans in what is now southern New Jersey, before any white settlement there.

Persecuted Quakers later founded Pennsylvania and, though they undoubtedly played a role in the displacement of native peoples, Quaker educators were instrumental in the survival of the Seneca Nation on the Allegheny River near the current city of Salamanca in New York State's Southern Tier following their devastating defeat during the Revolutionary War.

Benjamin Lay: A Quaker Voice against Slavery

Benjamin Lay, who was born during the lifetime of George Fox into a third-generation Quaker family, benefitted from the mercantile success of the Quakers and, having left his hometown of Essex at the age of 21, lived at sea for months at a time. As noted by historian Marcus Rediker, 'during an 18-month sojourn as a shopkeeper in Barbados, he saw an enslaved man kill himself rather than submit to yet another whipping; that and myriad other barbarities in that British colony both traumatised him and drove his passion for antislavery'.[12] He and wife Sarah Smith were both 'little people'. They eventually settled in Philadelphia in 1732 where he was shocked at the presence of slavery in William Penn's 'Holy Experiment', the largest city in North America, home to the world's second largest number of Friends. Lay began to stage protests of slavery in Quaker meetings. 'Conscious of the hard, exploited labor that went into making commodities such as tobacco and sugar… he protested slave labor, luxury, and the poor health caused by smoking'.[13] He smashed clay pipes in the midst of silent worship, one directed at the male elders, the other at

12 Marcus Rediker, 'The Cave-Dwelling Vegan Who Took on Quaker Slavery and Won', *Smithsonian* 48, no. 5 (2017): 40.

13 Ibid., 39.

female elders, and a third at all those gathered. In winter, he stood barefoot in the snow to protest poor treatment of slaves and, when ejected from one Quaker meeting for disruptive behavior, 'lay down in the mud, requiring every person leaving the meeting to step over his body'.[14] He wrote a book in protest of slavery called *All Slave-Keepers that Keep the Innocent in Bondage* that was published by his friend Benjamin Franklin. It includes such passages as: 'Your Fathers have built a Wall of Iniquity, and you are daubing it with untampered Mortar, for in Keeping Slaves & pleading for it; O vile and shameless practice, which we ought to be separated from... here the Leprosy spreads, and spreads more and more.'[15] This book became a 'founding text of Atlantic antislavery and an important advance in abolitionist thought. No one had ever taken such a militant, uncompromising, universal stand against slavery'.[16]

Spurned by leadership of the Quaker faith of his birth, Lay took up farming in Abington, Pennsylvania, where he and his wife cultivated an orchard of fruit and nut trees, grew vegetables, and crafted a cave home, surviving on fruits, vegetables, milk, and water. Similar to Gandhi, he refused to eat flesh and made his own clothes to avoid exploitive labour practices. When he was 76 years old, a delegation of Friends visited him to share that a resolution had been affirmed disowning slave-holding Quakers. He declared: 'I can now die in peace' and passed the following year.

---

14 Ibid., 39.

15 Benjamin Lay, *All Slave-Keepers that Keep the Innocent in Bondage* (New York: Arno Press and New York Times, [1746] 1969), 120.

16 Rediker, 'The Cave-Dwelling Vegan Who Took on Quaker Slavery and Won', 40.

Prisoners of Conscience

Gandhi endured numerous imprisonments, both in South Africa and in India. Having been inspired by the example provided by Ralph Waldo Emerson's 1854 essay 'Civil Disobedience', he saw being jailed as a public demonstration of conscience and used it repeatedly to draw attention to injustice. Eco-activist William Cottrell (b. 1980) was imprisoned for nearly five years for destroying gas-guzzling SUVs at a Southern California Hummer dealership in 2003.[17] His case brought heightened awareness to profligate lack of efficiency in SUVs. The Hummer, which was released by General Motors in 1992, was discontinued in 2010. Numerous other examples of environmentalists serving prison time could be cited, as well as horrific stories, particularly in the Amazon where eco-activists have been killed.

Gandhi also drew inspiration from John Ruskin (1819–1900), who wrote movingly of the plight of the working person in his book *Unto This Last* (1860) and Leo Tolstoy (1821–1910). Tolstoy had been in correspondence with Quakers. Tolstoy published *The Kingdom of God Is Within You* in 1894 and supported Gandhi's use of civil disobedience as a strategy to achieve change. Gandhi was put in jail or held in house arrest more than a dozen times and used these occasions for study and writing. By enduring these confinements without dismay he provided a living example of the *sthita-prajña*, a person of steady wisdom.

Gandhi, Fox, and Lay endured hardship due to their heartfelt commitment to the uplift of others. Like Arjuna, as advised

17 Ed Leibowitz, 'The Accidental Eco-Terrorist: How after a Night of Vandalizing SUVs a Gifted Caltech Student Became a Threat to Homeland Security', *Los Angeles Times Magazine*, 1 May 2005.

by Kṛṣṇa, they found inner strength in order to bring about change. Whereas Arjuna was impelled to take up arms to protect the peace, Gandhi and the Quakers found inner peace in order to, in the words of George Fox, go to the 'covenant of peace, which was before wars and strifes', a place from which one could speak with higher authority and which gave one the power to persevere in the face of great adversity.

Many passages in the *Gītā* describe the need for sacrifice, the need to perform austerity. These two key practices, *yajña* and *tapas*, generate the heat required to effect true change. Gandhi employed fasting and truthfulness as key tools in bringing attention to great injustice against his own personhood, the rights of Indians in South Africa, the rights of workers, women, and low-caste labourers in India. George Fox worked tirelessly against hypocrisy, speaking truth to power and living an example of a purified, perhaps perfected life, free from guile, free from all intoxicants, free from fear. Benjamin Lay used theatrical techniques to advocate for the freedom of slaves, allowing his own body to be stepped upon and abused, forgoing his own comfort so that others may flourish.

Each of these examples of the non-violent hero demonstrate through their life and labour the four forms of Yoga found in the *Bhagavad Gītā*: discernment, aplomb, devotion, and meditation. Discernment or Knowledge Yoga arose from apt observation of social ills that called for redress and correction. Aplomb or Karma Yoga gave each hero his sense of working for a higher purpose without regard for the pain and difficulty inflicted on his own body and mind in the process. Devotional Yoga can be found in each individual's staunch dedication to the transcendent, referred to by Gandhi as Ram, and by Fox and Lay as the Inner Light. And, finally, each nurtured a life oriented around and grounded in regular meditative practice. For Gandhi, the daily chanting and recitation of the *Gītā* nourished his sense of connection. The silent worship developed by George Fox as he created the Religious Society of Friends remains a rather unique example of Christian meditation that can be experienced and understood and shared by members of any faith.

The heroic journey on the path of non-violence combines the bravery required of a soldier with the insight cultivated within a sage. Great patience, forbearance and fortitude, and convincement of one's commitment to truth are all essential for success. Gandhi's heroic commitment to non-violent passive resistance has inspired generations of activists. Eleanor Roosevelt (1886–1962), moved deeply by the sufferings she witnessed in her childhood and through both World Wars, chaired the committee that issued the United Nations Declaration of Human Rights in 1948. Its preamble states that: 'recognition of the inherent dignity and of the equal and inalienable rights of all members of the human family is the foundation of freedom, justice, and peace in the world.' These words, which continue to inform and inspire people of good conscience worldwide, can be perhaps seen in the appeal to inclusivity from the *Bhagavad Gītā* that proclaims goodness 'in all women, in merchants, and in all workers'.[18] Gandhi, Fox, and Lay worked assiduously to cultivate this vision and steady wisdom.

Adapted with permission from Christopher Key Chapple. 'The Nonviolent Hero in the Bhagavad Gītā, Gandhi, and the Quakers'. *Journal of Vaishnava Studies* 26, no. 2 (Spring 2018): 99–114.

18 *Bhagavad Gītā*, ix, 32.

Discussion Topic: The Non-violent Hero

- Mahatma Gandhi, George Fox, and Benjamin Lay all endured periods of imprisonment due to their strongly held beliefs. Discuss parallel sacrifices made by contemporary climate activists. Consider researching the work of Julia Butterfly, who endured a self-imposed 'imprisonment' atop a 1500-year-old redwood tree for 738 days.

- How might equanimity be required as humans face ongoing climate catastrophes such as coastal erosion and forest fires?

- What parallels might be seen between the experience of *samādhi* in Yoga and the Inner Light of the Quakers?

Further Reading

Peter Ackerman and Jack DuVall. *A Force More Powerful: A Century of Nonviolent Conflict*. New York: Palgrave, 2000.

George Fox. *The Journal of George Fox*. Edited by Rufus M. Jones. New York: Capricorn Books, 1963.

Mahatma Gandhi. *The Bhagavad Gita According to Gandhi. Text and Commentary Translated from Gujarati*. John Stohmeier, ed. Berkeley: North Atlantic Books, 2009.

Benjamin Lay. *All Slave-Keepers that Keep the Innocent in Bondage*. 1736. Reprint: New York: Arno Press and the New York Times, 1969.

Thomas Merton, ed. *Gandhi on Non-Violence: A Selection from the Writings of Mahatma Gandhi. Edited and with an Introduction*. New York: New Directions, 1964.

Marcus Rediker, 'The Cave-Dwelling Vegan Who Took on Quaker Slavery and Won'. *Smithsonian* 48, no. 5 (2017): 34–41.

VI
Yoga and Ecology

In its various manifestations, Yoga includes practices and philosophical positions that accord with values espoused by modern ecologists. Unlike many other schools of thought in India, Yoga is thoroughly realistic. It builds upon the Sāṃkhya school of philosophy, attributed to the legendary sage named Kapila who is said to have lived in northeastern India or southern Nepal. The birthplace of the Buddha, Kapilavastu, is considered by some to be named after this philosopher. Kapila's teachings were later systematised by a philosopher known as Īśvarakṛṣṇa, who composed the *Sāṃkhya Kārikā* in the early centuries of the common era. In this seminal text, the author exerts great care to articulate the existence and importance of the natural world. He posits that the world is known to us through its effects, and the effects stem from a common cause, *prakṛti*, a term that many scholars choose to translate as 'nature'. Nature provides experience and liberation for her silent observer, the spiritual consciousness or *puruṣa*. According to the *Sāṃkhya Kārikā*, all things exist for the purpose of serving and liberating this consciousness. Through understanding the creative force known as nature, one advances toward a state of freedom. To understand the structures and purposes of things one must cultivate a state of nonattachment that, from the perspective of this philosophy, entails a state of appreciation and respect, not disdain and abnegation for nature.

The *Yoga Sūtra* of Patañjali (*c.* 350 CE) outlines an eightfold practice to ascend toward the state of self-realisation through which one realises one's connection with the universe. The underlying philosophy of Yoga places great value on feeling the connection between one's self and the larger world of nature. This continuity becomes celebrated in the term *samādhi*, the goal of Yoga, which describes an experience of non-difference between oneself, one's sensory and mental processes, and the world. As described by Patañjali, the practitioner of Yoga becomes like a clear jewel, with 'unity among grasper, grasping, and grasped'.[1] This state of consciousness allows one to melt into one's surrounding and in the process diminish and eventually reverse past tendencies (*saṃskāras*) bringing one to a state of clarity and immediacy.

The eight practices identified by Patañjali can be seen in light of environmental ethics. The beginning stage of Yoga includes five ethical practices (*yama*), held in common with the Jain tradition. First and foremost, Patañjali discusses nonviolence (*ahiṃsā*), which entails not harming any living being by thought, action, or assent to harmfulness. This precept advocates the protection of all forms of life, and certainly can be applied to cultivating an attitude of respect toward individual creatures as well as ecosystems. To support this discipline, Patañjali includes four additional vows. Truthfulness (*satya*) can be used to inspire acknowledgement of wrongdoing to the living realm. Not stealing (*asteya*) can be applied to remedy the imbalance of resource consumption in modern times. Sexual restraint (*brahamacarya*) can be used as a corrective to the crass commercialisation of sex as well as for population control. Non-possession (*aparigraha*) allows one to minimise the greed and hoarding that has plundered the planet. These five prac-

1 *Yoga Sūtra* I:41.

tices entail holding back, disciplining oneself, saying no to such behaviours as violence, lying, stealing, lust, and possessiveness.

The second stage of Patañjali's Yoga seeks to cultivate positive behaviours that can similarly be interpreted through the prism of heightened ecological awareness. Five practices are listed. Purity (*śauca*) can be seen in terms of keeping one's body, thoughts, and intentions clean in regard to one's surroundings. Contentment (*santoṣa*) encourages a philosophy of accepting what is 'enough' and not striving to gather more than one truly needs. Austerity (*tapas*) entails putting oneself in difficult situations for the purposes of purification and the building of strong character. Self study (*svādhyāya*) generally entails reading and reflecting on philosophical texts, which in the case of environmental applications might include reading poets. Surrender or devotion to god (*īśvara-praṇidhāna*) for an environmentalist might encourage regular forays into the wilderness to feel that important connection with the awe that nature inspires. Each of these serves as a touchstone for self-exploration and appreciation of one's place within the world.

The third phase of Patañjali's eightfold system, the practice of yoga postures (*āsana*) receives relatively scant mention in the *Yoga Sūtra*. Patañjali states that the purpose of performing the physical exercise of Yoga is to gain 'steadiness and ease, resulting in relaxation of effort and endless unity'.[2] In later centuries, this aspect of Yoga was adumbrated and expanded by later writers, who draw extensive parallels between the practice of physical Yoga and the ability to see one's relationship with the animal realm.

In order to understand the significance of animals as it develops in later Yoga traditions, we need to discuss briefly the nature of shamanism. Mircea Eliade describes the importance

---

2 *Yoga Sūtra* II.46–47.

of shamanic rituals that display intimacy with specific animals as follows:

> Imitating the gait of an animal or putting on its skin was acquiring a superhuman mode of being... by becoming this mythic animal, man becomes something far greater and stronger than himself.... He who, forgetting the limitations and false measurements of humanity, could rightly imitate the behavior of animals – their gait, breathing, cries, and so on – found a new dimension in life: spontaneity, freedom, 'sympathy' with all the cosmic rhythms and hence bliss and immortality.[3]

These remarks by Eliade underscore the important relationship cultivated between humans and animals from prehistoric times. Animals were noted for their particular abilities and accomplishments. To imitate these fine qualities was considered a sign of spiritual attainment.

In the later Yoga texts, animals play an important role. Many postures (*āsanas*) carry the names of animals. The *Haṭha-yoga-pradīpikā*, written by Svātmārāma in the fifteenth century, lists several poses named for animals. Some examples are the cow head's pose (*gomukhāsana*), the tortoise pose (*kūrmāsana*), the rooster pose (*kukkuṭāsana*), the peacock pose (*mayūrāsana*), and the lion's pose (*siṃhāsana*).[4]

Additionally, later Yoga manuals such as the *Gheraṇḍa Saṃhitā* include several additional poses named for animals, including the serpent pose (*nāgāsana*), the rabbit pose (*śaśāsana*), the cobra pose (*bhujaṅgāsana*), the locust pose (*śalabhāsana*), the crow pose (*kākāsana*), the eagle pose (*garuḍāsana*), the frog

---

3 Mircea Eliade, *Shamanism: Archaic Techniques of Ecstasy* (Princeton: Princeton University Press, 1963), 460.

4 *Haṭha-yoga-pradīpikā* 20, 24, 25, 32, 52–54, respectively.

pose (*maṇḍūkāsana*), and the scorpion pose (*vṛścikāsana*), to name a few.

Yoga practice does have an emotional effect that goes beyond mere strength or flexibility of the body. In the performance of the peacock pose, one feels a sense of balance, a sense of pride, an affirmation of one's ability to move competently in the world. In the eagle pose, one feels a sense of entwinedness and focus, a honing of one's vision and purpose. In the cobra pose, one feels both a tremendous gravity and a rising up, a sense of being weighted and glued to the earth, yet yearning and stretching to rise above. In the lion pose one feels positively regal, refreshed and energised. At the close of a Yoga session one feels renewed and in a sense redefined, prepared to encounter the world with greater agility and balance.

In India, animals are part of one's everyday reality, even in the cities. One encounters cows, goats, cats, dogs, and numerous other animals on a daily, sometimes continuous basis. People often feed birds before taking their own meal, birds that fly into the home at dinner time, expecting acknowledgement. Gurāṇi Añjali, a contemporary teacher of Yoga, has urged her students to observe animals, to learn from animals. One has a sense that the attention required to move into and sustain a yoga pose carries a connection with the ancient shamanic tradition of animal imitation.

However, it could also be argued that a danger lies in over-romanticising the mysterious or shamanic aspects of animal mimesis. For instance, Denise Kaufman, a prominent yoga teacher in Los Angeles, suggests that one adapt a largely empirical attitude toward doing yoga and relating with animals. In an interview she commented:

> Animals move; people can learn about movement from animals. House pets stretch all day long, creating space in their joints. Animals sit in different kinds of positions. Monkeys

> and apes do things with their hands. Perhaps as humans we need to reclaim our four leggedness. Getting down on all fours stimulates the pranic flow. Sitting in chairs tightens the hamstrings and the lower back. Animals don't sit on furniture; they have not built things contrary to their nature.[5]

From her perspective, Yoga involves recapturing our animal physicality, reconditioning the body to establish itself within a non-technologically enhanced modality.

The relationship between sacred power and the human cannot be divorced from harnessing the deep images evoked by intimacy with the animal world. Early peoples of India revered animals. They depicted animals in tableaus of adornment. They surrounded their early sacred meditating *yogī* with animals. Animals find prominence in classical literature. The later medieval Yoga texts explicitly prescribe animal poses as integral to mystical attainment.

We learn to be empathetic and connected from our experience of and relationship with animals. As Thomas Berry has noted, our consciousness as humans, as well as our development and affectivity, radically depend upon our openness and sensitivity to the natural order. To the extent that Yoga heightens our senses and brings us into visceral relationship with the non-human realm, our own sense of worth, well-being, and connectedness becomes enhanced.

Following the mastery of the physical realm through Yoga postures, one reaches the capacity to effectively control the breath (*prāṇāyāma*), the fourth phase of Yoga. As noted earlier, the breath plays an important role in the philosophy of the Upaniṣads, and in the *Yoga Sūtra* the mastery of the inbreath

---

5 Denise Kaufman, personal communication, February 1999.

and outbreath leads to 'dissolving the covering of light'.[6] The *Haṭha-yoga-pradīpikā* and the *Gheraṇḍa Saṃhitā* describe intricate techniques for manipulating the breath. Through this process, one reaches into the core of one's life force, sees the relationship between breathing and thinking, and cultivates an inwardness and stability. This leads to Patañjali's fifth phase, the command of the senses (*pratyāhāra*). This ability to draw one's energy into oneself opens one to the higher 'inner' practices of Yoga: concentration, meditation, and *samādhi*, collectively known as *saṃyama*. Construed through an ecological prism, the inner work from controlling the breath to *samādhi* can be seen as enhancing one's sensitivity to nature. This may produce an increase in empathy, and a willingness to stand to protect the beauty of the Earth. In a sense, the culmination of Yoga leads one to the very beginning point of non-violence, a sense that no harm must be allowed.

The beginning of this inner three-fold process requires sustained exercises of concentration (*dhāraṇā*). A standard concentration practice entails attention given first to the great elements (*mahābhūtas*), then to the sensory operations (*tanmātras*), the sense and action organs (*buddhīndriyas* and *karmendriyas*), and finally to the threefold operation of the mind (*manas, ahaṃkāra, buddhi*). By concentrating on the earth (*pṛthivī*) one gains a sense of groundedness and a heightened sense of fragrance. By reflecting on water (*jala*), one develops familiarity with fluidity and sensitivity to the vehicle of taste. Through attention to light and heat (*tejas, agni*), one arrives at a deep appreciation for the ability to see. Awareness of the breath and wind (*prāṇa, vāyu*) brings a sense of quiet and tactile receptivity. All these specific manifestations occur within the context of space (*ākāśa*), the womb or container of all that can be perceived or heard.

---

6 *Yoga Sūtra*, II:52.

Intimacy with the sensory process allows one to maintain focus on the operations of the mind. Thoughts (*citta-vṛtti*) generated in the mind lead one to question and investigate the source of one's identity and ego (*ahaṃkāra*). Probing more deeply into the constituent parts of one's personality, one begins to uncover the maze and mire of karmic accretions housed in the deep memory structures (*buddhi*), which can be lightened and released gently through reflective and meditative processes. However, in order for any of these purifications to arise, an intimate familiarity with the body and collection of habits must occur, an intimacy that takes place through an understanding of time and place. Yoga enables a person to embrace and understand the close connection between the body and the world. By understanding each, one attains a state of clarity.

From an ecological perspective, the practice of Yoga can prove beneficial. Through Yoga, one can begin to see the importance of the food we eat in constructing our bodies. One can find a calmness of mind through which to appreciate the stunning beauty of landscape, sunset, and sunrise. Through Yoga, one can understand that all things within the universe rely on the creative expression of the five great elements and that we gain access to all experience and all knowledge through our own sensuality and intuition. The practice of Yoga provides rich resources for persons to reconnect with the body and with the world. Through the insights and applications of Yoga, one can begin to live with the sensitivity, sensibility, and frugality required to uphold the dignity of life, stemming from a vision of the interconnectedness of all things.

Adapted with permission from Christopher Key Chapple. 'Yoga and Ecology'. In *Encyclopedia of Religion and Nature*, edited by Bron R. Taylor, 1782–1785. London: Continuum, 2005.

Discussion Topic: Yoga and Ecology

- Experiment with the Yoga poses described in this chapter. How might you relate to animals differently through their performance? How might your own moods change when doing Yoga postures and breathing exercises?
- How might the ethics of Yoga be engaged in relationship to sound ecological practices?
- How might the meditative aspects of Yoga foster a sense of nature connection?

Further Reading

Christopher Key Chapple, ed. *Yoga and Ecology: Dharma for the Earth*. Hampton, Virginia: Deepak Heritage Books, 2009.

Christopher Key Chapple. *Yoga and the Luminous: Patañjali's Spiritual Path to Freedom*. Albany, NY: State University of New York Press, 2008.

Raj Balkaran. *The Stories behind the Poses: The Indian Mythology that Inspired 50 Yoga Poses*. London: Leaping Hare Press, 2022.

VII
Dancing the World into Existence: The *Yoga-Vāsiṣṭha*

The *Yoga-vāsiṣṭha* (*c.* 1000 CE) includes glorious descriptions of how the goddess (Devī) dances the natural world into being. It includes descriptions of progressive meditations on the five great elements as well as encouragement to take up one's responsibilities in the world whole-heartedly. Several segments of this text resemble what has come to be known in American literature as nature writing, a genre distinct from its predecessor, Romanticism. This chapter will show how specific yogic practices described in the *Yoga-vāsiṣṭha* intersect with the emotionality generated by retreating into natural environments.

Many Americans revel in wandering fields and forests, exploring streams and ponds, visiting the beach and hiking in the mountains. The feelings brought forth by these nature encounters engender moments of spiritual connections. A genre known as eco-criticism celebrates an array of authors who write about such immersive moments in a variety of contexts: Terry Tempest Williams in Utah, John Muir in the Sierras, Aldo Leopold in Wisconsin, Mary Austin in Death Valley, Edward Abbey in the desert southwest, and Annie Dillard in the Blue Ridge Mountains. Each of these writers has helped shape American attitudes of appreciation for nature.

Nature literature values environment and the feelings that one experiences in the wild as important, transformative, and ethically formative. One improves oneself in nature. Emerging from nature, one feels restored and prepared, perhaps, to improve the world.

India holds a rich classical literature that glorifies the natural world, feminises nature not for exploitation but for celebration, and prods the individual into productive states of interiority. Emerson and Thoreau read the early translations of some of this material. We now have the benefit of 150 years of additional studies of Indian texts and traditions, as well as a renewed sense of the fragility of nature. Thoreau complained of a locomotive making too much noise, a problem that pales in comparison with the melting of the Arctic sea and the Antarctic ice shelf, not to mention the extinction of countless species and the stunning array of social ills that accompany wasteful contemporary lifestyles. Thoreau anticipated the tenor of these problems and the loneliness and alienation of modern peoples in his now-cherished essays.

The literature that inspired Emerson and Thoreau and indirectly a host of modern nature writers and activists can now be instructive not only on the American stage but it can prove useful for India herself as she grapples with post-modernity and post-colonialism and post-socialism. India faces the challenge of reclaiming her identity of place, of forging a forward-looking culture that recognises and relies upon its roots.

D.H. Lawrence, while living in New Mexico, wrote that:

> Every continent has its own great spirit of place...
> Different places on the face of the earth have difference vital effluence,

> Different vibration, different chemical exhalation, different polarity with different star: call it what you like.[1]

India's vibration, extending from the Vedas to the practice of modern Yoga, emphasises the human body and breath in relation to the elements and landscapes that hold the key to meaning within the world and suggest an ethic of minimising harm to oneself and others. Yoga brings a person to a state of inwardness (*pratyāhāra*), an inner understanding of the core of one's being. Yoga, bringing serenity to the body–mind continuum, allows one to feel deep connections with the breath, the senses, and the elements.

The Transcendentalists announced the need to shift from exploiting nature to cultivating its preservation. Perhaps the most-quoted passage that provides support for the emergence of a philosophy of American love for nature can be found in Emerson's essay 'Nature', published in 1836:

> Standing on the bare ground,
> My head bathed by the blithe air,
> And uplified into infinite space –
> All mean egotism vanishes.
> I become a transparent eyeball.
> I am nothing. I see all.
> The currents of the Universal Being circulate through me.
> I am part or particle of God.[2]

---

1 As quoted in John Gatta, *Making Nature Sacred: Literature, Religion, and Environment in America from the Puritans to the Present* (New York: Oxford University Press, 2004).

2 Ralph Waldo Emerson, 'Nature', as quoted in Gatta, *Making Nature Sacred.*

The Asian traditions such as Yoga that influenced Emerson and Thoreau, like the Quaker traditions of their peers, emphasise interiority and the immanence of God. In this view, the realm of spiritual experience does not reside in outward worship but in states of meditation and contemplation of the natural order. To love nature through Yoga seems like a natural expression born of fecundity as experienced upon the Indian subcontinent, with its wealth of flora and fauna, abundant monsoons, and warm climate.

The Feminine and Nature

The feminine plays an important role in the conceptualisation of the relationship between consciousness and material nature in Indian literature. Referred to in the *Devī Māhātmya* as Good Fortune, the Queen, Intelligence, Nourishment, Patience, and many other qualities, the goddess can be traced back to the Vedic and pre-Vedic times. The *Yoga-vāsiṣṭha,* an important eleventh-century Sanskrit text, presents a view that feminises the natural world, glorifying it as the entry point for transcendental experience. Without the story told by the mind and enacted by the body through the senses, there could be no reflection, no suffering, no spiritual journey. In one remarkable tale from the *Yoga-vāsiṣṭha,* Queen Cūḍālā attains freedom first and then leads her husband to insight, knowledge, and liberation. Most significantly, once the couple have had their fill of both experience and liberation, they return to rule their kingdom justly and in good spirits.

The sage Vasiṣṭha watches the goddess (named variously as Kālī, Devī, Sarasvatī, Lakṣmī, Jayā, and so forth) as she dances into existence the landscapes of hills and plains, rivers and ponds, the warming rays of the sun, and playful breezes. As he contemplates her munificence, he sees the powers of

Kālī in his own body. He ascends chapter by chapter from earth through water, fire, air, into space, and then returns, continuing his work in the world, just as Cūḍālā and her husband returned to rule.

As we examine how the *Yoga-vāsiṣṭha* describes nature and the elements, we see an unfolding that directly parallels the account given in Sāṃkhya philosophy regarding the progression and unfolding of the fundamental constituents of manifest reality. In Sāṃkhya, the *tattvas* exist in a symbiotic relationship. Consciousness (*puruṣa*) relies upon material reality (*prakṛti*) for experience and liberation, a theme echoed in the *Yoga Sūtra* as well:

> The Seer only sees; though pure it appears intentional.
> The nature of the Seen is only for the purpose of that (Seer).[3]

When the purpose of the Seen, also known as the realm of the manifest (*prakṛti*), has been accomplished, then it disappears, entering into a state of abeyance (*pralaya*). Patañjali's culminating *sūtra* describes this process as:

> The return to the origin of the *guṇas,*
> Emptied of their purpose for *puruṣa,*
> Is *kaivalya,* the steadfastness in own form
> And the power of higher awareness (*citi-śakti*).[4]

The *Sāṃkhya Kārikā* employs the metaphor of the dancer to describe the pivotal moment when the purpose of *prakṛti* has been accomplished, the realm of activity goes into abeyance, resulting in liberation:

3 *Yoga Sūtra* II.20.

4 *Yoga Sūtra* IV.34.

> Just as a dancer retired from her audience after performing,
> In the same way, *prakṛti* retreats... when she has been once
> Seen by the seer, she does not appear again.[5]

The term 'embarrassment' has been frequently employed to describe *prakṛti's* retreat, an image also found in the story lore of India when Kālī, on a destructive rampage, dances unwittingly onto the body of her supine husband Śiva. When she realises her mistake, out of deep embarrassment she sticks out her tongue and halts her deadly violence. These images of the 'restraint of the feminine' and the attendant association of manifest reality with the female gender emphasise the renunciation aspects of this tradition. However, the *Yoga-vāsiṣṭha* in contrast seemingly celebrates the feminine realm of the manifest world as the very occasion for liberation.

Vasiṣṭha's Liberation: The World within the Rock

Vālmīki, the author of the *Rāmāyaṇa*, wrote with a great depth of knowledge about the flora and fauna of India. In one set of verses, he describes twenty-five species of trees and plants from mangoes to sandalwood trees.[6] The *Yoga-vāsiṣṭha* also draws deeply from nature imagery and includes descriptions of India's lush, vast, and varied landscape, from the desert of King Lavaṇa's banishment to the listing of India's great mountain ranges. For most of the text, the natural world serves as a

5 *Sāṃkhya Kārikā* 59–61.

6 *Āraṇyakāṇḍa* 14.16–18, as quoted in David Lee, 'The Natural History of the Ramayana', in *Hinduism and Ecology: The Intersection of Earth, Sky, and Water*, ed. Christopher Key Chapple and Mary Evelyn Tucker, 245–268 (Cambridge, MA: Center for the Study of World Religions, Harvard University press, 2000).

backdrop and often as a metaphor for difficulty. However, toward the latter part its final section, nature becomes the context in which Vasiṣṭha describes his own experience of freedom, an experience that qualified him to become Rāma's teacher.

Nature has been articulated in Indian philosophy through the five great elements (*mahābhūta*): earth, water, fire, air, and space. These are carefully listed in the *Sāṃkhya Kārikā* and in various philosophical literature of the Hindus and Buddhists. They receive prominent mention in the Abhidharma literature of early Buddhism as well as in the later literature of Hindu and Buddhist Tantra. Each of these elements correlates to sensory processes as well as bodily functions. To know the elements, senses, and body constitutes an important foundation for knowledge in Indian thought and literature. Vasiṣṭha's spiritual journey leads him through the world of the five great elements into a reverie and from that reverie back into the world.

The *Yoga-vāsiṣṭha* consists of sixty stories within a frame narrative wherein the sage Vasiṣṭha offers words of wisdom to the young prince Rāma, whose mind has become overwhelmed at the prospect of armed conflict. In story after story, Vasiṣṭha seeks to stabilise Rāma's thinking and teach him about the ephemeral nature of all attachment.

In a tale entitled 'The World Within the Rock', Vasiṣṭha enters into a darkened cave where he sees Lord Śiva in meditation. A shadow calls his attention to the presence of the goddess. As he gazes upon her body, she dances, creating the world, carrying mountains and forests on her shoulders and arms. When she ceases to dance, the world stops and begins to dissolve. Her magical presence intrigues Vasiṣṭha. She instructs Vasiṣṭha about how she creates the material universe from her body. She inspires him to take up a sequence of concentration exercises (*dhāraṇā*) through which he sees how his own body is connected with the fundamental elements that comprise the world.[7] Contrary to a more Buddhist approach that would emphasise the putrid nature of decaying flesh, Vasiṣṭha celebrates all that emanates from and remains connected with his body. He enters into an experience of the anthropocosmic, a term used by Eliade from the 1940s through the 1970s 'to account for the correspondences between microcosm and macrocosm that appear throughout the history of religions', and more recently used by Tu Wei Ming 'to describe the dynamic interconnectedness of Heaven, Earth, and humanity'.[8] This episode occurs toward the end of the last book of the *Yoga-vāsiṣṭha* and indicates his own profession of enlightenment to Rāma. The examples given in other stories are about the experiences of other people. Because this is about Vasiṣṭha's own enlightenment, it merits close consideration.

There is a close relationship between the philosophy of Sāṃkhya and the process through which Vasiṣṭha reaches liberation. According to the *Sāṃkhya Kārikā* and the *Yoga Sūtra*, nature (*prakṛti*) serves two functions: providing experience and liberation.[9] In the story of Vasiṣṭha's realisation of liberation through his direct encounter with nature, we find that a goddess starts him on his quest, that he employs the Yoga technique of *dhāraṇā* to enter deep states of interiority, that his narrative takes the

---

7 This is the title of the story given in the translation in Swami Venkatsananda, *The Concise Yoga Vasistha* (Albany: State University of New York Press, 1985) and *Vasiṣṭha's Yoga* (Albany: State University of New York Press, 1993). This segment is referred to with various chapter titles in Ravi Prakash Arya's editing of Vihari Lal Mitra's 1890s translation, starting with 'Description of the Last Night of Death or General Doom' [VII.81] and ending with 'Description of the Current Air, as the Universal Spirit' [VII.92].

8 Sam Mickey, 'Contributions to Anthropocosmic Environmental Ethics', *Worldviews: Global Religions, Culture, and Ecology* 11, no. 2 (2007).

9 *Sāṃkhya Kārikā*, verses XXX and XXX; *Yoga Sūtra* II.20–22.

form of a personal confession. He seems delighted, surprised, and even overwhelmed as he discovers that the powers of the elements themselves reside in his own body.

The narrative begins when Kālī shuts down the world through her dance of cosmic dissolution. It then shifts to a reconstruction of the world within the body of Vasiṣṭha himself, celebrated element by element. It concludes (or rather transitions to yet another story) by placing Vasiṣṭha in dialogue with an ascended sage, who gives advice on how to maintain purified consciousness while moving about in the world. The sage tells him:

> The infinite consciousness (*cid-ākāśa*) is I,
> it is the three worlds,
> it is the *puruṣa* (cosmic being)
> and it is you.[10]

This philosophy affirms the validity of the constructed realm and hence forms a foundation for Vasiṣṭha to exhort Rāma to resume his duties.

In order to capture a sense of the rich imagery employed by the author in praise of nature, translations of portions of successive chapters describing Vasiṣṭha's encounter will follow. In this narrative, Vasiṣṭha undergoes a shift in awareness. He assumes the position of a sovereign king, overseeing the landscape of his domain from a birds-eye view. What begins as rhapsody about the beauties of nature becomes a celebration of the material powers contained within his own body. Vasiṣṭha, as we will see, becomes anthropocosmic.

10 *Yoga-vāsiṣṭha*, VII.96. Translation by author.

The Earth

In Volume VII Vasiṣṭha describes looking down upon the Earth. From this vantage point, he sees soil, plants, mountains, rivers and relates them to his own body:

58 Through performing concentration on the earth,
I dissolved into the form of the earth.
While still retaining this expanded consciousness,
I became like a universal ruler (surveying his domain).

59 And indeed, through my concentration on the earth,
I went to the mines at the root of the earth.
I came to understand my body as the trees,
the grasses, the mountains, the continents, and more.

60 As I took possession of the throne of the earth,
forests sprouted from my body.
I became adorned with cities
as if laced with strings of pearls.

61 I was endowed with forests separated by villages.
The regions of the netherworld were sunk deep in
my bowels.
My arms embraced the mountain ranges
and my continents were encircled with oceans like
bracelets.

62 I felt my body covered with grasses like hair,
as well as tree-tangled mountains,
held up by the heads of ten elephants
and the hundreds of heads of the primal serpent Śeṣa.

64 The beautiful ridges of the Himalayas and the Vindhyas,
the clouds high on Mount Meru,

the abundance of the rivers such as the Ganges:
all this evokes a delicate string of pearls.

65 Caves and thickets and marshes
appear to encircle the ocean.
The white salts of the desert
shimmer like a beautiful garment.

66 In ancient times (of the great flood)
the ocean purified all things.
When it receded, the flowery forests
were resplendent with fragrant pollen.

67 Repeatedly, the ground is plowed and turned:
cooled by the winds of the winter,
warmed by the heat of summer
and moistened by the waters of the rainy season.

68 My chest became the expansive plains.
My eyes became pools of lotuses.
My crown was the light and dark clouds.
My body (*mandira*) contained the ten regions.

72 Filled with floods, deserts, farms, kingdoms, as well as people,
on named continents of stone with rivers, forests,
and oceans to the end of the horizon,
the Earth is an assemblage of vessels and designs
connected with various adorning marks,
as if flecked with groups of lotuses in a raging river,
or like a pond laced with vines.[11]

11 *Yoga-vāsiṣṭha* VII.89.58–72. Translation by author.

Vasiṣṭha describes the planet with great precision and emotion. He sees mountains, forests, deserts, caves, plains, and oceans. He describes the seasons and, like the anthropocosmic sections of the *Bṛhadāraṇyaka Upaniṣad,* makes correlations between his body and the body of the world. He feels vegetation sprout from his body. His arms embrace the mountains. His chest becomes the broad plains, his eyes become lotus pools, and clouds gather around his head. He becomes entranced and absorbed into the beauty of the Earth.

Water

In the next chapter, Vasiṣṭha explores various forms of water. He again performs *dhāraṇā,* defined by Patañjali as 'the binding of the mind to a place' (*deśa-bandhaś cittasya dhāraṇā*).[12] This practice, when extended, moves one into a state of meditation (*dhyāna*) and ultimately into *samādhi*. Patañjali describes *samādhi* as a state of emptying (*śūnya*) that allows the higher self to shine forth.[13] Vasiṣṭha attains a state of transparency first to Earth and then to water, blending and merging with the experience of each:

> 9 Just as I experienced the earth-plane
> by earth contemplation (*pṛthivī-dhāraṇā*),
> then, just as I saw those many worlds
> held in the form of the earth,
> so also I became water, which was seen
> by me in the same way (as from above).
>
> 10 By concentration on water, I became water,
> as if this unconscious (substance)

12 *Yoga Sūtra* III.1.

13 *Yoga Sūtra* III.1–3.

took on consciousness
inside the abodes of the oceans with its quiet gurgling.

11 [The water] slowly rose up into the veins
and trunks of creeping vines, grasses, trees,
tendrils, and groves, as if a caterpillar
were mounting your limbs.

12 That [water] lifts everything like the [rising of sap in]
the trunk of a tree, cutting patterns like bracelets,
roiling the water worms gently
with undulating movements in its hollows.

13 Having rested, [the water] formed beautiful lines,
its full shape taking the form of the leaves and fruits
of vines, hardwood trees, and palm trees.

14 [Water] enters into the hearts [of plants]
as if through their mouths.
It lets the roots in the bodies [of plants]
hold firm during the adversity of the [monsoon] season,
[growing back] when cut, shaken, eaten, or harvested.

15 [Water] takes the form of drops of dew
asleep in the beds of leaves,
constant at all times,
tirelessly gleaming in all directions.

16 Along its endless journey,
[water] takes a home in various lakes and rivers,
occasionally resting gracefully by a bridge,
like an old friend.

17 Like the consciousness of a simpleton,
searching out a purpose but lacking support

due to his stupidity,
water swirls up into whirlpools, unaware of its brilliance.

18 By my bad deeds, I was lifted up
to a waterfall at the peak of a huge mountain
and then that self-same swirling whirlpool
was dashed into a hundred rivulets.

19 Having arisen from the woods in the form of mist
into the ocean of the sky,
this indwelling gem stuck
as tear drop jewels in the blue stars.

20 [Water] took rest in the thrones of the clouds,
accompanying Lady Lightning
whose blue sapphire light
illuminated Vasudeva on his Snake Throne.

21 Atoms of water gush forth in tiny drops.
Each holds its essential nature,
like Brahman is found in all souls.

22 Having reached a connection with the highest experience
through the taste buds, my soul was delivered
from the body to the singularity of knowledge.

23 That sweetness is not achieved by me,
nor by my body, nor by anything else.
It is revealed inside, to consciousness.
At that point, ignorance disappears.

24 The bee tastes and takes nectar from various flowers
in all directions across all seasons.
It takes this enjoyable elixir and
passes it along to the next bee.

25 In the connecting joints of the fourteen classes of beings,
water dwells as if it were conscious,
though by its inert nature it has no consciousness.

26 In the form of a rising mist,
[water] ascends on the chariot of the winds,
bestowing joyous fragrance in the channels
of the pure sky.

27 Rama, by dwelling in that [water concentration]
from the smallest particle
to the ultimate experience of it,
the whole world comes into existence.

28 Through this unconscious thing appearing as if conscious,
through the sameness of myself with this water,
all inner meaning of what is known
and unknowable was revealed to me.

29 I have seen the ascent of hundreds,
thousands, of worlds arising and falling there,
like layers of leaves in a banana tree.

30 Whether a world is beautiful
or a world is ugly,
all of them are consciousness only, like the sky.
Though [they seem] numerous, they are spacious and pure.

31 This knowledge shines forth as the highest purity.
It indeed appears to us as empty.
This vast space, in its expansiveness,
is who you were and who you are.[14]

14 *Yoga-vāsiṣṭha* VII.90.9–31. Translation by author.

Vasiṣṭha experiences water in its various forms. Just as he discussed the fragrance of the earth, he mentions the sense of taste in regard to water. In Sāṃkhya, foundational awareness of the earth arises from the power of smelling, and the capacity of tasting is known through and linked with water. He describes dew, drops of rain, the gathering of moisture in clouds, mist, rivers, and waterfalls. Vasiṣṭha talks of how sap rises in plant life. He also discusses how the beauty of water brought him again to a deep appreciation and awareness, stilling his thoughts and revealing vast empty space.

Fire

Fire (*agni, tejas*) finds an important role in the earliest literature of India. The very first hymn of the *Ṛg Veda* offers praise to the god Agni (cognate with the English word ignite) and more Vedic hymns address Agni than any other deity. Vasiṣṭha finds fire in a myriad of forms, from the sun and moon and stars to the simple oil lamp. Through light one experiences deep delight and a feeling safety and security. The correlated sense, seeing, can only function through the presence of light. For Vasiṣṭha, light becomes truly revelatory:

1 Then I disappeared into fire
through the brilliant concentration on fire.
I became linked with its various parts such as
the moon, lightning, stars, flames, and so forth.

2 From its essential nature as eternally luminous,
it spreads light like a beloved prince.
It makes all things visible. It makes all things right.
Thieves fail to conceal themselves in its glow.

3 Through its gentle, friendly lamps
it provides thousands of delights.

It allows all purposes to be seen
in every house, like a good prince.

4 It brings good cheer to all the world
through the sparkling rays of the moon and sun.
Through its singular delights it casts light
into the distance, lifting up and pervading
the circumference of the sky.

5 Light destroys the combined qualities
of blindness and affliction.
It possesses the quality of
revealing all truth and awakening.

6 The people proclaim with gusto:
'[Fire] is the axe [that cuts] the tree of darkness.
It provides the foothold for making things exceedingly pure.
It is golden, the ruby among gems.'

7 It [energises] reds, blacks, and whites;
it abides eternally through its gleaming limbs,
like a father gives shape to the bodies
of all his sons.

8 Fire, through its blessings, chooses
to spare the house of children from destruction.
It also protects [the people] from piercing winds
throughout the land.

9 I saw the master [burning] brightly
in the darkest forms of the hell region.
With eyes half open, I saw its active form,
on the surface of the earth and at the crown of existence.

10 I saw [fire] in the abodes of the gods,
where illumined souls are eternally in great splendour,
as well as the light on the ruined huts of the people
and in the recesses covered in great darkness.

11 [I saw] that stainless radiant virgin sky
become smeared with the colour of saffron [at sunset],
making way for the illumination of the moon and stars,
as well as the winds that bring night dew.

12 Her grace causes the fields of corn each day
to ripen and grow up out of the darkness.
Her radiance [draws water up] into the clouds
that fill the vast crystal dome [of the sky]
and bring cleansing rains.

13 By her, meaning is bestowed.
Through her, comes illumination.
Like a younger sister, she reveals the highest truth:
there is consciousness only.

14 Her luster on the lotus pool reflects
the actions of living beings on the earth and below,
just as from consciousness emerges
the wonderment of thought, perception, and form.

15 A necklace of innumerable jeweled stars
is called together from the mist.
Light increases with the days and seasons throughout the year
and froths in fires under the ocean.

16 The moon and sun move briskly
inside the great darkness of the night sky,

just as the one who stands deep in the great universe
is the one eternally moving and imperishable.

17 Fire is the brilliance in gold,
the strength in men,
the crystal gleam in all jewels,
and the flash in lightning storms.

18 It is the splendour in the phases of the face of the moon.
It is the mark of beauty in long eyelashes.
Its undying love flows abundantly.
It glitters in the laughter of friends.

19 Fire is in the love that arises and shines forth
and can be found in the innate allure of the movement
of a face, an arm, an eye,
an eyebrow, a hand, or a lock of hair.

20 Fire shows that these three worlds are as flimsy as straw.
It burns in the slap of one's worst enemies.
It starts the thunderclap
and dwells in the heart of the strong lion.

21 Among excellent, active warriors,
fierce fire can be found in the sound
of their clashing swords, breaking through armour,
and in their harsh, noisy battlecries.

22 It emboldens the gods to fight the Dānava demons
and the demons to resist the gods.
Fire is the force that moves all beings.
It causes plants to sprout upward.

23 Bright-eyed one, I experienced those things
in these coverings of space that make up the world
as if they were shimmering in the desert.

24 I saw the phoenix sun as its streams of light
scattered over all ten points of the horizon.
I saw its limbs flash on chosen mountains,
making them appear as if they were villages on the face of the earth.

25 The wheel of the sun is filled with treasure
like the desire within a flower's blossom.
Light sits within the universe like phosphorescence in the darkened sea.
Its continuous line of days unfolds just as fruits ripen on the tree.

26 The face of the moon in the sky
forms a pool of elixir.
Each evening it smiles cheerfully
on the people of the night.

27 (The moon's) power reflects all lovely good fortune in the world.
His wife, Rohiṇī, (shines) in the night
as the most beloved white lotus flower.

28 To me appeared a gentle trail of stars,
arrayed like nectar flowing through the heavens,
like a web of shining flowers on a vine,
twisted and heaped together.
(The Milky Way!)

29 I saw jewel-like waves in the hands of the oscillating ocean,
as if merchants' hands were tossing them
on their scales to weigh them.

30 I see whirlpools of fish in the water of the ocean,
multitudes of sunbeams on that water,

and in the delicate clouds,
[portents of] lightning igniting a forest fire.

31 I saw the beautiful burning of the sacrificial fire,
its tenacious flames devouring the wood,
spreading throughout all that can be burned,
roaring, strong, and crackling.

32 I saw the brilliance in gold and rubies
that is called great in things made of jewels.
I also saw things reduced to ash by fire
just as knowledge is destroyed by the wicked.

33 The wives of the rulers of men,
as well as those of the Asuras, Uragas, and Gandharvas,
are adorned, each of them, with strings of pearls
placed on the summits of their breasts.

34 Just as a bride applies the marriage mark to her forehead
delicately
as if treading a path without causing harm,
so also my wavering vision
catches glimpses of flickering fireflies.

35 I saw the gleaming flash of those little fish in the waves,
standing transfixed in the roar of the water of a beautiful
whirlpool.

36 Tender stalks of flowers engaged in amorous activities
in the women's quarters of the palaces, rising as if
illuminated by lamps.

37 Having given forth their radiance
under the cover of darkness,
they then retreated, exhausted, wilted,
like the steady turtle draws its limbs inside its shell.

38 Due to weariness at the end of these times,
when all the world wanes as if sinking into a whirlpool,
I sat as the clouds disappeared into space
with a flash like that of a roaring elephant.

39 The sun expanded at the end of the day
as its fires were absorbed into the waters,
into the skies at the end of the world's horizon,
dancing in endless waves of water.

40 With my teeth like kindling sparks
and my arms aflame, my tangled hair ablaze,
I generated a powerful roiling whirlpool of smoke.

41 I burned the towns made of wood.
My flaming mouth chewed on all creatures.
I devoured all things made of the eight forms of wood
and brought them to their ultimate dissolution.

42 Through striking forth fire as with axes, spears, and knives,
I caused a furious arc of sparks to fly forth,
giving vent to the purpose of fire.[15]

Vasiṣṭha explores various metaphors of fire and light including its ability to dispel ignorance, its ability to provide comfort 'like a good prince,' its ability to protect and illumine. Like a Buddhist, he proclaims that fires remind us that all things are fleeting. Like a Vedāntin, he hints that just as fire can be found in all manner of things, so also resides the soul. Through thinly coded language he applauds the sexual power associated with fire, and celebrates the beauty not only of the passing of each day at sunset, but the stark beauty of fire's destructive power.

15 *Yoga-vāsiṣṭha* VII.91.1–42. Translation by author.

Air and Breath and Space

When Vasiṣṭha practiced concentration on the wind (*vāyu-dhāraṇā*), he proclaimed:

1 Next I came to concentrate on the operations of the wind,
spreading my thoughts resolutely
to examine the world and satisfy my curiosity.

2 I rose up into the wind [that surrounds] the earth,
playing with the people, the trees, and the beautiful
blooming flowers,
protecting the water lilies.

3 Desiring to bring some relief
to the exhausted bodies of these amorous ones,
I sprinkled down drizzle and mist
with the higher purpose of bringing them joy.

4 I became the teacher of the dancing leaves
on grasses, trees, and tender vines.
I was adorned with the fragrance of flowers
and the splendour of medicinal plants and fruits.

5 At times of quiet and celebration
I fondly caressed the worlds of beautiful women.
At times of calamity (such as earthquakes)
I tossed rocks as if they were feather.

6 In heaven, I carry the earth's honey and pollen,
Arising from the jasmine that adorns the trees in paradise.
In hell, my gathered fires illuminate the thick fog.

7 In the ocean my undulating movements
can be seen in the pounding of the surf.

In the sky, I move the clouds to hide
and then reveal the mirror of the moon.

8 I support that beneficial vehicle,
the powerful army of stars,
moving perfectly through the three worlds
on their powerful, speedy chariot.

9 Closely resembling how thought quickly appears and disappears,
it touches the body though it has no body,
inducing bliss through its movement (*spanda*)
like the fragrance of sandalwood.

10 [The wind drives] the hard showers of rain and snow.
It brings infirmity to the old.
It makes the young drunken with joy.
For the gentle ones, it brings silence and innocence.

11 Its course lifts up sweetness,
and brings the nectar of happiness to the heavens.
The beloved [winds] of March take away
the fatigue that comes with long love making.

12 Though tired from the incessant
swinging and swaying and undulations of the Ganges,
the wind [in the mountains] does not recognise its own fatigue
and fends off extended exhaustion.

13 Through its caresses, it bends the abundant flowers
and the vines waiting like wives in springtime.
It incessantly shakes and moves the palm fronds.
It dislodges bees from the plants.

14 Having enjoyed pleasures for a long time under the face
of the moon,
the full cloud of sleepiness comes upon the bed.
Exhausted from making love, [the wind] is taken away
to that splendid lotus that throbs in the heart.

15 The wind, like a horse, moves through the sky,
established in and combined with the clouds.
It resembles a dancing elephant
in the throes of sexual desire.

16 [The wind] as herdsman of the clouds at the top of
the mountains
energetically casts down lightning and rain.
He extends soothing rain to the liberated ones
and destructive dust over the enemies of *dharma*.

17 The fragrance of flowers pervades
space as if it were sound.
Devoted to the limbs of each being as well as the earth
itself,
[the wind] rises up as the pulse of breath.

18 [This breath] is the one self behind all actions,
hidden in the heart of this splendid body.
It serves as the guide to eternal oneness.
Educated families know its essence.

19 [The wind] steals away the treasured fragrance
that traverses cities and rivers.
[It beckons] the cool moon, that orb shining in the
qdarkness,
rising from the ocean of milk.[16]

---

16 *Yoga-vāsiṣṭha* VII.92.1–19. Translation by author.

Swami Ventatesananda continues this translation as follows:

> I taught the grass, leaves, creepers and straw the art of dancing.
> Wafting a cool breeze, I became the dear friend of young ladies.
> At the same time I was dreaded for my heat wave, hurricane and tornadoes.
> In pleasure gardens I carried sweet scent; in hell I carried sparks of fire...
> I was operating the body-machine of all embodied beings
> by being their life-breath....
> Being the element air, I perceived within each molecule
> of air a whole universe.[17]

From this expansive moment, Vasiṣṭha roamed into vast space. In words that echo centuries later in Emerson's grand pronouncement quoted above, Vasiṣṭha claims:

> The netherworlds were my feet,
> the earth my abdomen,
> and the heavens my head...
> I was spread in all directions
> everywhere at all times
> and I did everything.
> I was the self of all.
> I was all.
> Yet I was pure space.
> I experienced being something and being nothing.
> I experienced universes within every atom
> and universes within the atoms of those universes.
> I myself became all these universes.[18]

---

17 *Vasiṣṭha's Yoga*, p. 582, VII.92.

18 *Vasiṣṭha's Yoga*, pp. 582–583, VII.92.

In this proclamation, Vasiṣṭha's body expands to encompass the universe. He has attained the pureness of space and, hence, liberation.

Conclusion

The description of the elements as expressed in the *Yoga-vāsiṣṭha* anticipates the best passages found in today's nature literature. These passages evoke the experience of what William James called conversion. In this narrative, nature speaks to and moves Vasiṣṭha to a place of deep connection. The bliss engendered by Vasiṣṭha's process of immersion in the elements and their correlative senses, one by one, culminates in a universal vision not unlike that experienced by Arjuna in the eleventh chapter of the *Bhagavad Gītā*. In the *Gītā*, Kṛṣṇa draws all the *Mahābhārata* warriors into their destruction, like moths to a flame. Vasiṣṭha's epiphany begins as Kālī performs her dance of destruction. This entices him into rarefied states of contemplation that culminate in universal consciousness, an immersion into the *cid-ākāśa*.

Vasiṣṭha's liberation takes place through the very tools of experience. Vasiṣṭha does not retreat from the earth or its smells; he does not disdain water or its tastes; he does not reject light and the forms it reveals; he does not recoil from the various forms of wind. He celebrates each with elation. Each condition becomes a moment for the expansion of consciousness, an important moment in the process of purification. The journey of Vasiṣṭha affirms, piece by piece, the vital importance of the creative powers of the goddess. By contemplating the elements, Vasiṣṭha comes to highest consciousness. By experiencing nature, he experiences liberation.

The poet Mary Oliver has written: 'I am sensual in order to be spiritual.' The human body, according to Sāṃkhya, is composed of five sense organs (nose, mouth, eyes, skin, ears) and five action organs (anus, genitalia, hands, legs, and voice) that allow one to perceive and operate in the realm of the five elements (earth, water, fire, air, space). Without the senses and the body there could be no engagement of the world. Without engagement, there can be no experience, and without experience, there can be no liberation. Without the story told by the mind and enacted by the body through the senses, there could be no reflection, no suffering, no spiritual journey. Rāma, at the very beginning of the *Yoga-vāsiṣṭha*, balks at being asked to venture forth from safety to defend the homeland of sages. Vasiṣṭha's advice points out to Rāma that one cannot avoid the unavoidable, but one can engage the world from a place of wisdom. This calls again to mind the poet Mary Oliver, who has written: 'There is only one question: how to love this world.'[19] Vasiṣṭha, having encountered the goddess, having seen the process of world creation emanate from his own body, having followed a great sage from space back into the world of subject and object, encourages Rāma to take up his duty. Knowing the world gives one power over the world; without the loss of innocence, there can be no knowledge, no liberation.

In one of the great descriptions of unmediated experience, Annie Dillard writes about an unexpected moment during a road trip:

> I am absolutely alone.... Before me extends a low hill trembling in yellow brome, and behind the hill, filling the sky, rises an enormous mountain ridge, forested, alive and awesome with brilliant blown lights. I have never seen anything so tremulous and live. Overhead, great strips and chunks of cloud dash to the northwest in a gold rush. At my back the sun is setting – how can I not have noticed before that the

19 Mary Oliver. *New and Selected Poems*. Boston: Beacon Press, 1992.

> sun is setting?... Shadows lope along the mountain's rumpled flanks, they elongate like root tips, like lobes of running water, faster and faster. A warm purple pigment pools in each ruck and tuck of the rock; it deepens and spreads, boring crevasses, canyons. As the purple vaults and slides, it tricks out the unleafed forest and rumpled rock in gilt, in shape-shifting patches of glow. These gold lights veer and retract, shatter and glide in a series of dazzling splashes, shrinking, leaking, exploding.... I am more alive than all the world.[20]

For Dillard, this moment contained all meaning in its poignant beauty and silence. This deeply religious encounter gave her a sense of fulfillment, as well as a wistfulness that regrets the inevitable intruding moment when self-consciousness returns and we lose intimacy and wander into thought and distraction.

Like Annie Dillard, Vasiṣṭha writes poetically about the beauties of nature. From nature he learns firsthand of immediacy and evanescence. He also learns intimacy through his successive encounters with the elements and the senses. One truth remains constant through the lessons taught by the great nature writers and by Yoga: once we learn of the ways of nature, we are confined only by our freedom to pay honour to her, to configure and reconfigure our lives as cultivators and agents of renewal. Like Vasiṣṭha and Rāma, we must return.

The narrative flow from the Vedas, the Sāṃkhya system, the Upaniṣads, and Tantra culminates in Vasiṣṭha's earnest praise for the creative powers of the goddess. As we have seen, this mode of meditation brought Vasiṣṭha to a state of immersion into the vast expanses of pure consciousness *(cid-ākāśa)*.

20 Annie Dillard, *Pilgrim at Tinker Creek*, Chapter Six, 'The Present', in *Three by Annie Dillard* (New York: HarperPerennial, 1990), 80.

This frame story provides a context for thinking about the land of India as sacred ground, the context for experiencing meaning, bliss, and deliverance into a state of full appreciation and connectivity.

Adapted with permission from Christopher Key Chapple. 'Liberation into Nature: Vasiṣṭha's Embrace of the Great Elements'. In *Engaged Emancipation: Mind, Morals, and Make-Believe in the Mokṣopāya (Yogavāsiṣṭha)*, edited by Christopher Key Chapple and Arindam Chakrabarti, 267–288. Albany: State University of New York Press, 2015.

Discussion Topic: The *Yoga-Vāsiṣṭha*

- Read aloud selected *Yoga-vāsiṣṭha* passages that describe each of the five elements. Which places come to mind when you read these descriptions?
- How might the manner in which Vasiṣṭha teaches Rāma to meditate on the elements enhance appreciation of the cosmos?
- Discuss elements held in common with the *Yoga-vāsiṣṭha* and the passages cited by Emerson, D.H. Lawrence, Mary Oliver, and Annie Dillard.

Further Reading

John Gatta. *Making Nature Sacred: Literature, Religion, and the Environment in the Americas from the Puritans to the Present*. New York: Oxford University Press, 2004.

Christopher Key Chapple. *Living Landscapes: Meditations on the Five Elements in Hindu, Buddhist, and Jain Yogas*. Albany, NY: State University of New York Press, 2020.

VIII
Animals in Literature and Activism

Animals suffuse the landscape of India. Every god and goddess has a companion animal. Diverse species of birds, mammals, and reptiles, large and small, abound in rural and urban areas. Chapter 6 discussed the shamanic process of animal imitation in the traditions of *haṭha-yoga*, a theme continued below. This chapter explores animal stories from the *Pañca-tantra* and the *Yoga-vāsiṣṭha* as well as briefly surveys the animal activism of the Bishnoi, noted even today for their protection of Blackbuck deer, and the work on behalf of elephants and tigers by Vivek Menon of the Wildlife Trust of India.

Animals in Hinduism

The Vedas serve as the foundation for various forms of Hinduism, extol the cow in dozens of hymns, likening the beneficence of the cow to the dawn, to speech, to the rain clouds, and creation itself. The Upaniṣads introduce the idea of reincarnation, with the *Kauṣītaki Upaniṣad* stating that '[One] is born again here according to [one's] deeds (*karma*) as a worm, or as a moth, or as a fish, or as a bird, or as a lion, or as a wild boar, or as a snake, or as a tiger, or as a person.'[1] In Chapter 3, we examined the ways in which animals instructed Satyakāma Jābāla, who later became a great sage. In the later Purāṇic period, animals themselves became elevated to deity status in Hinduism, such as the Eagle Garuda, the Monkey Hanumān, and the Elephant-headed Gaṇeśa. Additionally, each anthropomorphic deity has a companion animal: Gaṇeśa's rat, Durgā's lion, Sarasvatī's peacock, Lakṣmī's elephant, and Śiva's bull.

Yoga Training and Animals

During one memorable week in Yoga training, Gurāṇi Añjali asked her Thursday-night students to observe an animal keenly at least once each day. It did not matter if the animal were wild or domesticated and it could have been a cat or a dog or a bird or a rabbit. We were also encouraged to recollect past experiences with animals.

During my childhood we reared many litters of Labrador Retrievers, walking long distances through the fields behind our house, training them to fetch. Sadly, the Lab called Jeff, my steady companion on the long afternoons while my older siblings were in school, ran afoul of the local game warden. The warden shot and killed him in the dead of night under the light of the moon. Several months later, Mike, a thick coated Black Lab joined us, as well as a cat from the Adirondacks named Kenmore for the hotel where my sister had worked in the summer. Our family avidly followed birds, prowling the marshes and woods and country roads in search of geese, pheasants, robins, scarlet tanagers, woodpeckers, warblers, wrens, sparrows, vireos, and so many more. During my teen

1 *Kauṣītaki Upaniṣad* 1.2, in Robert Ernest Hume, *The Thirteen Principal Upanishads: Translated from the Sanskrit* (London: Oxford University Press, 1921. Revised edition 1971), 303.

years, my father and mother began to train standardbred horses, the ones that pull chariots at the races, and a stray dog joined our household, a Cockapoo we named Rover. Animals were an integral part of our childhood and have become the mainstay in the primatology career of my oldest sister, who has studied owl monkeys and lemurs for decades.[2]

Observing animals expands one's sense of self. The empathy felt in the company of a beloved dog, the calm experienced while petting a purring cat, the wonder stirred up by seeing the strength and speed of a mountain lion all call us to something larger. David Abram, who trained with a shaman in Nepal, describes connecting with a crow at the deepest of levels. Sonam, his teacher, trained Abram over the course of several weeks to practice *trāṭaka*, the yogic fixed gaze technique, honing his vision on the chest of a raven.

> 'Move into the bird', he said.... 'Keep your eyes open. Eyes open. Watch.' The bird is now hopping, not walking, toward the edge of the gorge, and I feel each hop as a slight jolt. Its shoulders expand as wings spread and lift, and then with a lunge we are aloft... the whole canyon opens beneath us... Now we're following the blue ribbon of water as it gets bigger and wider and *louder*, its many voices swelling as a freshness fills the whooshing air.... Then cliffs are slanting past and the river is falling away, and the cliffs [are] are close by again, then the river, then the cliffs, then that abyss and I finally realize we're spiraling up the side of the canyon, riding one of the warm updrafts like I've seen ravens do so many times.... And I'm balancing, floating, utterly at ease in the

---

2 See Patricia Chapple Wright, *High Moon Over the Amazon: My Quest to Understand the Monkeys of the Night* (New York: Lantern Books, 2013) and *For the Love of Lemurs: My Life in the Wilds of Madagascar* (New York: Lantern Books, 2014).

> blue air.... Falling, yet perfectly safe. Floating.... Among the rocks scattered near the chasm's edge there's a rectangular boulder we're falling toward.... And there, off past the other rocks toward the edge of the precipice is an odd creature – no, two creatures, two clothed people crouched together on the ground. Their faces are upturned, staring steadily at us even as we glide downward, their heads turning together as they track us perfectly with their gaze. The eyes of one are especially compelling, achingly so, staring straight toward, straight up into... me.[3]

This moment of yogic connection alters Abram's grasp of the world and the grasp of the living world upon Abram. Abram gained an intimacy with and sensitivity to the non-human realm that proved instructive for his sense of philosophical emplacement within the natural world.

Nepal and India abound with animals in many forms. I have encountered jackals and gaurs in Lumbini, Nepal; otters and elephants in the Periyar Preserve in Kerala; rhesus and langur monkeys along the roads and in the temples in Orissa and Uttarkhand; cows and pigs in the alleys and byways of Delhi and Jaipur; goats and Blackbucks in Rajasthan; thirteen different species of birds on the roadway from Varanasi to Bodh Gaya, and more. Animals can speak to us in many ways, regardless of our locale. To land on the Indian subcontinent places one in the company of abundant life. As D.H. Lawrence stated and was quoted in the prior chapter, each place has its own chemistry: 'Every continent has its own great spirit of place.... Different places on the face of the earth have dif-

---

3 David Abram, *Becoming Animal: An Earthly Cosmology* (New York: Vintage Books, 2011), 256–258.

ferent vital effluence, different vibration.'[4] In the literature that follows, we will explore India's distinct relationship with animals, a relationship that has produced hundreds of millions of vegetarians, a sophisticated philosophy of birth, death, and rebirth, and many fables wherein animals serve as the primary teachers.

Forests still blanketed India during the period of the composition of the Vedas, Upaniṣads, and the early texts of Buddhism and Jainism. Lewis Lancaster has noted that 'India of the time of the Buddha was composed of urban islands in the sea of the forest' and that 'the forest was a source of pain, danger, and struggle'.[5] In fact, the sage Tulādhāra recalls in the *Mahābhārata* a time when 'crops sprouted from the earth without cultivation;' people ate from the bounty of the earth before the advent of settled agriculture.[6] It might be said that the literature of this early period describes a simpler time, a time of attunement with the natural order (*ṛta*). It could also be surmised that this literature documents a radical transition from hunter-gatherer lifestyles to settled agricultural communities, and a consequent shift in relationships between humans and animals.

---

4 D.H. Lawrence, *Studies in Classic American Literature* (1923), as quoted in David Mazel, ed., *A Century of Early Ecocriticism*, Athens, GA: University of Georgia Press, 2001, 238.

5 Lewis Lancaster, 'Buddhism and Ecology: Collective Cultural Perceptions', in *Buddhism and Ecology: The Interconnection of Dharma and Deeds*, ed. Mary Evelyn Tucker and Duncan Ryuken Williams, 3–8 (Cambridge, MA: Harvard University Center for the Study of World Religions, 1997), 12.

6 *Mahābhārata* 9.262, as translated in Christopher Key Chapple, 'Ahiṃsā in the Mahābhārata: A Story, A Philosophical Perspective, and an Admonishment', *Journal of Vaishnava Studies* 4, no. 3 (1996), 110.

Animals in the Pṛthivī Sūkta of the Atharva Veda

In its celebration of the elements and the gifts of the Earth, the *Pṛthivī Sūkta* makes frequent mention of animals.[7]

5 She is the home of cows, horses, and of birds.
May that Earth protect us, grant us prosperity,
and bestow upon us vigor.

15 O Mother Earth!
Your progeny consists of not only bipeds but also quadrupeds.
Among the bipeds, there are the five races of humans
who are sustained by the Sun through its immortal light and rays.

This verse celebrates diversity of life, both human and animal. Even today, one encounters so many four-legged beings on India's streets and roads: camels, elephants, dogs, monkeys, goats, cows, and water buffalo. Additionally, India has been home to persons of African, European, and East Asian origin, as well as home to Caucasian peoples to the north and Dravidians in the south.

46 O Mother Earth!
Keep away from us venomous reptiles
such as snakes and scorpions which cause thirst when they sting;
keep away those poisonous insects which cause fever,

---

7 Following verses from O.P. Dwivedi and Christopher Key Chapple, trs., *In Praise of Mother Earth: The Pṛthivī Sūkta* (Los Angeles: Marymount Institute Press, 2011).

and let all those terrible crawling creatures
which are born in the rainy season keep away from us.
Be kind to us and grant us that which is beneficial.

48 The Earth which bears both the good and the wicked
permits wild animals such as boar and deer to move freely.

The world of nature includes danger. Thousands each year die from snake bite even today. Pestilence afflicts all communities, particularly during the monsoon, the season long awaited that also generate fear for one's safety, both for the punishing storms as well as for the abundance of life it unleashes.

49 O Mother Earth!
Although various wild animals
such as the lion, the tiger, the wolf, the jackal, the deer,
and others
are nurtured in your forests,
keep all menacing animals away from harming us.

Along with snakes and criminals, predatory animals, even today, threaten the well-being of humans in India. Hundreds lose their lives each year, particularly from tigers and elephants, as well as from rabid dogs.

51 The two-winged swans, falcons, eagles,
and birds of all kinds fly fearlessly above the Earth,
where the wind comes rushing,
raising dust storms and uprooting trees,
as well as fanning fires.

To complete this acknowledgement of the range of beings, the text describes the flight of birds, linking their feats and temperaments with wind and fire.

PAÑCA-TANTRA: *THE ṚṢI FINDS A SUITOR FOR HIS DAUGHTER*

Another genre of Indian literature can be found in the narrative story tradition. The *Pañca-tantra,* a collection of lore that dates from at least 1500 years ago, includes several animals parables.[8] In the story that follows, we see a fluid boundary between non-human animals and humans. We are reminded of the importance of recognising kinship with all life forms and are taught about the power and limitations of parental care.

One day a *ṛṣi,* presumably a composer of Vedic hymns, performed his ablutions as usual at the nearby river. A falcon flew overhead. It released from its talons some freshly caught prey, a mouse that fell into the river, unharmed. The *ṛṣi* cupped the mouse in his hands and placed it safely onto a leaf on the shore and then, having finished his morning bath, began walking home. Midway he was struck with a feeling of immense responsibility toward the mouse. It dawned on the *ṛṣi* that this encounter was somehow auspicious and that his task was not yet complete. He returned to find the mouse still drying off in the sun. He invoked a special *mantra* and transformed the mouse into an infant human girl. The *ṛṣi* placed her in swaddling and then brought her home to his wife. The couple had been childless; now they devoted their doting attention to rearing this little girl.

---

8 The following sources were consulted for the retelling of this story: Patrick Olivelle, tr., *Pañcatantra: The Book of India's Folk Wisdom* (New York: Oxford University Press, 1997); McComas Taylor, *The Fall of the Indigo Jackal: The Discourse of Division and Pūrṇabhadra's Pañcatantra* (Albany, NY: State University of New York Press, 2007); Franklin Edgerton, tr., *The Panchatantra Reconstructed: Volume 2. Introduction and Translation* (New Haven, CT: American Oriental Society, 1924).

In traditional India, the task of the parent includes arranging for the marriage of one's children. The *ṛṣi*, who clearly had developed a deep love for his daughter, took this responsibility very seriously and sought out the most appropriate match for this miracle given from the heavens. Because of her propitious origins, the *ṛṣi* aimed very high, choosing as her first suitor the Sun himself. He approached Sūrya and explained that his daughter came from the sky itself and therefore was his equal. The Sun demurred and remarked, 'Yes, I am powerful, but there is one more powerful than I. The clouds, which seem so soft and gentle, nonetheless occlude my rays and mute my power. Ṛṣi, approach the clouds; they will make a better match for your girl.'

The *ṛṣi* then approached the cloud, made of water vapour. The cloud also demurred. 'Yes, I can be billowy, light or dark, thin or thick and yes I can overpower the sun. But there is one better than I. The wind slices me into pieces, forces me to give up my form into countless drops of rain, destroys the magnificence of my form. Ṛṣi, approach the wind.'

The *ṛṣi* called out to the wind. 'Come here, O great Vāyu. You will meet your match in this daughter of mine, arisen from the sky and the river, beautiful, and ready for marriage.' Vāyu, like the others, explained his own limits. 'O *ṛṣi*, it is true that I can travel the face of the earth and that my power courses through the veins of all that lives. But I also have limits. Whether in the heat of the day or the darkness of night, one great force stops my wanderings: the mountain. The mountain, with its great majesty, is the most powerful and the most worthy suitor for your beloved daughter. Approach the mountain and offer to him the hand of your daughter in marriage.'

The *ṛṣi* traveled along the base of the mountain and looked up at its immense grandeur, covered with forests, boasting spectacular granite boulders. Certainly, nothing could be grander.

However, the mountain too spoke from a place of humility. He grumbled, 'You flatter me and, yes it would be nice to think that I am above all other beings. But look closely and you will see that one being always gets the best of me, tunneling into hillocks, lacing passages underneath the roots of my forests and around the boulders that adorn me like massive jewels. The smallest of beings can also be the most powerful. Behold the greatest being of all: the mouse!'

The *ṛṣi* approached a hole in the face of the mountain. He called out to the best of mice to step up and meet his future spouse. The best of the mice stepped forward and proclaimed: 'Indeed, your daughter is lovely. However, she is too large for my lair. How can she fit inside when it is time to sleep?' With that, the *ṛṣi* reversed his original spell. His daughter, for whom he had cared for a period of twelve years, returned to her original form and then joined the best of mice as his wife and queen.

This story explains interactions between three realms: the elements of fire, water, air, and earth; the human world of the *ṛṣi* and his wife; and two forms of animal, the falcon, powerful and air bound, and the mouse, humble yet tenacious. The *ṛṣi* evokes deep sentiment repeatedly in the story: love for the vulnerable mouse and love for his daughter. He beholds the great elements with awe, holding a sense of reverence for the powers of nature. And just as he himself took on the responsibility of rearing a child, he tenderly attends to her future happiness, arranging for her transfer from childhood to adulthood, knowing that he will lose her constant company in the process. As noted above, this story highlights the emotions of parenthood: care, attention, and eventually dispassionate love and surrender. Interestingly, the story focuses almost exclusively on the emotions of the father. Neither wife nor daughter exerts agency. Nonetheless, the deep feelings of the *ṛṣi* speak to the supreme values of responsibility and a care that well up from within the heart of an individual and go far beyond external mandates. This might also be seen as a call to compassion for all orphans, for all vulnerable beings, whether heaven-sent, animal, or human.

In terms of landscape, this story is cyclical. It begins at the banks of a river. Its narrative soars with the offending hawk who carried the mouse aloft into the air. It transitions to a human village. Successive encounters with the sun, the clouds, the wind, and the mountain bring the story back to humble origins, within the furrows of the earth.

THE STORY OF PUṆYA AND PĀVANA FROM THE YOGA-VĀSIṢṬHA

The *Yoga-vāsiṣṭha,* discussed in the last chapter, includes a story about two brothers who grapple with the death of their parents. In a playful cascade of poetic description, this story describes the process of reincarnation. It suggests that because all humans have once been animals, insects, and even trees, that we can feel empathy for each of these life forms. Through reflecting on these other existences, we can lessen our attachment to this particular precious human birth.

Puṇya, the older brother, has attained the state of liberation (*jīvan-mukti*). Their father, a holy man named Dīrghatapas, dies. His wife and the mother of the boys, using yogic techniques, follows him in death. Pāvana, the younger brother, is inconsolable in his grief. Puṇya instructs him regarding the fleeting nature of the body and eventually frees his brother from his affliction, bringing him to liberation through tales of birth and rebirth. His teachings admonish Pāvana to remember his past births as a myriad of beings. By reflecting on the joys and pains of various past births, Puṇya prompts his brother to gain a new perspective on his current circumstance. Ultimately, this insight liberates Pāvana.

19.1 Vasiṣṭha said: Indeed, now they tell an old story
about two brothers on the banks of the Ganges,
said to be the two sons of a sage.

2 Listen, O Rāma, to this wonderfully good story
remembered as a tale about
who is related and who is not.

3 On the continent of Jambudvīpa,
there is a moist mountain covered with forest.
This highest mountain is called Mahendra.

4 Within its peaks extending into space,
with abundant forests rising up,
peaceful sages and musicians can be found
in the shadows of the wishing tree forest.

5 Having obtained the inner heavenly realm,
these sages hum the songs of the *Sāma Veda*,
which echo through the peaks and caves.

6 On the peak of the mountain
which is covered with vines and flowers,
water from dense, playful clouds
shimmers like locks of hair.

7 Rain resounds from thunder clouds and lightning,
like the open mouths of Śarabhas
flying straight out from their caves.

8 The roar generated by the torrents of water
moving through these caves
is equal to that of the resplendent surf
in the ocean's waters.

9 Spread out from that singular place
on the beautiful jewel encrusted mountain,
the Ganges descends from the sky,
to be used by the sages for bathing and drinking.

10 On the banks of that three path Ganges
radiant trees catch flashes of light up against the slope
of the jeweled mountain, illuminated by golden river fog.

11 A highly intelligent sage lived there, called Dīrghatapas,
endowed with noble vision due to his abundant *tapas*.
In fact, due to his *tapas*, his body was unexcelled.

12 This sage had two sons, Puṇya and Pāvana, handsome as the full moon,
as brilliant as those two sons of the father of speech (Bṛhaspati).

13 He, his wife, and his two sons all lived together as one
on the bank of the river under a fruit tree.

14 In due time, one of the two sons became knowledgeable.
The elder brother named Puṇya had superior qualities, O Rāma.

15 Pāvana was only half awakened, like a lotus at twilight.
Due to his slow-mindedness, he had not attained anything and was stuck in doubt.

16 The inevitable passage of time – 100 years, in fact –
caused Dīrgha's vitality to diminish and his body to grow old.

17 Having experienced repeated rounds of wealth and pleasure

as well as difficulty and decline, his life, wracked with senility, drew to an end.

18 The sage Dīrghatapas left his body like a bird flies from the nest.
He died in his house hidden on the mountain, laying down his heavy load.

19 With death, he flew into *samādhi*, free from thought,
into the abode of consciousness.
He went to the stage free from passion,
like the scent of a flower wafts up into the sky.

20 His wife, having seen the body of the lifeless sage,
fell to the earth, like a lotus without a stalk.

21 Through the discipline of Yoga taught to her by her husband over many years,
she renounced her delicate frame, like a bee flying from a lotus.

22 She followed her husband, departing to the place unseen by people,
the light of her soul fading in the sky like the half moon at sunset.

23 With mother and father gone, Puṇya steadfastly focused
on the funeral ceremonies, while Pāvana descended into grief.

24 His mind afflicted with grief, he wandered the forest paths.
Having lost sight of his brother, Pāvana wailed: 'Aaaaah!'

25 Having performed the appropriate funeral rites
for the bodies of his mother and father,

Puṇya ventured into the forest after Pāvana, who was
afflicted with great sorrow.[9]

26 'Why, boy, this thick cloud of sorrow? It is making you
blind and ignorant.
Your violent cloud of tears is like a monsoon season filled
with rain.

27 Your mother and father, of great wisdom, have gone
together to heaven,
indeed, to that highest Self, that place called Mokṣa.

28 That place is the goal of all people who have overcome
this world of form.
Why mourn your parents? They have attained their true
nature.

29 You are really bound to this state that is born of delusion.
You mourn for things in *saṃsāra* that should not be
mourned.

30 She is not your only mother nor is he your only father.
Nor are we the only two sons of the many who have been
born of those two.

31 Child, our mother and father have passed through
thousands of births,
as numerous as the streams running deep in each and
every forest.

32 Honored son, we are not the only two sons.
Our parents have had countless children.
Multitudes of sons have passed through the generations
like rapids in a river.

9 Translation by Griffin Guez.

33 Our parents had innumerable distinguished sons
who have passed away long ago,
just as the branches of a creeping vine give forth many
flowers and fruits.

34 Just as a great tree gives forth an abundance of fruits
with the passage of each season,
So also our many friends and relatives have experienced
many births.

35 Son, if parents and children are to be mourned out of
affection,
Then why should the thousands who die continually
not also be mourned?

36 From your perspective of worldliness,
the affairs of wandering people are deemed important.
But from the highest perspective, knowledge reveals that
there is no lasting friend, no lasting relative.

37 On the other hand, brother, from the perspective of
absolute truth,
no destruction is known either.
Everything happens only in the mind and then
evaporates like water in the desert.

38 The beautiful things that you see are none other than
a dream,
fluttering like feathers on a parasol, lasting three or
five days in the great mind.

39 By seeing things from the perspective of the ultimate
reality, son,
You must regard this truth: 'There is neither you nor we.'
You must renounce all your confusion.

40 Realize that all your previous negative views are now
dead and gone.
Such tortures arise in your own imagination and must
not be seen as true.

41 In a death characterized by ignorance,
The rolling waves of pure and impure vibrations
Cause past impressions to manifest without interruption
into the realm of name and form, like moonlight on water.

20.1 Who is the father? The friend? The mother? The relatives?
One's conception of them can be swept away as if they
are dust in the wind.

2 Love, aversion, and delusion in regard to our friends,
relatives, and offspring
are merely accomplished by the projection of our
own conceptions.

3 The quality associated with 'relative' makes a relative.
The quality associated with 'stranger' makes one a stranger,
just as the conditions of poison or nectar
depend upon the appearance of fixity (in the mind).

4 How can this notion arise that 'this one is a friend, that
one is a stranger'
when the mind of wisdom sees the oneness of the
all-pervading soul?

5 Son, reflect on yourself through your mind.
Ask, 'Who am I? What could I be? Something other than
the body?
A bony skeleton? A heap of blood, flesh, and bones?'

6 From the perspective of highest truth, there is no 'you',
there is no 'I'.

Only in delusion and ignorance do Puṇya and Pāvana
spring forth.

7 Who is your father, who is your friend?
Who is your mother? Who is your enemy?
In regard to the endless luminosity of space,
What can be proclaimed to be the Self? Or not the Self?

8 You are consciousness in the midst of many other
prior births
where you have had friends and properties.
Why do you not grieve for them also?

9 Those many deer in the flowery meadow,
born of their mother does, were your relatives.
Why do you not grieve for them?

10 Regard the swans in the bouquets of lotuses on the
riverbank.
Why do you not grieve for those swans who were
your relatives?

11 Those fine trees in the splendid beautiful forests were
also your relatives.
Why do you not grieve for them?

12 Those lions on the awe-inspiring peaks of those
mountains
were also your relatives. Why do you not grieve for them?

13 Those fish among the beautiful lotuses in the clear lakes
were also your relatives. Why do you not grieve for them?

14 You were a monkey in the brown woods of the
Ten River Land,
a prince in the land of snow, and a crow in the forest
of the Puṇḍras.

15 You were an elephant among the Haihaya people,
a donkey in the company of the Trigartas,
a puppy with the people of Śalva, and a bird in that tree.

16 You were a fig tree in the Vindhya range, and an insect in a great tree.
You have been a hen on the Mandara Mountain.
You were born also as a Brahmin in Kandara.

17 You were a Brahmin in Kosala. You were a partridge in Bengal.
You were a horse in the land of snow.
And you were the beast killed at the Brāhmaṇa sacrifice.

18 The one who was an insect inside the root of a palm tree,
who was a mosquito on a big ficus tree,
the one who was previously a crane in the forest,
that one is now you, my son, my little brother.

19 That small red ant that lived for six months
in the hollow of the thin knotty birch tree bark
on the cliffs of the Himalayas is now you, my little brother.[10]

20 You were the beetle living for a year and a half
in cow dung at the edge of a frontier village.
O Sādhu, that was you, little brother.[11]

21 The child who sat on the six petalled lotus throne of the Pulinda tribal woman,
hidden in the forest, that one was you, little brother.

---

10 Translation by Kija Manhare.

11 Translation by Erika Burkhalter.

22 For thousands of prior births in these many woods
you were born of various wombs, my son,
And now you are born on Jambudvīpa.

23 By the purified clear vision of my subtle intellect,
I see the previous successive lives of your self.

24 I remember today my many past lives, born of
many wombs
due to ignorance and indolence. This insight has
arisen due to knowledge.

25 Having been a parrot in Trigarta and a frog on a
riverbank,
and having been a lumberjack in the woods, now
I am born here in this forest.

26 I ravished a royal woman in the Vindhyas.
I have been fashioned as a tree in Bengal as well as
a camel in the Vindhya range.
I am now born in this forest.

27 That bird in the Himalayan town, that king in the
Pauṇḍra region,
that tiger in the Śalya region... that one is now me,
your elder brother.

28 I was that vulture who lived for ten years,
that shark who lived five months, and that lion who lived
a full century.
That one indeed is now your older brother.

29 Can you believe it? I lived as a prince of a village
in Andhra,
as a sovereign king in the Tuṣāra region, and as the
son of the Śailācārya.

30 I remember from long ago all the various incarnations
and all the various customs
that have arisen into manifestation due to confusion.

31 There, in that place [of memory], so many thousands
of relatives
were born in those worlds that have now gone:
fathers, mothers, siblings, and friends.

32 Whom shall we two grieve? Whom shall we not grieve?
We grieve all relatives that die. This is the way of life
in the world.

33 Like the endless passing of fathers and mothers in this
world of *saṃsāra*,
souls drop like leaves, falling off the trees in the forest.[12]

34 Who can measure the varieties of pleasure and pain,
O brother?
Therefore, renounce all of them. Let us take our place
in the light.

35 Having renounced all cultivation of outward
manifestation in the mind,
abiding in the Self, go happily to that place,
that place where the wise ones go.

36 Inactive beings fall away. Active persons rise again.
Those with good thoughts do not grieve They move
gradually toward freedom.

37 Be free of confusion. Be free of [attachment to] existence
and nonexistence.

---

12 Translation by Natalé Ferreira.

Escape from old age and death. Be cool, always
remembering your true Self.

38 You are not your suffering. You are not this birth.
You are indeed the Self, not this intellect.
Indeed, how could you be other than true Self?

39 Sādhu! Ignorant people performing various dramas
in this journey of *saṃsāra*
attach themselves to the sentiments of existence.

40 One can attain the goal of being the witness,
self-possessed in the midst of all that can be seen.
Such persons are established in the dharma of the
observer,
being the knower and spectator at all times.

41 Whether engaged in action or inactive,
such persons regard actions as if they were the
fading light
at the start of the night. The knower stands
unperturbed by the world.

42 Those who have arrived at the illumination of the
true Self
no longer see the reflection [as real], just as the jewels
reflected in the mirror
are taken to be mere reflections by those with wisdom.

43 Through moving away from all this self-made darkness,
dwell in your true Self, which is like the radiant
moon in the middle of your heart.

44 Son, find the Self in the Self. Be a sage like the great sages.
Having renounced all impure perplexity, be content!

This narrative, told over two chapters of the *Upaśama-prakaraṇa* of the *Yoga-vāsiṣṭha*, holds many insights relevant for the topic of this book. Like the Abram narrative of 'becoming animal', it reminds the listener that we are not limited beings. We carry unfathomable histories and experiences; according to Hinduism, Buddhism, and Jainism, we have taken birth countless times. By appreciating the landscape perspective suggested by Puṇya, that is, being cognizant of the beauty of the meadow, the river, the mountain, and all the many lives contained therein, we can move beyond the petty dramas that trap the mind and emotions in negativity. This does not mean that grief is to be avoided; Pāvana channeled his grief into the performance of the funeral rituals. Pāvana suggests that we must always take the wider view, surrendering attachments in favour of contentment and peace.

Humans as Animals

In the Indian system of reincarnation, all beings are said to be equal. As famously stated in the *Bhagavad Gītā*: 'People of learning view with equal eye a Bramhin of knowledge and good learning, a cow, an elephant, and even a dog and an out-caste.'[13] The preparatory lessons from past lives shape and guide an individual into the present and future lives. Recognition of innate animal impulses can work for good and for ill; a good animal might be regarded as superior to a bad human. To have been an animal and to have recalled past animal experiences indicates a sign of greatness, an acknowledgement of one's ongoing connections and kinship with other species.

13 *Bhagavad Gītā* V.18.

Implications

The animal stories give voice to the prevailing ethic of non-violence, the keystone of yogic practice. Animals are teachers. Satyakāma Jābāla learns truthfulness and humility from them. Because of his attunement to the natural world, he is able to receive sixteen truths regarding the four directions, the nature of elements, the specific qualities of light, and the operations of the human body and mind. He receives these teachings not from a human but from elements and animals. Due to his receptivity to these other-than-human entities, he returns to the realm of humans with the glow of deep knowledge, a knowledge of connectivity and emplacement and embodiment, a knowledge that qualifies him to become one of India's most renowned sages.

The story of the *ṛṣi* and the mouse daughter demonstrates the power of parental love. The sense of care exhibited by the *ṛṣi* and his wife extends from the everyday nurturing of basic needs to planning for the eventual marriage of their adopted daughter. Furthermore, though he had great plans for her future, he also accepted her eventual fate, a return to her original innate state. This story presents both a lesson in *dharma* in that parents must do everything for their children, and, in a perhaps modern way of viewing *svadharma*, the realisation that all individuals must follow their own path.

Puṇya's friendly advice to his grieving brother outlines a way of understanding human emplacement within the round of birth, death, and rebirth. Kinship defines this story in a radical way: brothers deal with the passing of their parents each in his unique way, with Puṇya expanding the definition of kinship to include all manner of beings: trees, ants, beetles, bees, mosquitoes, scorpions, frogs, crocodiles, cranes, parrots, hawks, swans, eagles, donkeys, deer, camels, elephants, tigers, and lions. By connecting with the broader web of life, Pāvana moves from despair to calm.

Bishnoi Animal Activism: Protecting Personhood

Perhaps the most famous animal activism movement in India can be found in the work and life of the Bishnoi. The founder, Jambheśvara, also known as Jambhoji, was born in Pipasar, a rural region of Rajasthan, in 1451, and died in 1536. According to some accounts, his father was a Rajput prince and his mother was a Muslim. Both Hindu and Muslim communities lay claim to his story. Though they self-identify as Hindu, the Bishnoi maintained practices associated with Islam; they bury their dead and keep no images of deities in their temples. Before partition, the shrine table devoted to his memory was covered with a green cloth, indicating a connection with Islam. Since partition, the colour of the cloth has been saffron. Having served as a cowherd for more than twenty years before receiving a religious vision, Jambheśvara established the Bishnoi community in 1485 for the protection of humans, animals, and plants. He composed twenty nine rules to be followed by all members of this community, which include the following:

18 Be compassionate towards all living beings;

22 Provide common shelter for goats and sheep to avoid them being slaughtered in abattoirs;

23 Do not castrate bulls;

28 Do not eat meat or non-vegetarian dishes.[14]

---

14 See www.worldatlas.com/articles/india-s-bishnoi-community-have-fearlessly-protected-nature-for-over-500-years.html.

Another of his works, the *Jambha Sāra*, lays out six rules to avoid violence:

> First is the *Jhampari Pāl* that prohibits the animal sacrifice. Second is the *jeevani vidhi* to filter water and milk. Third is putting the water-creatures back into the water. Fourth is to make sure that the firewood and the cowdung for fuel do not have any creatures or insects that might be accidentally burnt. Fifth is the *badhiyā,* to avoid harming the bullocks, to not sell them to the butchers, or to send them to animal shelter centers. Sixth is the protection of deer in forests like cows, goats and other non-violent beasts.[15]

According to traditional lore, the Bishnoi commitment to the protection of plants and animals has cost hundreds of them their lives since the fifteenth century, including a group of 363 Bishnoi who, under the leadership of Amrita Devi, resisted deforestation in 1730. Because of this tragedy, the ruler of Jodhpur, Maharaj Abhay Singh, apologised and issued the following decrees that would prevent such slaughter in the future. All cutting of green trees and hunting of animals within the revenue boundaries of Bishnoi villages was strictly prohibited. If by mistake people violated this order, they would be prosecuted by the state and severely penalised. Even the members of ruling families were not permitted to shoot animals in or near the Bishnoi villages.

---

15 Suryashankar Parik, *Jāmbhojī kī Vāṇī, Jīvanī, Darśana, aur Hindi Artha Sahita Mūlavāṇī-pātha* (Bikaner: Vikāsa Prakāśana, 2001), as translated by Pankaj Jain in *Dharma and Ecology of Hindu Communities: Sustenance and Sustainability* (Surrey, UK/Burlington, VT: Ashgate, 2011), 60.

Amrita Devi inspired the Chipko tree protection movement in the 1730s. To this day, the animals within the Bishnoi area, which includes most of Rajasthan and parts of Gujarat and Haryana, are afforded extraordinary protection. In 2000, the Amrita Devi Award was given to the family of Gangaram Bishnoi, who lost his life while protecting a Chinkara deer. In 2004, the same award was bestowed on the family of Chhailuram Singh Rajput, a Bishnoi who lost his life saving a Blackbuck. In 1998, Hindi film actor Salman Khan was sentenced to five years in prison for killing a Blackbuck in Bishnoi territory. In modern times, Bishnoi have established the Community for Wildlife and Rural Development Society, and the All India Jeev Raksha Bishnoi Sabha, a wildlife protection organisation. The Bishnoi maintain an active website, which includes the posting of an award winning film about their movement, *Willing to Sacrifice*.

Wildlife Trust of India

In October 2019 my wife and I visited the offices of the Wildlife Trust of India in Noida for a conversation with its founder and director, Dr. Vivek Menon. I first met Vivek at a Global Buddhist Congregation sponsored by Aśoka Mission in New Delhi in 2011. The topic of the conference was 'Environment and the Natural World: A Buddhist Response'. We both participated on a panel about the work of the Gyalwa Karmapa on behalf of the Tibetan antelope as inspired by renowned conservation ecologist George Schaller, who also presented a talk. We next met at a Minding Animals conference that convened in Utrecht, the Netherlands, in 2012 where I learned more details about his remarkable work on behalf of tigers and elephants. The next year he regaled my students on a service learning alternative break in India with news that had come in earlier that day regarding a rogue tiger that had been captured in the Sundarbans, and then released back into the wild. His book *Mammals of India* has become a major resource for naturalists in India, alongside Pradip Krishen's *Trees of Delhi: A Field Guide*.[16]

My wife and I recently had returned from a trip to Rishikesh where we noted a new transportation innovation: a flyover between Rishikesh and Dehradun that allowed hitherto impossible night travel. As we described the flyover on the way to Rishikesh, noting that it will allow safe passage of elephants and tigers, Vivek smiled and… yes, this was his idea and required a great deal of effort to implement! The flyover also helps humans, whose risk will be reduced. Five hundred humans are trampled to death each year by elephants.

Vivek told of one recent fortuitous meeting with Prince William, Princess Kate, and Prime Minister Modi. William, very much his father's son, has long been concerned with and a fervent advocate for the protection of nature. As he asked the Prime Minister about future plans, it was clear that Modi probably had not been briefed on this particular topic. However, Vivek Menon made the case for nature protection in India as vital to heritage preservation and by the end of the conversation everyone was agreed about the importance of protecting India's elephants and tigers.

16 Vivek Menon, *Mammals of India* (Delhi: Penguin, 2003); Pradip Krishen, *Trees of Delhi: A Field Guide* (Delhi: Dorling Kindersley, 2006).

Conclusion

From earliest recorded history, through the advent of Buddhism and the Jaina tradition, with such notable practices as Yoga, and the perdurability of resistance movements such as the Bishnoi, animal advocacy has been an integral part of Indian culture. Animals have been accorded respect. They are said to carry an innate dignity. Each human person has endured and experienced countless lives as an animal, and each human can most likely look forward to a future non-human animal birth. The core philosophies of India hold animals in great regard, not only for their gifts, but for their very being. From India, the world can learn a great deal about building an ethic of animal advocacy. Lively stories of past animal births, philosophies that emphasise the interconnectedness of life, and a long history of women and men willing to make sacrifices to protect trees and animals constitute a substantial reservoir of inspiration. Personhood dwells not only in human form and not only with the higher primates. All beings can be seen as companions, placing the human in place of humility and great responsibility.

Portions of this chapter are excerpted from Christopher Key Chapple. 'Animal Stories'. In *Living Landscapes: Meditations on the Elements in Hindu, Buddhist, and Jain Yogas*, 126–150. Albany: State University of New York Press, 2020.

Discussion Topic: Animals and Ecology

- Discuss the possible therapeutic benefits to accepting a worldview that includes reincarnation as found in the story of Puṇya and Pāvana.
- Share a story of an animal encounter. In what ways did your animal serve as a guide or inspiration?

Further Reading

Sir Edwin Arnold. *The Book of Good Counsels: From the Sanskrit of the Hitopadesa*. London: Smith, Elder & Co., 1861.

Pankaj Jain, *Dharma and Ecology of Hindu Communities: Sustenance and Sustainability*. Surrey, UK: Ashgate, 2011 (for a comprehensive study of the Bishnoi).

Pradip Krishen. *Trees of Delhi: A Field Guide*. Delhi: Dorling Kindersley, 2006.

Nanditha Krishna, *Sacred Animals of India*. New Delhi: Penguin Books, 2010 (for a collection of Hindu animal fables).

Vivek Menon. *Mammals of India*. New Delhi: Penguin, 2003.

Patrick Olivelle. *Pañcatantra: The Book of India's Folk Wisdom*. New York: Oxford University Press, 1997.

Artist.
Ghasi Ram. Sharma
Nathdwara

IX
Gandhi and Two Gandhi-Inspired Eco-Activists

From the time of Gandhi, a constant refrain has been sung in India: live simply so that others may live! Starting with an examination of the lifestyle advocated by Gandhi, we will look at two leaders inspired by his example who continue to advocate for environmental causes: Vandana Shiva and M.C. Mehta.

Mahatma Gandhi and the Enduring Challenges of the Twenty-first Century

Gandhi championed three values that remain important as we confront the many ecological and economic challenges of the twenty-first century: *satyagraha* (holding to truth), *ahiṃsā* (non-violence), and *aparigraha* (non-possession). In this chapter, three applications of Gandhian thought will be explored: its relevance for resolving environmental issues, his own stated attitude toward the 'engine' of modern economies: transportation and increased globalisation, and the pressing issue of deciding the most ethical way to allocate medical treatments.

Thomas Merton articulated one aspect of *satyagraha* as follows: 'The whole Gandhian concept of non-violent action and *satyagraha* is incomprehensible if it is thought to be a means of achieving unity rather than as *the fruit of inner unity already achieved.*'[1] For Gandhi, appropriate action can only take place from a place of direct encounter of a transcendent reality, of the sort described in the Vedic term *ṛta* and the Yoga meditation term *samādhi*. By seeing our unity with the adversary, we can hope to understand, empathise with, and convert that enemy. The enemy facing the twenty-first century goes beyond enemies of times past. Cataclysmic climate change in past eras was precipitated by cosmic events such as meteors or comets. Today, we have come to the slowly dawning truth that humans have been responsible for a shift of weather patterns, and that the very behaviours that have brought great comfort are becoming our own worst enemy. As an increasingly global society, we must grapple with the truths of climate change, species extinctions, and the ongoing heath problems (animal and human) caused by human-induced industrial pollution. In the words of Thomas Berry, we must take responsibility for the emergence of the Ecozoic age, wherein humans become community partners in the web of life beyond, though not excluding, anthropocentric concerns. Through non-violent appreciation of all forms of life, from landscapes to non-human animals, we might be able to recover from the nature-deficit syndrome caused by being caught in the technological and consumerist trance.

Gandhi's non-violence required vegetarianism as well as a willingness to engage and converse and ultimately have compassion and even love for one's antagonists. In our current situation, we must learn to even better love nature, love animals, and, for the purposes of change, even love the corporations that must transform their habits to bring about a sustainable economic environment. Gandhi also emphasised

1 Thomas Merton, ed., *Mahatma Gandhi on Non-violence* (New York, New Directions, 1965), 10.

that 'we must become the change we want to see in the world'. By practising the lessening of possessions, we can move toward reversing the obsession with material accumulation, in the words of John Cobb, the 'religion of economism', and restore balance to modern lifestyles worldwide. Our ecological moment of reckoning might once more make relevant several of Gandhi's key insights into the nature and function of human work. Young people in contemporary India, benefitting materially from the new globalised economy, are fond of relegating Gandhi to a retrograde past, seeing him as irrelevant. However, in the words of Lloyd and Suzanne Rudolph, we might now need to heed 'Gandhi's postmodern emphasis on human capital, decentralised production, and "appropriate technology"'.[2] As Gandhi himself stated, there is enough in the world for 'everyone's need, not everyone's greed.' The ethical anchor of Gandhi's teachings can help people worldwide make a shift to a common-sense, and truly human-sized, footprint on planet Earth.

Gandhi and Vegetarianism

Mahatma Gandhi was born into a family that practiced vegetarianism, as remains common among Vaiṣṇavite Hindus and Jainas throughout the subcontinent. During the period during which he studied law in England from 1888 to 1891 he came to understand his vegetarianism and commitment to non-violence in a modern context. He was a mere nineteen years old when he embarked on this journey. It was a time of remarkable self-discovery and undoubtedly shaped ideas and attitudes to take form over the case over several years,

2 Lloyd and Susanne Rudoph, *Postmodern Gandhi and Other Essays* (Chicago: University of Chicago Press, 2006).

culminating in the publication of his core work, *Hind Swaraj*, in 1909.[3]

Three primary written sources were influential on Gandhi during his years in London that helped shape his views toward the role of vegetarianism in the development of personal ethics: Henry Salt's *A Plea for Vegetarianism, The Ethics of Diet* by Howard Williams, and *The Perfect Way in Diet* by Anna Kingsford. Gandhi became deeply involved with the Vegetarian Society while in England and contributed nine articles to a periodical titled *Vegetarian*.[4]

When Gandhi landed in England, he endured hunger, not knowing where to find food that sufficiently provide complementary nutrition. Finally, he learned of a vegetarian restaurant on Farringdon Street. It was here that he discovered the works of Henry Salt (1851–1939):

> Before I entered I noticed books for sale exhibited under a glass window near the door. I saw among them Salt's *A Plea for Vegetarianism*.[5] This I purchased for a shilling and went straight to the dining room. This was my first hearty meal since my arrival in England.... From the date of reading this book, I may claim to have become a vegetarian by choice. I blessed the day on which I had taken the vow before my mother. I had all along abstained from meat in the interests of truth and of the vow I had taken, but had wished at the

3 Gandhi wrote 50,000 published pages in *The Collected Works of Mahatma Gandhi*, which spans 98 volumes. *Hind Swaraj* is recognized as his core manifesto. Mohandas Gandhi, *Hind Swaraj and Other Writings*,. ed. Anthony J. Parel (Cambridge University Press, 1997).

4 Tara Sethia, *Gandhi: Pioneer of Nonviolent Social Change* (Boston: Pearson, 2012), 17.

5 Henry Salt, *A Plea for Vegetarianism* (Manchester: The Vegetarian Society, 1886).

> same time that every Indian should be a meat-eater, and had looked forward to being one myself freely and openly some day, and to enlisting others in the cause. The choice was now made in favour of vegetarianism, the spread of which henceforward became my mission.[6]

Gandhi delivered these words more than forty years after first obtaining Salt's book, recalling his happiness at finding support for his vegetarianism. Salt himself, at the time of the speech an octogenarian, was present at Gandhi's talk.

> Mr. Chairman, Fellow Vegetarians, and Friends, when I received the invitation to be present at this meeting, I need not tell you how pleased I was because it revived old memories and recollections of pleasant friendships formed with vegetarians. I feel especially honoured to find on my right, Mr. Henry Salt. It was Mr. Salt's book, *A Plea for Vegetarianism,* which showed me why apart from a hereditary habit, and apart from my adherence to a vow administered to me by my mother, it was right to be a vegetarian. He showed me why it was a moral duty incumbent on vegetarians not to live upon fellow animals. It is, therefore, a matter of additional pleasure to me that I find Mr. Salt in our midst.[7]

The tract that so inspired Gandhi with its elegant, elevated, engaging, and entertaining prose sets forth an argument for vegetarianism that Gandhi found quite bracing. Salt wrote that

---

6 Speech delivered by Gandhi at a Social Meeting organised by the London Vegetarian Society, 20 November 1931, cited at https://ivu.org/history/salt.

7 Speech delivered by Gandhi at a Social Meeting organised by the London Vegetarian Society, 20 November 1931, cited at https://ivu.org/history/salt.

'future and wiser generations will look back with amazement on the habit of flesh-eating as a strange relic of ignorance and barbarism'.[8] Gandhi, in his early twenties, no doubt took solace in this affirmation of the lifestyle in which he was raised. At the same time, Salt acknowledges that vegetarianism, though the norm in many Indian households, ran counter to mainstream British sensibilities at the time, noting that many regarded it to be an 'impious absurdity and dangerous hallucination of modern times, to be classed with Mormonism, Spiritualism, Anglo-Israelism, Socialism, and possibly Atheism itself'.[9] The rhetoric employed by Salt was simultaneously humorous and insightful, demonstrating the truly counter-cultural aspects of the vegetarian lifestyle.

Gandhi visited Howard Williams (1837–1931) on the Isle of Wight in 1891. He wrote of being moved by Williams' research into the historical aspects of vegetarianism. Howard Williams' *The Ethics of Diet*[10] provided dates and details regarding eighty-four men (and one woman) throughout history who have written positively about the practice of vegetarianism. These include Hesiod, Buddha, Pythagoras, Empedokles, Plato, Aśoka, Ovid, Seneca, Apollonius of Tyanna, Plutarch, Tertullian, Clement of Alexandria, Porphyry, Rousseau, Adam Smith, Jeremy Bentham, Schopenhauer, Shelly, Byron, Lamartine, Wagner, and Thoreau. In the 1896 edition he added a detailed profile of the next major influence on Gandhi's view on vegetarianism and vivesectionism, Anna Kingsford.

---

8 Salt, *A Plea for Vegetarianism*, 20.

9 Salt, *A Plea for Vegetarianism*, 10.

10 Howard Williams, *The Ethics of Diet* was first published as a series of articles in the journal *The Dietetic Reformer and Vegetarian Messenger* (1878 ff.), later as a book in 1883 and reissued in several subsequent editions. Tolstoy wrote the preface to the 1892 Russian edition.

Anna Bonus Kingsford (1846–1888) was born into a wealthy merchant family, was highly educated from childhood, and married an Anglican priest at the age of 21. She converted to Catholicism with his blessings at the age of 26. Kingsford, at the age of 28, traveled to Paris in order to receive medical training. She collaborated with Edward Maitland during her six-year stay in France. She took a strong stand against vivisection, considered at the time to be a concoction of the French, and apparently went to France to get a firsthand view of what to her and Maitland was an abhorrent practice. She was the only medical student at that time to earn her degree without performing animal dissection.

Her dissertation, 'De l'Alimentation Vegetal chez l'Homme', was translated into English and published as the book *The Perfect Way in Diet: A Treatise Advocating a Return to the Natural and Ancient Food of Our Race*. Its fifth edition was published in 1892.[11] It opens with a 'Proem', a lengthy verse quote from Edwin Arnold's *Light of Asia* recounting the episode in which the Buddha forbids animal sacrifice: 'Henceforth none shall spill the blood of life nor taste of flesh, seeing that knowledge grows, and life is one, and mercy comes to the merciful.'[12]. Her argument for vegetarianism begins with an anatomical analysis of the human mouth, noting its similarities to 'orangs, chimpanzees, and the gorilla' whose teeth stomach, and saliva are adapted for a herbivorous, frugivorous diet (5–16). She devotes several pages to the dietary habits of various peoples, including Romans, Hindus, Buddhists, Egyptians, Chinese, 'Indians of the New Spain', Turks, Chinese,

11 Anna Kingsford, *The Perfect Way in Diet: A Treatise Advocating a Return to the Natural and Ancient Food of Our Race* (London: Kegan Paul, Trench, Trübner, & Co., 1892).

12 Kingsford, *The Perfect Way in Diet*, xii.

Algerians, extolling the vegetarian diet in each instance. She writes that in regard to Palestine, 'the diet of both Christian and Muslim is strictly vegetarian' (31). She describes in great detail the suffering inflicted on cattle and warns of the dangers of parasites in meat. She gives several case examples of cures brought by about by changing to a vegetarian diet. She also writes about the superior farming efficiency gained by the cultivation of vegetables rather than the grazing and feeding of animals (100–104). In short, she advances various scientific and social reasons for adopting a vegetarian diet, all in colourful, elegant rhetoric. She closes the book as it begins, with a poem that concludes: 'Let your mouths be empty of blood, and satisfied with pure and natural repasts' (121).

These three thinkers affirmed for Gandhi the principles and premises of India's long-standing commitment to nonviolence and vegetarianism. Some aspects of Indian thought that informed Gandhi's worldview can be summarised as follows. The Vedas, the Sanskrit literature that arose from 1500 BCE, articulate an unformed foundation, a realm of nonexistence (*asat*), a mist from which arise distinct worlds, depending upon human desire. Through desire, humans craft their world, creating boundaries and distinctions, separating heaven from earth, light from darkness. In this constructed world, sustained by sacrifice, meditation, and prayer, individuals gather into community, moving from the unformed to the formed. Intention and desire direct communities and individuals to select various options, symbolised by various deities, all seen as provisional tools for attaining a goal, whether worldly or sublime. This process connects the individual with the cosmic flow of life (*ṛta*). Practitioners of Yoga in its various forms strive for an elevated sense of connection, known as *samādhi*. For both the worldly and the spiritually inclined, five precepts must be followed:

non-violence, truthfulness, not stealing, sexual propriety, and non-possession. These guarantee harmony between the ongoing flux or flow between the unspeakable realm of origin and the realm of manifest activity. These precepts, observed by Vaiṣṇavas, *Śaivas,* Jainas, Buddhists, and Sikhs in India, include respect for all forms of life, a mandate to be truthful and honest, and cautions against the dangers of greed and lust. These precepts shaped both Gandhi's personal and social ethics.

Drawing from this worldview, Gandhi championed non-violence and a commitment to truth, as well as non-possession. In his life work, he constantly reminded his followers of the importance of *satyagraha* (holding to truth), *ahiṃsā* (non-violence), and *aparigraha* (non-possession). For Gandhi, appropriate action can only take place from a place of direct encounter of a transcendent reality, of the sort described in the Vedic term *ṛta* and the Yoga meditation term *samādhi*. By seeing our unity with the adversary, we can hope to understand, empathise with, and perhaps find fellowship with that enemy. For Gandhi, the adversary was not only the British but also any form of injustice toward the downtrodden, whether impoverished low-caste Hindus, women of all faiths, and disadvantaged Muslims.

For Gandhi, non-violence entailed kindness to animals, both human and non-human. Gandhi's non-violence required vegetarianism, as well as a willingness to engage, converse with, and ultimately have compassion and even love for one's antagonists. Gandhi advocated a village economy. This involves the consumption of local foods and the wearing of clothes spun and woven by each individual. He also encouraged small-scale technologies, which, for instance, involve solar cook stoves, locally generated electricity, and self-transport using bicycles.

Self-Rule, Transportation, and Health Care in Gandhi's Hind Swaraj

Hind Swaraj, published in 1908, encapsulates the core ideas that propelled Mahatma Gandhi onto the world stage. Three items stand out as holding relevance for our times and into the future. The first has to do with its general philosophy of self-effort, indicated in the title *Hind Swaraj* which means 'India's Self-rule' and attested to by the reading list that influenced the Mahatma. The title refers not only to Hind/India as a country but also to the people of India themselves. Gandhi proclaimed that by mastering themselves individually and collectively, Indians will find the will to govern themselves and cast off their colonial oppressors, which in fact transpired some thirty-seven years after the publication of *Hind Swaraj*. The second area to be examined has to do with Gandhi's abiding critique of transportation, and his related call for maintaining a slow-paced life. The third topic that I will discuss is Gandhi's critique of physicians and his general approach to health care.

Self-Rule

First, in regard to self-rule, I would like to share a translation that I rendered many years ago from the *Mumukṣu-prakaraṇa* of the *Yoga-vāsiṣṭha*, one of the texts recommended to Gandhi by his Jaina teacher Raichandbhai, also known as Rajchandra Ravjibhai Mehta (1868–1901).[13]

> There are some who, due to their desire,
> have incapacitated themselves to such an extent
> that they cannot squeeze their fingers together

13 Mohandas Gandhi. *Hind Swaraj and Other Writings*, ed. Anthony J. Parel (Cambridge University Press, 1997), xlix.

> sufficiently enough to hold water
> without scattering several drops.
> On the other hand, there are some who,
> by efficacious actions, take on the responsibility
> of seas, mountains, cities, and islands,
> as well as families, for whom even the earth itself
> would not be too much.[14]

Gandhi struggled to find strength within India and within the Indian psyche. In the *Yoga-vāsiṣṭha* he found a philosophy that regales one into action, that rejects any form of submissiveness. This strength must be directed inward, however, and not against an external enemy. From Rajchandra and his own mother, Gandhi learned and lived an undying commitment to non-violence. Nonetheless, he advocated inner warfare, heeding the advice of the second chapter of the *Bhagavad Gītā*. As I learned from his personal secretary, Narayan Desai, in 2008, Gandhi recited the last eighteen verses of the Yoga of Knowledge daily, adhering to the ideas encapsulated in verse 64: 'With the elimination of desire and hatred, even though moving among the objects of the senses, the one who is controlled by the self through self-restraint attains tranquility.' Combining strength, adherence to non-violence, and self-control, Gandhi set himself and others on a path that changed the course of world history.

Transportation

The railroad roiled Gandhi, unlike Thoreau, who extolled the punctuality and progress and support of commerce offered

14 Christopher Key Chapple, *Karma and Creativity* (Albany, NY: State University of New York Press, 1986), 105–106.

by the 'iron steed'.[15] First, in regard to allocation of resources, Gandhi makes an apt comment on the nature of the railroad. Although common wisdom states that England united India through its railroads and hence improved the general situation in the subcontinent, Gandhi suggests that a better use of public funds would have been to improve irrigation systems, allowing local areas to flourish. He suggests that railways facilitate the spread of disease and that 'Good travels at a snail's pace – it can have little to do with the railways'.[16] In his critique of railroads, Gandhi calls into question the very premises of progress and speed. He writes: 'Honest physicians will tell you that, where means of artificial locomotion have increased, the health of the people has suffered.... I cannot recall a single good point in connection with machinery.'[17] Although we hesitate to think in categories of either/or and recognise that both irrigation and transportation result in positive outcomes, daily life through improved access to water would have been a good use of imperial resources. Today, alongside the railways, both air travel and automotive transport have increased exponentially, resulting in a faster pace of life, and, to an extent, an increase in disease. The AIDS problem has been exacerbated in India by truckers, patrons of sex workers, bringing the disease home to remote villages.

Railways, steamships, private cars, and airplanes have accelerated the flow of goods in ways nearly unimaginable in 1910. Gandhi could not have imagined the new colonialism brought about by reliance upon oil, which powers the bulk of

---

15 Henry David Thoreau, *Walden and Other Writings*, ed. Brooks Atkinson (New York: The Modern Library, 1937), 101–111.

16 Gandhi, *Hind Swaraj*, 47.

17 Ibid., 110.

our electricity, drives the engines of our automobiles, provides the fertilisers for our crops, and lies at the root of ongoing wars and turmoil worldwide. Yet, in his critique of the railroad, he imparts an enduring wisdom. Gandhi asks himself:

> What, then, of tram-cars and electricity?' He responds, 'If we are to do without the railways, we shall have to do without the tram-cars. Machinery is like a snake-hole which may contain from one to a hundred snakes.... where means of artificial locomotion have increased, the health of the people has suffered.... Nature has not provided any way whereby we may reach a desired goal all of a sudden.[18]

He advocates the slow-paced life of the village, wherein all needed goods and services and provided locally. The simplicity advocated by Gandhi would entail little or need for transportation of goods or persons. By adhering to a village economy, and by remaining content within one's community, basic human needs could be fulfilled.

Today, great virtue is seen in scaling back our modes of transportation. Emphasis is being placed upon mass-transit options and ride sharing. In quiet ways, Gandhian principles are being reasserted by individuals who compost, grow their own vegetables, and minimise their own transport and oil consumption needs by living close to work, who drive rather than fly when possible, purchase low-emission vehicles, and preferably walk or bicycle frequently. Though Gandhi could not have anticipated the massive looming problem of global warming, he certainly saw the ills that accompany complexity. His call for simplicity and abstinence from reliance on machinery remains relevant.

---

18 Ibid., 110–111.

As the planetary population continues to urbanise, a host of difficulties arise: reliance on agribusiness, alienation from the rhythms of nature, and a loss of a sense of community. In the developing world, which now provides the bulk of manufactured goods, we see the increase of what Gandhi lamented in Europe a century ago, when he wrote: 'Machinery has begun to desolate Europe. Ruination is now knocking at the English gates. Machinery is the chief symbol of modern civilisation: it represents great sin.'[19] With great prescience, Gandhi wrote: 'And those who have amassed great wealth out of factories are not likely to be better than other rich men. It would be folly to assume that an Indian Rockefeller would be better than the American Rockefeller.'[20] In China, labour now balks at working conditions. Within the next two decades, India will most likely absorb more manufacturing jobs, and similarly struggle with issues of justice, seeking to avoid what Gandhi lamented: 'The workers in the mills of Bombay have become slaves.'[21]

Health Care

Health care has been an issue of great discussion in the past few years. On the one hand, advances in medical research and delivery systems have helped humans overcome countless diseases and allow for greater longevity. On the other hand, the defeat of the microbe in the past seventy-five years has resulted in exponential rates of population growth, stressing the carrying capacity of the planet. Though the global trend indicates a leveling of population by mid-century, nine billion people will occupy and seize the

19 Ibid., 107.

20 Ibid., 108.

21 Ibid., 108.

resources of the planet as never before, imperiling the viability of life systems worldwide. This comes at a great cost, economic and spiritual. For each individual to maintain health in the developed world, particularly in the United States, vast sums are expended each year, consisting of a significant percentage of the gross domestic product. The rise of modern medicine ushered in medicines and technologies that allow the postponement of death. Accompanied with what has been termed the Denial of Death, what once was known as inevitable now seems unfair.

For Gandhi, growing up in an era before antibiotics and in the proximity of the Jaina community, death was not a mystery nor were extraordinary measures employed to avoid death. In fact, the tradition of fasting unto death (*sallekhanā/santhara*) undoubtedly informed his worldview, a practice still enacted by monastic and lay Jainas worldwide today. Hence, death with dignity would be an essential part of a Gandhian approach. He considered the manner of death far more important than the avoidance of death, advocating a spiritual approach. He considered medicine to be a 'parasitical profession'[22] and wrote that 'Doctors have nearly unhinged us'.[23] His attitude toward medicine was highly suspicious, and he regarded reliance on physicians as feeding human weakness:

> How do these diseases arise? Surely by our negligence and indulgence. I over-eat. I have indigestion, I go to a doctor, he gives me medicine, I am cured, I over-eat again, and I take his pills again. Had I not taken the pills in the first instance, I would have suffered the punishment deserved by me, and I would not have over-eaten again. The doctor intervened

22 Ibid., 62.

23 Ibid., 63.

> and helped me to indulge myself. My body thereby certainly felt more at ease, but my mind became weakened. A continuance of a course of medicine must, therefore, result in loss of control over the mind.... Had the doctor not intervened, nature would have done its work, and I would have acquired mastery over myself, would have been freed from vice, and would have become happy.[24]

Though this approach seems to arrogate all illness to the mind without taking into account truly debilitating conditions beyond human control, Gandhi nonetheless offers insight and wisdom. The rise of diabetes worldwide is due in part to the increase of caloric intake. Many diseases, including those related to alcoholism and smoking, arise due to human behaviour.

Gandhi, as a vegetarian, considered the life of animals to be sacred and advocated for the protection of animals. He was a vocal anti-vivisectionist. He wrote:

> European doctors are the worst of all. For the sake of a mistaken care of the human body, they kill annually thousands of animals. They practise vivisection. No religion sanctifies this. All say that it is not necessary to take so many lives for the sake of our bodies. These doctors violate our religious instinct. Most of their medical preparations contain either animal fat or spirituous liquors; both of these are tabooed by Hindus and Mahomedans.... The fact remains that the doctors induce us to indulge, and the result is that we have become deprived of self-control and have become effeminate.... To study European medicine is to deepen our slavery.[25]

---

24 Ibid., 63.

25 Ibid., 64.

Anticipating the rapaciousness of pharmaceutical companies, he also observed:

> Doctors make a show of their knowledge, and charge exorbitant fees. Their preparations, which are intrinsically worth a few pennies, cost shillings. The populace in its credulity and in the hope of ridding itself of some disease, allows itself to be cheated.[26]

As one reflects on the disproportionate compensation given to physicians, particularly in the United States, and the extreme expense of both medicine and insurance, Gandhi's homespun remarks continue to be poignant.

In his nineteen-point call for action, he proclaimed that a doctor, in order to exert the strength needed for *swaraj*, 'will give up medicine, and understand that, rather than mending bodies, he should mend souls'.[27] He called all physicians to abjure vivisection:

> it is better that bodies remain diseased rather than that they are cured through the instrumentality of the diabolical vivisection that is practised in European schools of medicine.

In a radical acceptance of the inevitable, he considered it more noble for patients to succumb rather than subject themselves to drugs:

> if any patients come to him, [the doctor] will tell them the cause of their diseases, and will advise them to remove the cause rather than pamper them by giving useless drugs; he will understand that, if by not taking drugs, perchance

26 Ibid., 65.

27 Ibid., 117.

> the patient dies, the world will not come to grief, and that he will have been really merciful to him.[28]

Although this advice would often be imprudent today given the advances of modern medicine, the adoption of a less interventionist approach would help reduce the modern doctor's propensity for ordering expensive tests and prescribing too many medications. This of course would need to be complemented by a less litigious attitude in the health care field.

Gandhi advocated simple living. He held deep suspicions about the benefits of European civilisation, including its insistence on mechanised transport and its fetish for medicines of dubious efficacy. The wisdom he shared regarding self-reliance remains relevant for the contemporary post-modern world, though with modifications. Our economy has become globalised and greed-based. It no longer is manipulated by governments, but by corporations. If Gandhi were alive today, he no doubt would stand in awe of cell phones, the internet, and so many other accoutrements of daily life. He would be relieved at the number of nations that have cast off the shackles of colonialism and remain concerned about the host of social justice issues that remain unresolved, not only in India, but in China, the nations of Africa, and elsewhere. He would, however, still bear witness, as do modern Gandhians such as Satish Kumar, Vandana Shiva, and many others, against the power of corporations, the unbridled greed of business, and the frivolous embrace of materialist consumerism that now pervades the globe.

---

28 Ibid., 117.

The Wisdom of Gandhi as Summarised by Narayan Desai

The late Narayan Desai served as Chancellor of Gujarat Vidyapeeth, the university that Mahatma Gandhi established in Ahmedabad, India. He spoke throughout the USA in 2008, presenting stories of Gandhi in Gujarati and English. Desai, who served as Gandhi's personal secretary, reminded his audiences of Gandhi's core message: holding to truth in a spirit of non-violence. Simply stated, we need to overcome our all-too-human greed and fear with love and cooperation. Before the crash of 2008, an enticing ad by Citibank inviting everyone to 'Live Richly', but without warning of the eventual dire consequences of debt poorly managed. Signs of greed can be found throughout the world in obesity and other food-related crises, and in lumbering, energy-guzzling cars, trucks, and overbuilt houses. Likewise, fear can be seen in a deepening split between red and blue, Muslim and Christian, rich and poor, leading to increased bellicosity and mistrust.

Few political figures today dare to suggest that Americans should alter their lifestyle willingly for the sake of a common good. Desai offered one radical personal solution: Live within one's means, occupy your hands with creative work, and be open to the ideas and views of others. Even when engaged in world travel, Desai, following the model of Gandhi, spins tufts of cotton into thread, adding to his spool each day. After several weeks or months, he weaves this thread into homespun cloth and wears only self-crafted clothing. All the students and faculty at his university do the same, engaging head, heart, and hands. This simple act helped India cast off its colonial oppressors. Gandhians today continue to espouse the ideals and realities of self-control, moving toward self-sufficiency and self-respect.

As the American economy retracts, each of us needs to ask the question: How much is enough? How much food? How much entertainment? How large a car? How large a house? We might surprise ourselves with the realisation that true happiness comes with ingenuity and restraint, not through unbridled consumption.

Vandana Shiva

Gandhi-inspired activist Vandana Shiva has become one of the world's most outspoken critics of globalisation and has provided a trenchant critique of 'patenting' traditional knowledge for economic gain by corporations. Her activism in the realm of seeds serves as a paradigm for exposing the excesses of the human attempt to manipulate nature. She takes a broad historical view in developing her analysis of 'enclosure' or the marketing of what was once held in common, to be commoditised and controlled by industrial and commercial forces.

Shiva's advocacy of sustenance economy would require a shift from a corporate model to one in balance with nature, valuing relationships over and above commodities. She has taken up food production as her primary arena for activism. Shiva writes:

> I launched a national program to save seed diversity in farmers' fields. We call it Navdanya, which literally means nine seeds.... The farmers [had] become mere consumers of corporate seed. This excludes the farmer from the critical role of conserver of genetic diversity and development of seed. It robs farmers of their rights to their biological and intellectual heritage.... Navdanya wanted to build a program in which farmers and scientists relate horizontally rather than vertically, in which biodiversity and production of food to hand

> in hand, and which farmers' knowledge is strengthened, not robbed.[29]

The corporatisation of agriculture, including the patenting of seeds and the mass marketing of herbicides, pesticides, and petroleum-based fertilisers, has created a horrific situation, turning farmers away from organic practices and into debtors.

Shiva, citing government statistics, notes that 'According to India's National Crime Bureau, 16,000 farmers in India committed suicide during 2004. During one six-month span in 2004, there were 1,860 suicides by farmers in the State of Andhra Pradesh alone' (120). During the first decade of the twenty-first century, 250,000 farmers committed suicide in India.[30] This great tragedy has received scant attention from the international press. Shiva advocates for individual farmers and their families, and has helped urge legislation to help India's rural poor.

M.C. Mehta

In 1996, Supreme Court lawyer M.C. Mehta won the Goldman prize for his advocacy on behalf of protecting the Taj Mahal. For years, the industrial grime generated by the city of Agra had degraded the once-gleaming marble of the famous building. Through his efforts, several industries relocated and a stringent programme for reducing air pollution was enacted, including a ban on non-electric vehicles within several hundred yards of the Mughal masterpiece.

On 1 April 2001, Mehta achieved another landmark victory. On that day, all public transport vehicles in the Delhi capital

29 Vandana Shiva, *Earth Democracy: Justice, Sustainability, and Peace* (Cambridge: South End Press, 2005), 92.

30 Vandana Shiva, Loyola Marymount University, 1 November 2011.

region converted from gasoline, diesel, and kerosene fuels to compressed natural gas. The air quality improved overnight. The new buses, taxis, and auto-rickshaws are brightly painted in yellow and green, celebrating the light of the Sun and the bounty of the Earth.

M.C. Mehta, with support from the Ford Foundation, has developed a training camp to equip lawyers from throughout South Asia to face the challenges presented by environmental conditions. While visiting this camp, Eco Ashram, near Rishikesh in 2006, I witnessed a dozen young brilliant lawyers from Nepal, India, Bangladesh, Bhutan, Sri Lanka, and Pakistan being taught by Mehta as part of a six-week residential course. Everyone lived in straw huts, shared simple food, and attempted to keep warm, even when pelted by Himalayan hail. The lectures on industrial pollution included heartbreaking tales of miscarriages, birth defects, and early death.

One of Mehta's first environmental cases included the protection of children working in 'electro plating, chemical industries, mining, so many different industries'. If he succeeds in his legal efforts, 40 million children will be removed from these work places and be able to begin an education.

The rivers of India are sources of inspiration and consternation. Abundant literature extols the beauties of rivers. For instance, Paṇḍitarāja Jagannātha's *Gaṅgā-laharī* praises the Ganges River:

> Your water is bliss incarnate.
> Your water is forever pure.
> The glory of your waves, Mother,
> is unequalled anywhere in the world.[31]

---

31 John E. Cort, tr., *Paṇḍitarāja Jagannātha: The Saving Waves of the Milk-White Gaṅgā* (Calcutta: Writers Workshop, 2007), 42.

Rūpa Gosvāmin's *Yamuna-śataka* offers similar praise for the Yamuna River:

> She beautifies the spacious forests with her flow of alluring
> water;
> She dances with the birds and bees flying around her lotus
> fields;
> She completely destroys all disease, sickness, and sin
> For those who desire to bathe in her;
> May the Daughter of the Sun always purify me.[32]

Sadly, we know that both rivers carry dangerously high levels of pollution and 'Action Plans' have been developed for each to help improve their current degraded state.

Mehta became involved with the rehabilitation of the Ganges River in 1986. He said:

> I fought this case when I came to know that Gaṅgā caught fire. I came over and investigated and fought that case first against two industries. Now more than 150,000 industries in 300 towns are all affected by this case; 600 [leather] tanneries were closed down in Calcutta. And now, similarly the court has directed other industries to use air pollution control and water pollution control. The monitoring process is going on.

The rivers of India not only suffer from pollution but from canalisation and siphoning for irrigation. Mehta said:

> I am fighting for the rights of the rivers. The rights of the rivers mean that the river has a right to live, to exist. One

32 Gosvāmin, in David L. Haberman, *River of Love in an Age of Pollution: The Yamuna River of Northern India* (Berkeley: University of California Press, 2006), 197–198.

> should not touch the river bed because there are too many species that live in the river or near the river bed, like birds, that live along the riverbed. Now you only see the river when there is a monsoon. The river is channeled through the canals so it goes everywhere.

Mehta claims that:

> Gandhi was a true environmentalist. He said 'we should not live in debt, we should help others to grow.' I like Gandhi for his spiritual values, and for his cultural values, and for his vision about India. He said 'don't put up all the big industries, there is no need, we should try to give a job to each hand.' In India we are lucky that way, we have more than two billion hands. It was Mahatma Gandhi's vision to give jobs to the people. India is unique because of its magnetic power and vibrations that go deep into our mind and soul. Each country, each continent has its own uniqueness, so in my view we should respect that.

Mehta spoke of three primary concerns:

> Health, the environment, and education, these three things are important. A push should be given so that people feel more secure. Apart from the unemployment, I am worried about the food security, because the way housing projects are going in the country. The industries are taking over the land, and the land is limited, it cannot be expanded. So if India has a limited land, then we should see how in the best way we should give the maximum amount for the growth of food only, and that is agriculture, and that is what 70% of India should be. So in India we need organically-made foods. People can export it, it can improve the economy. And the youth should be involved in so many areas, like instead of cutting the trees; I always tell the states that they should be put in

> forestation programs. Don't cut the trees, make more trees, all medicinal plants, all that are here in the Himalayas, grow them and see that the economy will grow. So there are many ways where the youth can be put up for this, to do constructive work.

Global warming worries Mehta, who had a direct encounter with the collapse of a glacier while hiking in the Himalayas:

> I think only if we sensitize the people all over the world, then only we can reduce greenhouse gas emission and we can bring back the climate. Otherwise it is too late. The glaciers are melting on the Himalayas, yet nobody is bothered. I saw it myself when I went 14,000 feet high there. It was so sad that the glaciers are melting so fast. In the morning I went this way and by the evening the people said don't go this way. I asked what happened and the people said that the water in the glaciers had already caused a huge area to collapse. We have to be sensitive.

Mehta shared that his next project will be to initiate and support legislation within India that will help slow climate change.

Mehta has acknowledged that India's traditional environmental wisdom can provide a valuable resource for moving the public will into supporting the steps necessary to improve air quality, deal with water pollution, and slow global warming. He has commented:

> The elements of nature such as air and water are being overtaken by greed. Greed has overtaken us, leaving us under the cloak of greed. For people wearing the cloak of greed, it is very hard to come out and see real life. With correct understanding they will be in a position to respect law, and enforce it. Then we have sustainable elements.

Conclusion

South Asian systems of knowledge recognise a continuity between human well-being and the well-being of nature. Negative actions will produce suffering; positive actions will result in harmony. When the scientific method of Descartes found application in technology and manufacturing, unimaginable resource exploitation resulted. Timber, petroleum, natural gas, and minerals are being quickly fed into the production line to produce consumer goods that have as their by-products many toxic wastes that affect the atmosphere, the soil, and the water. According to some thinkers, this is simply the law of *karma*. Unintended consequences have resulted. We must look to the root cause of these troubles. The causes are myriad and are rooted in human greed and delusion. Science, in addition to bringing great comfort and long life to human beings, when married to a consumerist ideology, can create suffering. By employing Gandhian wisdom, a path may be created to move forward toward healing.

Portions of this chapter are adapted with permission from the following resources: Christopher Key Chapple. 'Nonhuman Animals and the Question of Rights from an Asian Perspective'. In *Asian Perspectives on Animal Ethics: Rethinking the Nonhuman*, edited by Neil Dalal and Chlöe Taylor, 148–168. London and New York: Routledge, 2014; Christopher Key Chapple. 'Mahatma Gandhi and Some Enduring Challenges for the 21st Century'. In *World of Philosophy: A Harmony (Acharya Prof. Dr. Yajneshwar S. Shastri's Felicitation Volume)*. Delhi: Shanti Prakashan, 2011.

The section on vegetarianism was presented at UC Berkeley and has not been published elsewhere. The quoted lectures and interviews cited are listed as follows: Narayan Desai. Lecture. Loyola Marymount University. 9 October 2008. M.C. Mehta. Interview. Eco Ashram. Dehra Dun, India. 12 December 2006. Vandana Shiva. Lecture. Loyola Marymount University. 1 November 2011.

Discussion Topic: Gandhi and Eco-activism

- In what ways do you find Gandhi's critique of modernity prescient? Unsettling?
- What lifestyle changes would you deem possible within the context of current economic systems?

Further Reading

Mohandas Gandhi. *Hind Swaraj and Other Writings*, edited by Anthony J. Parel. Cambridge University Press, 1997.

Rajmohan Gandhi. *Mohandas: A True Story of a Man, His People, and an Empire*. New Delhi: Penguin Viking, 2006.

Homer A. Jack. *The Gandhi Reader: A Source Book of His Life and Writings*. Madras: Samata Books, 1956, 1984.

Thomas Merton, ed. *Gandhi on Non-Violence: A Selection from the Writings of Mahatma Gandhi. Edited and with an Introduction*. New York: New Directions, 1964.

Lloyd I. Rudolph and Susanne Hoeber Rudolph. *Postmodern Gandhi and Other Essays: Gandhi in the World and at Home*. Chicago: University of Chicago Press, 2006.

X
Hinduism and Deep Ecology

The grammar not only of language, but of culture and civilization itself, is of the same order as this mossy little forest creek, this desert cobble.[1]

Deep ecology speaks of an intimacy with place, a sense of being in the world with immediacy, care, and frugality. Gary Snyder, drawing from an American tradition that stretches back to Thoreau, writes of how the wild enriches the human spirit and sacralises the process of survival. Establishing oneself within in a sense of place gives meaning to one's existence; for a deep ecologist, this becomes a way of life, encompassing 'an attempt to uncover the most profound level of human–nature relationships, stressing the need for personal realisation as accomplished by integrating the self with nature'.[2] Deep ecology also urges the examination of the underlying political and economic structures that work against intimacy with nature and thwart the development of a sustainable society.

---

1 Gary Snyder, *The Practice of the Wild* (San Francisco: North Point Press, 1990), 76.

2 Mitchell Thomashow, *Ecological Identity: Becoming a Reflective Environmentalist* (Cambridge, MA: MIT Press, 1995), 58.

Ecological thinkers in India proclaim the need for social change that includes the sustenance and uplift of the masses as integral to the process of environmental healing. They have been somewhat reluctant to embrace the concept of deep ecology as expressed through American authors, largely due to the particular situation of India's overwhelming population and suspicions that the deep ecology rhetoric smacks of neocolonialism, romanticism, and religion. The environmental movement on the part of India's intellectuals has been largely a secular movement; deep ecology moves into the realm of affectivity and a ritualisation of life. Its near (i.e. near-religiosity) religiosity would render deep ecology suspect for many contemporary Indian thinkers, for whom religion connotes fundamentalism, nationalism, and a return to a castebound past.[3]

In recent years, some scholars and activists within the Hindu tradition, inspired by industrial tragedies such as the Bhopal explosion, the depletion of forests, and the fouling of India's air and water, have started to reconsider traditional Hindu lifeways in terms of ecological values. In earlier writings, I have explored various modalities of environmental activism in India, including educational programmes, the emphasis on social ecology by the post-Gandhians, and Brahminical and renouncer models for the development of an indigenous Indian

3 One reason for the underdevelopment of deep ecology in India lies in the absence of both religious and environmental studies as academic disciplines in the universities of South Asia. Religious instruction takes place in the observance of home rituals, story telling, and media presentations such as the literatalist television versions of the Rāmāyaṇa, Mahābhārata, and other religious tales. The rote and somewhat static nature of the conveyance of religion in South Asia has resulted in its rejection by many of the educated elite, who prefer to embrace secularism as their primary world view.

environmentalism.[4] In this chapter I will more fully explore how the Hindu tradition, broadly interpreted, might further its contribution to both a localised and a globalised sense of deep ecology.

Defining Hindu Religion

To look at deep ecology in light of Hindu religion, we must probe the term *Hinduism*. First of all, the term *Hindu* is inherently a non-Hindu construct, first coined by Persians to describe those persons living on the other side of the Indus River. Another definition of Hinduism links the term to a cluster of religious faiths and theological schools that ascribe truth to the earliest of India's sacred texts, the Vedas, and the various texts and traditions stemming therefrom. Such persons might call themselves followers of Viṣṇu (Vaiṣṇavas), Śiva (*Śaivas*), or the Devī or Goddess (*Śakti*) or some other deity, or a follower of no deity in particular. This definition would include several million persons living outside India in such places as Sri Lanka, Singapore, Britain, and the United States. It would, in a sense, also include many persons of non-Indian descent who ascribe to the monistic Vedānta philosophy and to the many practitioners of Indian physical and spiritual disciplines such as Yoga.[5] The term Hindu could also refer in

4 See Christopher Key Chapple, *Nonviolence to Animals, Earth, and Self in Asian Traditions* (Albany: State University of New York Press, 1993); 'India's Earth Consciousness', in *The Soul of Nature: Celebrating the Spirit of the Earth*, ed. Michael Tobias and Georgianne Cowan, 145–151 (New York: Plume, 1996); and 'Toward an Indigenous Indian Environmentalism', in *Purifying the Earthly Body of God: Religion and Ecology in Hindu India*, ed. Lance E. Nelson, 13–38 (Albany: State University of New York Press, 1998).

5 A.R. Victor Raj, *The Hindu Connection: Roots of the New Age* (Saint Louis: Concordia Publishing House, 1995), 62–119.

a general way to the people who live in the subcontinental region. This would include Jains, Buddhists, and Sikhs, as well as Indian Christians and Muslims, all of whom exhibit at least some common cultural traits associated with 'Hindustan'.

Hinduism does not operate in the manner of many traditional religions. It includes multiple doctrines, multiple deities, and many different types of people from various levels of society. Hence, rather than attempting to present a monolithic view of Hinduism and deep ecology, I prefer to suggest some ways in which I have discovered that Hinduism, broadly defined, espouses a philosophy akin to the core sensibilities of deep ecology. This chapter begins with a discussion of the importance of the five elements in the Hindu world view and the relationship between meditative practices and the natural world. Ritual worship will be explored as providing a context for understanding the function of 'embedded ecology' in Hindu life, with special reference to the Mannarassala Temple in Kerala. I will then turn to a discussion of sacred groves in India, with mention of some of the successes and difficulties encountered by those involved with tree planting in India. The chapter will close with reflections on the challenge posed by contemporary consumer pressures in India and the suggestion that the meditative and ritual deep structures of Indian life and culture can help support an indigenous form of Hindu deep ecology.

The Five Elements (*Pañca-Bhūta*)

Hindu religious literature, from the Vedas to contemporary theorists, takes up a discussion of the natural world through a systematic approach to the five elements. This tradition provides an analysis of material reality in terms of its manifestation through earth (*pṛthivī*), water (*āp*), fire (*agni*), air (*vāyu*), and space (*ākāśa*). These elements find mention not only in the earliest of India's oral texts, the *Ṛg Veda*, but also play a prominent role in the later philosophical systems of Sāṁkhya and Vedānta, as well as the non-Hindu systems of Jainism and Buddhism. For instance, the *Vāmana Purāṇa* states:

> Let all the great elements bless the dawning day: Earth with its smell, water with its taste, fire with its radiance, air with its touch, and sky with its sound.[6]

These elements are not seen as abstractions or metaphors but literally compose the reality of the world and of one's own body. The *Mokṣa-dharma-parvan*, one of the books of the *Mahābhārata* epic, summarises the relationship between body and cosmos first articulated in the *Ṛg Veda* and the *Bṛhadāraṇyaka Upaniṣad*:

> The Lord, the sustainer all beings, revealed the sky.
> From space came water and, from water, fire and the winds.
> From the mixture of the essence of fire and wind arose the earth.
> Mountains are his bones, earth his flesh, the ocean his blood.
> The sky is his abdomen, air his breath, fire his heat, rivers his nerves.
> The sun and moon, which are called Agni and Soma, are the eyes of Brahman.
> The upper part of the sky is his head.
> The earth is his feet and the directions are his hands.[7]

This vision of the relationship between the body, divinity, and the order of the things becomes both descriptive and prescrip-

---

6 *Vāmana Purāṇa* 12.26.

7 *Mokṣa-dharma-parvan* 182:14–19, adapted from O.P. Dwivedi and B.N. Tiwari, *Environmental Crisis and Hindu Religion* (New Delhi: Gitanjali Publishing House, 1987), 126.

tive in terms of the human relationship with nature in India. The world cannot be separated from the human body nor can the human body be separated from the world.

In the traditional Hindu view, the world exists as an extension of the body and mind; the body and mind reflect and contain the world. In describing the women of the Garwhal region of the Himalayas, Carol Lee Flinders notes that they 'enjoy a connection with trees, rivers, mountains, livestock, and plants that is simultaneously their connection with divinity, and that connection is seen as absolutely reciprocal'.[8] From the texts above, we can understand this continuity as an expression of what Vandana Shiva calls 'embedded in nature' and Vijaya Nagarajan refers to as 'embedded ecology'. This notion of intimacy with the natural world, culturally supported by an anthropocosmic vision of the Earth, instantiates a person in immediate and intimate contact with one's surroundings. Just as the Hymn of the Person (*Puruṣa Sūkta*) in the *Ṛg Veda* identifies human physiology with the cosmos, correlating the feet with the Earth and the head with the sky, so also a vision of deep ecology in the context of Hindu faith will seek to integrate and include its understanding of the human as inseparable from and reflective of nature.

Meditative Mastery

Hinduism, while revering the five elements and venerating many gods and goddesses, places ultimate importance on the attainment of spiritual liberation (*mokṣa*). The path toward liberation requires a skillful reciprocity between spirit and materiality. Yogic practice (*sādhana*) cultivates an awareness of and intimacy

8 Carol Lee Flinders, *At the Root of This Longing: Reconciling a Spiritual Hunger and a Feminist Thirst* (San Francisco: Harper SanFrancisco, 1998), 260.

with the realm of manifestation and materiality (*prakṛti*). Just as the *Bṛhadāraṇyaka Upaniṣad* proclaims a relationship between the body and the universe, so also the Yoga system urges one to gain mastery over how the body stands in relationship to the cosmos. The *Yoga Sūtras* of Patañjali state: 'From concentration on significance and connection of the subtle [body] and the essence of gross manifestation, there is mastery over the elements.'[9] This statement acknowledges a linkage between the realm of bodily sensation and the experience of the physical world. By concentrating on this relationship, one gains an intimacy with the elements that results in an understanding of one's embeddedness with one's environment.

The yogic accomplishment of mastery over the elements (*bhūta-jaya*) entails a detailed training that focuses on the elements over a period of several months. In this regimen, one begins with concentration on the earth, moving toward an appreciation of the special relationship between the sense of smell residing in the subtle body (*sūkṣma-śarīra*) and the earth (*pṛthivī*). Moving up in subtlety, the practitioner then concentrates on the link between subtle taste (*rasa*) and water (*āp*); between visible form (*rūpa*) and light and heat (*tejas*); between touch (*sparśa*) and the wind (*vāyu*); and between sound (*śabda*) and space (*ākāśa*). Beginning with earth, the heaviest aspect of manifestation, one progresses to the lightest and most subtle. This insight into the relationship between the senses and the elements leads to an ability to acknowledge and withhold the outflow of the senses (*prapañca*). Through this mastery, one gains freedom from compulsive attachment; this lightness (*sattva*) ultimately leads to liberation (*mokṣa*).

---

9 Christopher Key Chapple and Yogi Anand Viraj (Eugene P. Kelly Jr.), *The Yoga Sūtras of Patañjali: An Analysis of the Sanskrit with English Translation* (Delhi: Satguru Publications, 1990), 99.

On the one hand, it might be argued that this process leads one away from intimacy to an introspective distancing from nature. On the other hand, it could also be stated that this meditative practice entails a greater rapport with nature, an entry into a purified, immediate state of perception freed from residues of past attachment. In the words of David Abram:

> The recuperation of the incarnate, sensorial dimension of experience brings with it a recuperation of the living landscape in which we are corporeally embedded. As we return to our senses, we gradually discover our sensory perceptions to be simply our part of a vast, interpenetrating webwork.[10]

By entering fully into a reflection on the workings of the senses through the practices of yogic meditation, one gains an intimacy with the foundational constructs of objects that transcends their specificity, leading one to a state of unity with the natural world.

Ritual Worship (*Pūjā*) and Ecology

Ritual worship performed by meditators and temple priests includes a veneration and internalisation of the elements, a sanctification of the body that leads to identity with divine power. Anthropologist James Preston describes the experience of one temple priest at the Chandi Temple in Cuttack, Orissa:

> One of the first steps in the puja is for the priest to transform his body into a microcosm of the universe. This is accomplished by combining the five elements represented within it. Kumar Panda explained the correspondences between

---

10 David Abram, *The Spell of the Sensuous: Perception and Language in a More-Than-Human World* (New York: Pantheon Books, 1996), 65.

> nature and the human body: *earth* is equated with that part of the human body below the waist; *water* is symbolised by the stomach region; *fire* is represented by the heart; *wind* is equivalent to the throat, nose, and lungs; *sky* corresponds to the brain. As these elements are mixed together in symbolic rites, the priest is filled with divine power or *śakti*, which is the goddess herself.... Kumar Panda describes his inner vision during meditation: 'After performing meditation and the ritual for two or three hours, lightning flashes before my eyes.... I become the goddess. She who is Ma (Mother) is me.... Water and the coldness of water, fire and the burning capacity of fire, the sun and the rays of the sun; there is no difference between all these things, just as there is no difference between myself and the goddess.'[11]

This journey through the relationship between the body and the elements to the point of unity with the goddess brings the meditator to a point of visionary immersion, a form of profound and deep ecological awareness.

Within the context of celebrating the special relationship between the human person and nature, each region of India has developed an extensive ritual cycle. These festivals often coincide with times of harvest or renewal. For instance, the Pongal festival in South India takes place each January to acknowledge the rice harvest. Many Hindu rituals include reverence for sacred traditional plants such as the Tulsi tree; many explicitly invoke the elements as mentioned above and many celebrate the earth goddess or Bhū Devī. Vijaya Nagarajan has extensively described how the practice of the Kolam morning ritual establishes in Tamil women a sense of connectedness

11 James J. Preston, *Cult of the Goddess: Social and Religious Change in a Hindu Temple* (Prospect Heights, IL: Waveland Press, 1985), 52, 53.

with their environment.[12] Madhu Khanna writes about how rituals practised in the urban context maintain significant agricultural and hence ecological meanings. Ritual acknowledges and invokes one's position in the order of things and connects the worshipper directly with fecundity cycles.[13]

I would like to describe a fertility ritual in South India that provides a living example of embedded ecology in the state of Kerala. In 1997, I visited the Mannarassala Temple, between the cities of Cochin and Trivandrum. We spent many hours in the cool shade of this sylvan retreat and learned, through observation and friendly informants, of the mythic history and ritual cycles associated with this temple. My companion, Professor Surinder Datta, a retired biologist from the University of Wisconsin, Parkside, sought out this particular site because of its renowned sacred grove. Adjacent to its buildings, behind a walled enclosure, the temple maintains a fourteen-acre preserve of forest. No one is allowed to enter these towering woods except a small group of Brahmin priests who enter once each year to gather medicinal herbs, to be used in Ayurvedic treatments. The forest stretches as high as the eye can see, a remarkable remnant of the tropical forests that once covered the entire state of Kerala. Though not far from the main road, this compound stands in stark contrast to the densely populated and cultivated surrounding landscape which, though green and lush with rice paddies and coconut groves,

---

12 Vijaya Rettakudi Nagarajan, 'The Earth as Goddess Bhu Devi: Toward a Theory of "Embedded Ecologies" in Folk Hinduism', in *Purifying the Earthly Body of God: Religion and Ecology in Hindu India,* ed. Lance Nelson, 269-296 (Albany: State University of New York Press, 1998).

13 Madhu Khanna, 'The Ritual Capsule of Durgā Pūjā: An Ecological Perspective', in *Hinduism and Ecology: The Intersection of Earth, Sky, and Water,* ed. Christopher Key Chapple (Cambridge, MA: Harvard University Center for the Study of World Religions, 2000).

has been thoroughly domesticated by the many people that live in Kerala. Similarly, even in the mountains, what at first glance appears to be wild forest at a closer examination turns out to be terraces of spice and coffee trees, creeping vines of black pepper, and bushes of cardamon, all under cultivation.

According to the local tale, this particular temple arose on the spot where Paraśurāma, an incarnation of Viṣṇu, met with the snake god Nāgarāja to obtain blessings to ensure the fertility of Kerala's soil. Years prior, the mountains of Kerala were formed when Paraśurāma had thrown his ax (*paraśu*) into the ocean. The plain below the mountains, though seemingly rich, was too salty to support life. Paraśurāma pleaded with the snake king to purify the land. Now, in return, offerings are made to the snake king to thank him for granting Paraśurāma's request and snakes, particularly in the wild areas, are protected. This story divinises the land of Kerala and offers a local rationale for preserving both forest and wildlife in honour of and respect for a viable ecosystem.

The Mannarassala Temple serves as a sacred place for human reproduction. Our visit to Mannarasalla Temple coincided with a fertility thanksgiving in the form of a first name and first solid food ceremony to bless several babies. For several decades, one woman, Valia Amma, served as priestess of the temple. She was born in 1903 and, according to our informants, she married a temple priest when she was thirteen or fourteen years old. At the age of fifteen, in 1918, she renounced the carnal aspects of her marriage and dedicated her life to serving the temple. She instituted *pūjā* or worship ceremonies at the temple that continue to the present day, including weddings and the Kalasam tantric rite.[14]

---

14 Moozhikkulam Chandrasekharam Pillai, *Mannarassala: The Serpent Temple*, tr. Ayyappa Panikker (Harippad: Manasa Publication, 1991), 33.

During our visit, we witnessed a portion of the special rituals known as the Choronu ceremony associated with the successful birth and nurturance of babies. Young couples come to the temple priestess for fertility blessings when they decide it is time to bear children. After the birth of a child, the family returns when the baby reaches six months, for the naming and first solid food ceremonies. The parents first place the baby in a basket attached to a scale and fill the opposite basket with grain. When the scale balances, the proper payment is accepted by the temple staff. Midst the smoke and light of the oil lamps and the blaring trumpets of a circumambulating band of musicians, we saw several children receive the name acknowledging their survival through the first six months of life. We also witnessed these babies being fed their first meal of cooked rice. A woman temple musician playing a onestringed instrument held with her toe then sings a song in honour of the baby and the family proceeds to receive *darśan* or blessing from the temple priestess, who greets people from the family quarter within the temple compound. Valia Amma died in 1993; we received blessings from her husband's brother's wife, who assumed the priestess duties upon her passing.

The ritual life of this temple complex exhibits the qualities of embedded ecology in its story of cosmic origins, its grounding in nature, and its function as promoting the good health and wellbeing of future generations.

Sacred Groves

In her work on sacred groves, Frederique Apffel-Marglin describes such ritual centres as source of rejuvenation. She writes that 'the network of sacred groves in such countries as India has since time immemorial been the locus and symbol of a way of life in which humans are embedded in nature.... It stands for the integration of the human community in nature....

The sacred grove, with its shrine to the local embodiment of the Great Goddess, is the permanent material sign of these periodic processes of regeneration.'[15] Though Apffel-Marglin writes of her experiences in a sacred grove in northeast coastal Orissa, the grove parallels and mirrors that of Kerala, more than 1000 miles to the southwest. Both affirm the process of fertility. Both celebrate feminine powers of reproduction. Both serve as symbols of community and continuity, a place where, in Apffel-Marglin's words, 'culture and society are embedded in nature, and the spiritual is embedded in the material'.[16]

Ramachandra Guha notes that 'sacred groves and sacred ponds... protection of keystone species and the moderation of harvests from village woodlots have persisted in Indian society over the historical period, sometimes to the present day'.[17] He tells the story of the Bishnoi sect, a group in the Rajasthan desert for whom the Khejadari tree became sacred. This tree, described as a 'multipurpose leguminous tree of great utility to the villagers' was never to be uprooted or killed.[18] In the 1650s a prince of Jodhpur attempted to cut a grove of Khejadari trees to fire a kiln to manufacture bricks for a new palace. The Bishnois revolted, laying down their lives to protect the sacred tree. Even today, the Khejadari serves as the backbone for desert subsistence; I have seen women in Rajasthan lopping its limbs to provide food for their goats; they also harvest its leaves and pods. Unlike the Joshua tree of the western

15 Frederique Apffel-Marglin, 'Sacred Groves: Regenerating the Body, the Land, the Community', in *Global Ecology: A New Arena of Political Conflict*, ed. Wolfgang Sachs (London: Zed Books, 1993), 198.

16 Ibid., 206.

17 Madhav Gadgil and Ramachandra Guha, *This Fissured Land: An Ecological History of India* (Delhi: Oxford University Press, 1992), 106.

18 Ibid., 108.

United States which has lost its utility since the decimation of indigenous populations, the Khejadari reciprocally supports the people who sustain it through their protective customs.

Water Harvesting

Anil Agarwal and Sunita Narain have written of water catchment systems employed throughout India that have allowed human life to flourish in what otherwise would be arid wastelands. This system, like the prudent pruning of the Khejadari tree by desert women, works with the immediate available resources on a small scale. They note that '[a]ncient texts, inscriptions, local traditions and archaeological remains refer to a wide range of techniques – canals, huge tanks, embankments, wells and reservoirs – to harvest every possible form of water: rainwater, groundwater, stream water, river water and flood water.'[19]

One of the tragic consequences of the British colonial period was a dismantling of many traditional water catchment systems. Before the British period, each village supported the workers who maintained the irrigation systems. The British, in an attempt to increase revenues, deemed these to be merely 'religious and charitable allowances' and discontinued allocation for these functions. In time, the systems fell into disrepair, leading to 'the disintegration of village society, its economy and its polity'.[20]

Following independence from Britain, India initiated huge irrigation projects inspired by the example of the Soviet Union.

---

19 Anil Agarwal and Sunita Narain, 'Dying Wisdom: The Decline and Revival of Traditional Water Harvesting Systems in India', *Ecologist* 27, no. 3 (1997): 112.

20 Ibid., 115.

Massive water projects have been and continue to be destructive to traditional life in India, disrupting indigenous ways of desert survival, as in the case of the Narmada Dam project in western India.[21] As the dry lands of Gujarat open to wetter styles of cultivation through the various planned irrigation channels, and as more desert dwellers and displaced tribals from the flooded valleys flock to the cities in search of employment in a cash-based economy, the age-old deep ecology based on a traditional economy of living within available means will disappear. Some have argued that progress is inevitable, that the benefits of wealth and increased nutrition outweigh clinging to an outdated lifestyle. However, from a religious point of view and from the perspectives of deep ecology, a sense of connectedness with the land becomes lost when largescale development prevails.

Nature as Romance?

Guha has argued against the romanticisation of Western-style deep ecology, claiming that it merely extends the imperialism of a culture of abundance that can afford to set aside vast tracts of land in convenient preserves. Guha's position, unfortunately and probably unintentionally, can play into the hands of modern developers who would argue for 'Wise Use', taking the position that progress is desirable and inevitable. However, for traditional India, Wise Use would entail protecting the sacred grove. For Nehruvian, progress-oriented contemporary India, Wise Use has led to the uprooting of people from their habitats, increased urbanisation, and ultimately increased pollution.

21 William F. Fisher, *Toward Sustainable Development: Struggling over India's Narmada River* (Armonk, NY: M.E. Sharpe, 1995).

In a probing analysis and critique of colonialism, Guha notes that British land use policies marginalised and impoverished the hunter-gatherers of India. The British usurped many common lands and required they be converted to food production and the production of cash crops for export such as indigo. Guha explains that the literate castes of India were able to move into clerical jobs and to operate as trading partners, but that 'the others – hunter-gatherers, peasants, artisans, and pastoral and nonpastoral nomads – had all to squeeze into the already diminishing niche space for food production. And they, we have seen, suffered great impoverishment.'[22] The emotional and material toll of this upon great masses of the Indian population has been devastating. He writes:

> The consequence has been a scramble for resources and intense conflict, in the countryside and in the cities where people who have been driven out from elsewhere are flocking .... Endogamous caste groups remain cultural entities [in the cities] but have no common belief system to hold them together. No longer functional entities in the present scenario of shrinking niche space, castes and communities are set up against each other, with frighteningly high levels of communal and caste violence being the result.[23]

The cities of India teem with millions of street dwellers displaced from rural life who, having flocked to the cities without the benefit of education, perform menial tasks to eke out a survival living.

---

22 Gadgil and Guha, *This Fissured Land,* 243.

23 Ibid., 244.

Establishing a New Grove

Australian environmental activist John Seed paints a somewhat sobering picture of on-the-ground conservation in the Indian context. In 1987, Seed received a plea from Apeetha Aruna Gin, an Australian nun living near Arunachala mountain in Tiruvannamalai, Madras. She lived at Sri Ramana Ashram, a spiritual hermitage named after the famed Indian sage Ramana Maharshi, whose life energised spirituality in India during the first part of the twentieth century. She noticed that the surrounding areas had become stripped clean of vegetation due to local scavenging for firewood and fodder to feed the goats. Seed raised money for the development of a new NGO established by Apeetha: the Annamalai Reforestation Society. Through the efforts of this organisation,

> The space between the inner and outer walls of the vast 23-acre temple complex has been transformed from a wasteland into the largest tree nursery in the south of India. Hundreds of people have received environmental education, and a 12-acre patch of semidesert was donated to the project and transformed into a lush demonstration of permaculture and the miraculous recuperative powers of the earth, Hundreds of Tamil people have been trained in reforestation skills – tree identification, seed collection, nursery techniques, watershed management, erosion control, sustainable energy systems. Shiva's robes are slowly being rewoven.[24]

However, despite Seed's enthusiasm, this project has not been universally well received. Guards must be maintained

24 John Seed, 'Spirit of the Earth: A Battle-Weary Rainforest Activist Journeys to India to Renew His Soul', *Yoga Journal,* 138 (January/February 1998):135.

to prevent local people from scavenging for fuel and fodder in the preserve, a practice that is enforced in various of India's national preserves and at other temple sites. Pilgrims to the sacred mountain complain that the trees block their view of the sunset. Clearly, the affection for trees in the Anglo-Australian love for nature movement does not necessarily work in the Indian context, where trees are seen as an economic resource necessary for human survival.

Seed himself speaks and writes of his own affirmation of the importance of this preservation work through a special quiet moment he experienced in the Arunachala forest with a troop of scores of monkeys:

> They groomed each other, they made love, mothers breastfed their babies, children played and cavorted, utter unselfconsciously living their everyday lives in my astonished and grateful presence… I had never felt more accepted by the nonhuman world. I knew that Shiva had answered my prayer, had acknowledged my efforts, and was giving me his sign of approval.[25]

For Seed, this shamanic moment established a link between his work and the life of the mountain. For others, this fencing of the forest might be seen as an extension of colonialist attitudes that seek to ban *ādivāsī* or aboriginal peoples from their source of livelihood, an example of 'the colonials having saved the forests of South Asian from certain destruction by indigenous forest users'.[26]

---

25 Ibid., 136.

26 Mahesh Rangarajan, *Fencing the Forest: Conservation and Ecological Change in India's Central Provinces 18601914* (Delhi: Oxford University Press, 1961), 5.

Recognising the encroachment of desert lands in areas that were once forested and then under cultivation, the Indian government and several NGOs have promoted tree planting. Balbir Mathur, founder of Trees for Life, has planted thousands of trees in India.[27] Visheswar Saklani, recipient of the Vrikshamitra or Friend of Trees award bestowed by Indira Gandhi in 1987, has planted more than 200,000 trees.[28] Banwari, a contemporary environmentalist writer in India, attributes India's abundance and traditional economic strength to its magical forests, its sacred groves, and its medicinal trees. He writes of the care for forests and trees in India's ancient cities and towns and celebrates the forests that once stood in India as 'the land of no war'.[29] The tree and the grove provide a foundation through which some ideas akin to deep ecology might be appreciated or understood in the Indian context.

In my own travels to India over the past several years, I have been alarmed by the increase in air pollution, saddened by the lack of resolve to effectively clean India's rivers, and heartened by the extensive planting of trees on the northern plains. In 1980, one could gaze over lentil and vegetable fields for what seemed like miles, with no hedgerow, only a raised furrow to separate one field from another. Twenty years later, the same landscape vista now offers tall Asokha and Champa trees along the roadsides and throughout the fields. These new trees are not sheltered within sacred groves nor does one see them adorned or revered. Their quiet and pervasive presence nonetheless bears witness to a regreening of the landscape.

---

27 Ranchor Prime, *Hinduism and Ecology: Seeds of Truth* (London: Cassell, 1992), 90.

28 Carolyn Emett, 'The Tree Man', *Resurgence: An International Forum for Ecological and Spiritual Thinking* 183 (July/August 1997): 42.

29 Banwari, *Pañcavaṭī: Indian Approach to Environment*, tr. Asha Vora (Delhi: Shri Vinayaka Publications, 1992).

The Contemporary Challenge

In this chapter, we have surveyed meditative and ritual practices, and the ancient tradition of preserving sacred groves, as possible models for deep ecology within Hinduism. However, just as we mentioned that deep ecology might be a hard sell for secular intellectuals in India, so also it might be difficult to champion the old ways in light of modern consumerism. The automobile has arrived in full force in India. Vehicles contribute more than 70 per cent of India's urban air pollution. According to the Tata Institute, 'air pollution in India caused an estimated 2.5 million premature deaths in 1997 – equivalent to wiping out the entire population of Jamaica or Singapore.'[30] Consumerism can be seen in all its splendour and allure. And with consumerism come the accompanying difficulties of waste disposal, air pollution, and water pollution. Can a deep ecological sensibility inspired by the Hindu tradition help counter these recent harmful developments? Most likely it will not for the urban peoples who have little touch with traditional ways and little interest in the meditative model presented by the wandering *sādhu* or renouncer.

The rising prevalence of urban life (and the imitation of urban life in rural areas) threatens to undermine the very embeddedness that has so characterised the underlying Hindu ecological sensibility. Vasudha Narayan laments that 'a burgeoning middle class in India is now hungry for the consumer bonbons of comfortable and luxurious living.... The rich in India can easily surpass the middle class and the rich of the industrialised nations in their opulent lifestyles... unbridled

---

30 Payal Sampat, 'What Does India Want?' *World Watch* 11 (July/August 1998): 36.

greed reigns.'[31] Informants have told Vijaya Nagarajan that since inorganic substances (plastic, stone) are used in the Kolam (household threshold artistry) in place of rice paste,

> We do not know why we do the Kolam anymore. We have forgotten. If we had not, we would not make the kolam out of plastic or white stone powder. Now everything is modern, modern, modern. Before we would make it with rice... to feed a thousand souls... ants, birds, small worms, insects, maggots... How ungenerous we are becoming![32]

Just as modernity moved the American masses from the countryside to the cities and suburbs, robbing its populace of operative barnyard metaphors and knowledge of basic pastoralism, the Indian urbanised population potentially will lose touch with some of its embedded relationship with nature. A woman from India, observing a fully lit football field at night, once commented that such uses of electricity 'rob the sun of its power', a poignant statement laden with multiple meanings.

On a more optimistic note, environmental writer Bill McKibben has suggested the world consider the state of Kerala as a model for sustainable development. We have already discussed one ritual aspect of life in Kerala that seems to indicate a living example of embedded ecology. Melinda Moore has written about how even the architectural design of a house

---

31 Vasudha Narayanan, 'One Tree Is Equal to Ten Sons: Hindu Responses to the Problems of Ecology, Population, and Consumption', *Journal of the American Academy of Religion* 65, no. 2 (January 1997): 321.

32 Ibid., 275.

in Kerala takes into account one's place in the cosmic scheme.[33] Along with maintaining ancient rituals, sacred places, and an integrated sense of the human's niche in nature, Kerala has developed a society that in quality of life equals that of most First World countries, but with a Third World economy. Specifically, of the twenty-nine million living in the state of Kerala, nearly 100 per cent are literate, though the per capita cash income in Kerala is low.[34] The seventy-year life expectancy of the Keralese male nearly equals that of a North American male (seventy-two years), and during a recent visit one Kerala promoter boasted that home ownership in Kerala stands at over 90 per cent. Essayist Bill McKibben, who has spent time in Kerala, writes:

> Kerala demonstrates that a low-level economy can create a decent life, abundant in things – health, education, community – that are most necessary for us all.... One recent calculation showed that for every American dollar spent or its equivalent spent anywhere on earth, half a liter of oil was consumed in producing, packaging, and shipping the goods. One-seventieth the income means one-seventieth the damage to the planet. So, on balance, if Kerala and the United States manage to achieve the same physical quality of life, Kerala is the vastly more successful society.[35]

Unlike most of the subcontinent, two monsoons visit Kerala each year, which allows for denser foliage than most of India.

---

33 Melinda A. Moore, 'The Kerala House as a Hindu Cosmos', *India through Hindu Categories*, ed. McKim Marriott, 169–202 (New Delhi: Sage Publications, 1990).

34 Department of Economics and Statistics, Government of Kerala, *Kerala Review 2003*, 23.

35 Bill McKibben, *Hope, Human and Wild: True Stories of Living Lightly on the Earth* (Saint Paul: Hungry Mind Press, 1995), 121, 163.

Consequently, women spend less time collecting fodder and firewood, allowing time for educational pursuits, a hallmark of Kerala's success. And its abundant spices have provided ready cash in the world economy for nearly three millenia. Nonetheless, the region's ability to maintain harmony with the land despite great population density, and to balance three powerful religions (Hinduism, Islam, and Christianity) stands as a beacon of hope for an operative, simple, deep ecology.

In India, the issues of social context, historical realities, and survival in a country with huge population pressures demand a different definition of deep ecology. Hundreds of millions of people in India live by subsistence, without certain access to clean water or adequate food. In some ways, this population lives according to the precepts of deep ecology. These people do not consume petroleum; their diet is largely grain- and vegetable-based; they own next to no consumer products or luxuries. India's middle class (of several hundred million), on the other hand, has developed an elaborate urban lifestyle replete with packaged foods, private scooters and automobiles, and numerous consumer luxuries. India's poor live in a deep ecology mandated by circumstance not design. The middle class has embraced all that America can offer; many Indians have joined wholeheartedly the American consumerist model.

Between these two extremes of utter material poverty and material excess lies the possibility of a deep ecology that improves health, nutrition, and education for the poor and offers thought ways, perhaps along the Gandhian model, to inspire restraint from overconsumption. Deep ecology in India must be linked to sustainable development with a focus on universal education (as in Kerala), adequate food supplies, and the development of appropriate technology and transportation systems.

People overpower the landscape of India. Even in remote rural areas, stay still for a minute or two and a person will appear, off on a distant hill or in a hedgerow nearby. Ecologist Patricia C. Wright has commented that China and India have not willfully stumbled into pollution and overpopulation; they simply have been settled and civilised far longer than Europe or the Americas, which has led to a greater density of people. Consequently, any 'nature policy' or sensitivity to the core values of deep ecology as outlined in this book must by necessity be instrumental. The human person will not disappear from the subcontinent, nor can one effectively escape from people into a pristine forest; even the sacred grove exists in reciprocity with human use. Gary Snyder has suggested that 'some of us would hope to resume, reevaluate, recreate, and bring into line with complex science that old view that holds the whole phenomenal world to be our own being: multicentered, "alive" in its own manner, and effortlessly self-organizing in its own chaotic way.'[36] In a sense, India and the Hindu approach to environmental issues operates in a careening, inventive fashion, drawing from the tradition, yet recognising the complexity of distinguishing between human need and human greed.

---

36 Gary Snyder, *A Place in Space: Ethics, Aesthetics, and Watersheds* (Washington, DC: Counterpoint, 1996), 241.

Conclusion

Deep ecology in the American context requires personal struggle to resist the temptations of overconsumption. For a middle-class American, a move toward an ecological lifestyle might include riding a bicycle to work and adopting a vegetarian diet. Such changes reduce harmful emissions into the air, improve one's health, and allow one to consume fewer natural resources by eating low on the food chain. One might also find inspiration in beautiful landscapes and in reading literature from the burgeoning field of nature writing.

In a Hindu context, deep ecology can be affirmed through reflection on traditional texts that proclaim a continuity between the human order and nature, through ritual activities, and through applying meditative techniques that foster a felt experience of one's relationship with the elements. Long ago, India developed yogic techniques for self-awareness, self-control, and the cultivation of inner peace. These techniques have been practiced by Hindus, Buddhists, Jainas, Sikhs, and Sufis throughout the world, and, as mentioned at the beginning of this chapter, have been embraced by many individuals in the Americas and Europe. The principles of abstemiousness and harmlessness associated with these meditative practices can help cultivate an awareness of one's place in the ecosystem and inspire one to live within the confines of a wholesome ritual simplicity.

These features of Indian thought can also inspire an environmental approach that acknowledges the significant needs of a large and growing population. Deep ecology in a Hindu context must take into account the harmful effects of urbanisation due to pollution and use its insights to encourage earthfriendly attitudes in the villages and the cities.

Adapted with permission from Christopher Key Chapple. 'Hinduism and Deep Ecology'. In *Deep Ecology and World Religions: New Essays on Sacred Grounds*, edited by David Landis Barnhill and Roger S. Gottlieb, 59–76. Albany: State University of New York Press. 2001.

Discussion Topic: Deep Ecology

- Deep ecology suggested the need for radical systemic change. What areas for possible improvement do you see?

Further Reading

Bill McKibben. *The Flag, the Cross, and the Station Wagon: A Graying American Looks Back at His Suburban Boyhood and Wonders What the Hell Happened*. New York: Henry Holt, 2022.

XI
Hindu Ecology, Yoga Ecology: A Fifty-Year Retrospective

Prologue

We need every resource, including our own stories, to restore, renovate, and re-energise our commitments to the Earth. What follows is part auto-ethnography, part confessional, part an endeavour at cross-cultural discernment. My professional scholarly work over the past forty years has sought to clarify possible linkages between the contemporary call for ecological awareness and how the Hindu, Jain, and Yoga traditions might enter the conversation. As indicated in my book *Living Landscapes: Meditations on the Five Elements in Hindu, Buddhist, and Jain Yogas*[1] this interest arose from childhood encounters with nature; high school, college, and graduate studies of world cultures; and a committed practice to meditation and Yoga since the age of thirteen.

---

1 Chapple, Christopher Key, *Living Landscapes: Meditation on the Five Elements in Hindu, Buddhist, and Jain Yogas* (Albany, NY: State University of New York Press, 2020).

First Earth Day, 22 April 1970

We were high school sophomores and co-editors of the student newspaper the *Supernova*. Annie Oldershaw (1954–2010) and I spearheaded the Earth Day events at Avon Central Junior-Senior High School, located in the Finger Lakes region of New York State. We organised teach-ins and the planting of roses and poplar trees along the northern boundary of our newly built school building. The New York State Department of Environmental Conservation District 8 headquarters, a couple miles east on Routes 5 and 20 in Avon, gave us the root stock for the roses and the saplings for the trees. The rose brambles remain; the poplar trees, almost on schedule, started to die in the year 2000, the short end of their life expectancy of thirty to fifty years. And sadly, Annie, a National Merit Scholar at William Smith College and a children's librarian for twenty-five years in Irondequoit, succumbed a decade ago, taken, like so many of our friends, by cancer.

We knew the earth was in danger. Six years later after the first Earth Day, the Love Canal debacle hit the news in nearby Niagara Falls. Carol Joyce Oates, who was born in Niagara County, once wrote of the high rates of birth defects and cancer deaths in her hometown. It gives one pause: did our village also harbour chemicals in the water or soil that took the lives of Annie and our friends and classmates, Jeff Dewey, and Cann Clary? Rachel Carson's *Silent Spring* (1962)[2] had prepared us to expect the worst. Earth Day carried much hope and promise that, through heightened awareness, corrective measures would be taken, and many were. The passing of friends due to cancer and the devastating effects of climate change serve as poignant reminders that the warnings of Rachel Carson, who herself died of cancer, must be heeded.

---

2 Rachel Carson, *Silent Spring* (New York: Fawcett Publications, 1962).

Yoga Anand Ashram, 1972–1985

Philip Kapleau, author of *Three Pillars of Zen*, was invited by Chester Carlson (1906–1968, founder of Xerography) and Harriet Lee Gratwick (1907–1999, founder of Linwood Music School) to establish the Zen Center of Rochester in 1966, with donations from Carlson. Two years later, my good friend Kenneth Ketwig (1954–1991) and I, having read the book and started a daily *zazen* practice, interviewed him. This conversation became the foundation for my first scholarly presentation on the religions of Asia, to my ninth-grade world cultures social studies class. In 1971, Richard Alpert, also known as Ram Dass, published *Be Here Now*, and the routine of Yoga postures in the back of the book became the warm-up routine before Zen practice. At the Religious Society of Friends (our default weekend meditation practice; Kapleau said we were too young to become part of his Zen community) we met Maureen Shannon. Four years later, Maureen and I married at the same Quaker Meeting House, with Kenneth and Annie among our many witnesses.

In 1972, having landed after quite some discernment at the State University of New York at Buffalo, four courses shaped the fall semester: Spanish, Anthropology, Philosophy, and the chanting, in Sanskrit, of the *Bhagavad Gītā*. The senior graduating class had occupied the administration building during campus revolts in protest of the Vietnam War three years prior. This resulted in a momentary capitulation of hierarchies: parking became first-come-first-parked for all, regardless of status, and anyone was deemed qualified to teach a four unit class, provided that the class always convened. The *Gītā* 'moment' did not last very many years. However, Oren Lyons, an elder of the Onondaga Community and standout lacrosse player at Syracuse University, helped establish one of the very first majors in American Indian Studies, which continues to the present day. He served on the University of Buffalo faculty for 35 years, achieving the highest rank and honours.

In the 8 a.m. philosophy class, Carole Zeiler shared frequently about her Yoga teacher on Long Island, Srimathi Añjali Inti. In the late afternoon *Gītā* class, we did call-and-response, verse by verse, of the Sanskrit text and ended the class with chanting the Hare Kṛṣṇa Mantra, dancing, and sharing food prepared at the local ISKCON farm in Clarence. Though the mood generated was sweet, the exclusivist Gauḍīya Vaiṣṇavite theology taught in Buffalo clashed with the 'impersonalist' epiphanies experienced in the silence of Rochester *zazen* and Quaker meeting. During a Thanksgiving visit to my sister, a social worker in Brooklyn and now a professor of anthropology at Stony Brook, Carole welcomed me to meet her teacher, Añjali, at Yoga Anand Ashram, which had just been dedicated in a former hayloft and artist studio on Merrick Road in Amityville. Añjali also invited me to her home on Eden Avenue in Massapequa Park. I attended a Yoga class and a Sunday Service. On the way back to Buffalo, I resolved to transfer universities and start a new life on Long Island. Maureen joined me for a visit to Amityville over the Christmas break and we both filed paperwork to study at SUNY Stony Brook. For twelve years we trained at the Ashram, performing daily Yoga *sādhana*, including weekly fasting and silence. We helped build multiple businesses including a bookstore and a restaurant as we completed our degrees and we eventually started a family.

Gurāṇi Añjali (1935–2001) taught what, in retrospect, might be called an earth-friendly form of Yoga. She trained us to meditate on the elements, two times each day for a month, dedicated in turn to earth, water, fire, air, and space. Decades later I discovered that this practice is central to the Yoga taught in the *Gheraṇḍa Saṃhitā*. Raised in India during the halcyon years of Mahatma Gandhi, Añjali frequently lamented about the waste inherent in the American lifestyle. She lived frugally, setting an example for others. She often reflected on the sad state of the environment, always in the news in the 1970s. During her three decades of teaching, she wrote more than seven dozen songs, including this anthem to the Earth, sung in call and response, alternating between men and women:

> The earth is burning, the sky is ablaze.
> The earth is burning, the sky is ablaze....
> Pollution on the land, in the waters, in the air
> Where are the fathers, where are the mothers?
> Like little children we scream now and then.
> To be heard once again, we scream now and then.
> Hypocrites abound, all around and around.
> Taking issue everywhere, no one cares, who will care?
> Where is the embrace and the loving care?
> We keep looking for that place with that embrace.
> Stranded in this world, you and me, all alone.
> You are my hope. I am your hope.
> The earth is burning, the sky is ablaze.
> The earth is burning, the sky is ablaze.

This song speaks to a place of urgency and a need for personal and community responsibility.

During our time on Long Island, we grew to love both the south shore and north shore beaches, the Nissequogue and Amityville Rivers, the fertile farmland on the eastern end of the Island, and so much more. However, the ground water of Long Island, the only source for drinking water, was laced with industrial effluent. In the 1970s and 1980s Long Island experienced elevated rates of breast cancer and miscarriage, causing many to invest in reverse osmosis carbon filters.

India 1981 and 1989: Non-violence to Animals, Earth, and Self in Asian Traditions

Many if not most scholars doing India-related research spend a year or two doing field research or working with pandits. Being part of an Ashram was a bit like living in India. Two of my major professors at Fordham University, Jose Pereira (Sanskrit) and John Chethimattam (Philosophy), were of Indian origin. Hence, I finished graduate school without traveling to India, benefitting from mentorship from people of Indian origin while living in New York. In the following year, 1981, my doctoral advisor at Fordham University, John Chethimattam, arranged for me to present a paper at an international conference in Cochin, Kerala, South India. It was during this trip that I became sensitised to the dire environmental destruction taking place. A dystopic visit to a fertiliser factory surrounded with a quarter mile of dead forest destroyed any romance about India's love of nature. A travel essay first published in the *Ashram Journal* eventually prompted a long-term inquiry into environmental issues in India. Interrogating the praise of nature in the *Ṛg Veda* and the *Atharva Veda* and reflecting on our own earth-friendly Yoga training at the Ashram resulted in the first of many conference presentations on Hinduism and Ecology.

A return visit to India in 1989 included conversations with the Gandhi Foundation and the Centre for Science and Environment (CSE) in New Delhi. The CSE, which remains active, serves as an information clearing house for the multiple non-governmental agencies that arose after the tragic Bhopal Union Carbide explosion in 1984. The CSE brings public awareness to the many threats to human flourishing within the subcontinent through its multi-platform site, Down to Earth. I also visited the Nehru Centre for Environment Education in Ahmedabad, which had recently experienced success in implementing a nation-wide curriculum to educate children about the perils of pollution.

From the capital city, I traveled to the Pink City of Jaipur, home of Dr. S.L. Gandhi, founder of Anuvibha, a nonprofit dedicated to the popularisation of adherence to Jain values, particularly non-violence (*ahiṃsā*). We ventured to the western Rajasthan town of Ladnun, passing through Bishnoi villages renowned for their defense of trees and the black buck deer. We stayed a few days at Jain Vishva Bharati, a 100-acre seminary college dedicated to the study and practice of the Jain faith. Over the course of several conversations with Acarya Tulsi (1914–1997), I heard first-person descriptions of how one might cultivate an environmentally friendly lifestyle through Jain principles and practices. Jain ethics, also at the core of Patañjali's Yoga, begins with the vow of *ahiṃsā*, to do no harm. In Jain practice this generally means vegetarianism and avoidance of any involvement with animal byproducts such as leather. Acarya Tulsi extended this into an overall concern for the well-being of the planet. In response to the direct question: 'how might Jain practice inform environmental action?' he pointed to his only worldly possessions: simple clothing, his bundle of books, and his water pot. He commented that the way to prevent harm to the planet is to simplify one's lifestyle through the minimisation of possessions, the Jain art and science of *aparigraha*.

Non-human animals were central to the unfolding of this research project on religion and ecology. Vegetarianism and animal shelters are found throughout India adhered to and maintained by both Hindus and Jains. One cannot visit India without a sense of continuity between animal life and human life, if only due to the sheer presence of animals in the public sphere, whether cows, goats, camels, or the abundant wandering dogs and ever-present species of so many different birds. One wonders about the psychic effects of the sixth great extinction, caused by human callousness toward non-human species. What if our places become bereft of birdsong? Even in India, some urban neighborhoods proudly proclaim themselves to be modern and 'cow free'. A world sanitised of animals becomes an impoverished world. Thinking and writing about intimacy with place as well as depth encounters with the 'animal other' has informed much of this work.

Ecological Prospects: Scientific, Religious, and Aesthetic Perspectives, 1991

Emplacement within a supportive university community brings many blessings. Landing at Loyola Marymount University in 1985 was fortuitous. A fund had been established in honour of Charles Casassa, S.J., who served as President of LMU from 1949 to 1969. Casassa insisted upon highlighting social justice issues throughout all aspects of the university and provided regional leadership for interfaith dialogue and the advancement of women. Serving as Casassa Chair, a title that I held for two years, brought abundant resources and support for convening a major conference. Gathering university faculty leadership from the humanities, sciences, and arts, we issued a call for papers. From dozens of proposals we assembled a magnificent group of scholars, including Lynn Margulis who spoke on Gaia theory, Patricia Chapple Wright who shared her work to save the Golden Bamboo Lemur in Madagascar, J. Baird Callicott on wilderness, Mary Evelyn Tucker on cosmology, Rosemary Radford Ruether on Ecofeminism, and Bron Taylor on the religious radicalism of Earth First! From this seminal event, a methodology emerged that helped shape the emerging field of religion and ecology: learn how things work in the landscape, large and small (science), explore human affect in regard to the natural world (spirituality), and examine the call to action inherent in the process of discovery (ethics). From there, one can hope to influence policy at the local, state, federal, and global level. Our dinner speaker, Tom Hayden, (1939–2016) a member of the California Assembly, shared his success in implementing Proposition 65, a ubiquitous public reminder of the toxic chemicals that lurk in and suffuse our surroundings.

Purifying the Earthly Body of God

Through the American Academy of Religion and the Southern California Seminar on South Asia, Professor Lance Nelson of the University of San Diego convened a series of meetings (1994 and 1996) that resulted in the publication of *Purifying the Earthly Body of God.*[3] Ann Gold, Rita Sherma, Kelly Alley, and Vijaya Nagarajan, shared their research into the local wisdom of village-based moral ecology, Hindu ecofeminism, the Ganges River, and the earth-grounded daily ritual of Kolam in Tamil Nadu, respectively. I shared an analysis of how the traditional ethics of Yoga and Jainism can be applied to issues of environmental concern, particularly non-violence (*ahiṃsā*) and non-possession (*aparigraha*). Collaborations emerged that carry into the present day, continuing and expanding the process of observation (every village and municipality seeks to ensure a clean environment), sources of guidance (whether local folk wisdom or formal textual prescriptions), and implementation (action plans). Knowing the sorry state of the water and air in India, we shared insights, explored causes, and celebrated the good work being implemented, some of which will be described below.

3 Lance E. Nelson, ed., *Purifying the Earthly Body of God: Religion and Ecology in Hindu India* (Albany: State University of New York Press, 1998).

Harvard University Conferences and Book Series

Mary Evelyn Tucker, John Grim, and I studied together with Thomas Berry at Fordham University in the 1970s. John did his Ph.D. on shamanism informed by fieldwork with the Ojibway peoples. After earning the M.A. in the History of Religions, Mary Evelyn moved over to Columbia and did her Ph.D. on the Japanese neo-Confucianism of Kaibara Ekken, a nature philosopher. They took leave from their positions at Bucknell University from 1996 to 1998 for an extended fellowship at Harvard's Center for the Study of World Religions. With support of the Rasmussen and other foundations, they launched a series of conferences on religion and ecology, starting with Buddhism, and eventually including Christianity, Islam, Judaism, Hinduism, Jainism, Confucianism, Taoism, Shinto, and indigenous traditions. In collaboration with Arvind Sharma, I convened the Hinduism event and with support from the Jaina Academic Foundation of North America, the Jaina event.

Each of the conferences sought to include voices from the realm of religious practice and leadership as well as from academia. Srivatsa Goswami, head of Vrindavan's Gambhira Ashram presented at the Hinduism and Ecology Conference and Sadhvi Shilapi of the Veerayatan Institute at the Jainism and Ecology conference, among others. The resulting two volumes have been published both in the United States and India and have been widely acknowledged as important resources.[4] Furthermore, the website of the Forum on Religion and Ecology, now based at Yale University, contains updated information and serves as a resource for religious leaders, scholars, students, and activists worldwide.

Green Yoga Association

Laura Cornell, while completing her doctoral dissertation at the California Institute for Integral Studies in San Francisco, came across a stunning fact: the sticky Yoga mats that had gained popularity in the 1990s with the advent of Yoga studio businesses, are suffused with phthalates, a highly harmful and carcinogenic plastic. She began a small business importing and distributing organic mats made of rubber and jute and launched a global information campaign. Having trained in Yoga at Kripalu Center for Yoga and Health in Massachusetts, she arranged to interview several Yoga teachers about environmental issues, discovering a deep well of creativity and concern. She decided to start a non-profit organisation, the Green Yoga Association, for which I served as a founding board member. The activities included board retreats, large residential retreats, newsletters, and the implementation of a university continuing education certificate programme in Yoga and Ecology, renamed Yoga, Mindfulness, and Social Change, conducted annually at Loyola Marymount University since 2003. Before the formal non-profit dissolved, hundreds of studios participated in the Green Yoga Certification process and hundreds of Yoga teachers from

4 Christopher Key Chapple and Mary Evelyn Tucker, eds., *Hinduism and Ecology: The Intersection of Earth, Sky, and Water* (Cambridge, Massachusetts: Center for the Study of World Religions, Harvard University Press, 2000); Christopher Key Chapple, ed., *Jainism and Ecology: Non-violence in the Web of Life* (Cambridge, MA: Harvard University Press, 2002).

around the world participated in the trainings at Pema Osel Ling, the Mount Madonna Center in the Santa Cruz Mountains, and at Loyola Marymount University.

The Dharma Academy of North America convened two sessions at their 2006 annual meeting in Washington, D.C. that were edited into a book called *Yoga and Ecology: Dharma for the Earth*.[5] The final chapter, 'Green Yoga: Contemporary Activism and Ancient Practices: A Model for Eight Paths of Green Yoga' encapsulates Laura Cornell's dissertation. She articulates the need for the following Yogas to enhance human-earth relations: Jnana/Knowledge, Bhakti/Reverence, Aranyaka/Nature Immersion, Hatha/Sacred Embodiment, Raja/Conscious Evolution, Karma/Action, Sangha/Community, and Tantra/Embracing Opposites.

Centres for Environmental Learning and Immersion in India

Countless environmental advocacy organisations have emerged in India, from the science-based TERI School of Advanced Studies in New Delhi which offers doctoral degrees in the area of sustainable development to Fireflies Ashram on Kanakapura Road near Bengaluru which emphasises community development and artistic expression. Mention has been made early in this chapter of the Centre for Science and Environment in New Delhi, established by Anil Agarwal (1947–2002) and the Centre for Environment Education in Ahmedabad, established by Kartikeya Sarabhai (b. 1947).

Three organisations modeled on the traditional Ashram must also be noted: Eco Ashram, also known as Swastigram,

5 Christopher Key Chapple, ed., *Yoga and Ecology: Dharma for the Earth* (Hampton, VA: Deepak Heritage Books, 2009).

operated by the M.C. Mehta Environment Foundation near Rishikesh; Navdanya, also known as Bija Vidyapeeth, founded and directed by Vandana Shiva, located near Dehradun; and Govardhan Ecovillage, founded by Radhnath Swami and located northeast of Mumbai. Brief descriptions follow of each.

The stated mission of Swastigram 'is to create harmony between human beings and Nature through an eco-friendly and ethical way of life'. M.C. Mehta (b. 1946) assembles people from a wide range of professions including lawyers, politicians, real estate developers, as well as representatives from the NGO community to learn about the threats posed by pollution and global warming. Through the case study method, they learn of the suffering caused by industrial tragedies and explore remediation, including legal recourse. Mehta has been awarded the Goldman Environmental Prize (1996), the Ramon Magsaysay Award for Public Service (1997), and the Padma Shri, Government of India (2016). His major accomplishments have included protections for the Taj Mahal (1984), wastewater treatment for the Ganges River (1985), and the implementation of compressed natural gas (CNG) throughout all modes of Delhi public transit (court case, 1992; full implementation, 2001).

During a visit to Eco Ashram in 2006, Mehta, who had just helped with the birth of a calf at the Ashram, brought us to a nearby *Śaivite* temple in honour of the Goddess, revealing the religious roots of his life's work. Originally from the region of Jammu, Mehta is gravely concerned about climate change. He had just recently witnessed the collapse of a massive glacier in the Himalayas near Gangotri. Himalayan glaciers provide waters that sustain more than a billion people, feeding the Indus, Yamuna, Ganges, Brahmaputra, Irrawaddy, Yellow, and Mekong Rivers. Global agricultural cycles are in peril. The Foundation seeks to establish common ground and collaboration though educating people on environmental issues throughout the South Asian region.

Navdanya, founded by Vandana Shiva (b. 1952) in 1987, provides residential training in organic farming. She received LMU's Doshi Bridgebuilder Award in 2011 and returned to LMU the next year to share her insights and analyses, both times to a packed audience. A group of LMU students organised an Alternative Break to Navdanya supported by Loyola Marymount University's Center for Service and Action in 2014. The diverse group of students, with a profound interest in agricultural justice, included the founders of the LMU organic garden. While in residence for more than a week, we learned, under the able guidance of Navdanya staff, seven forms of composting, including vermiculture and pit burial; cleaned turmeric root for several hours; and worked in the kitchen. Workshops about food sustainability through organic methods, and treks into the forest and to the local potter enriched this immersion experience. We also met with Dr. Shiva at the Navdanya restaurant in south Delhi where food produced at Navdanya can be purchased.

Vandana Shiva earned her Ph.D. in the history and philosophy of science at the University of Western Ontario in Canada. She has eschewed a traditional academic career in favor of direct activism. Her searing analyses of agro-industrial crops have shaken the global establishment. *The New Yorker* employed the services of a GMO industry advocate to 'debunk' her studies in 2014, but the most Michael Specter (who acknowledges that he has 'often written favorably about agricultural biotechnology') could muster was a critique of her educational background, noting that her degree was in the history of science, not hard research into quantum physics. The article claims that glyphosate is 'not so toxic'. However, since the publication of the article in 2014, Monsanto, its manufacturer has lost multiple lawsuits that proved otherwise. Monsanto no longer exists, having been absorbed into the larger German conglomerate, Bayer. Shiva's organisation has provided direct instruction to more than a million farmers in India. She is a staunch advocate for the cultivation of barley and millet. These overlooked grains hold great potential for withstanding the stresses of climate change due to their hardiness.

In the tradition of the Bishnoi (sixteenth century) and Chipko (twentieth century) movements, Vandana Shiva advocates direct action against exploitation of resources. In her most recent book[6] she asserts that vested industrial interests, the 'empire of the 1%' breed 'separation, violence, colonisation, extractivism, extinction'. Committed to the Gandhian principles of simplicity, self-reliance, and holding to truth (*satyagraha*), she writes that 'Our only option is to heal the earth, and in so doing, heal and reclaim our humanity, creating hope for our only future – as one humanity on one planet.'[7] Written months before the Covid-19 pandemic, her words have proven prophetic. Global cooperation has become essential in this time of great loss.

The Govardhan Ecovillage seeks to replicate village life on the far reaches of the metro Mumbai region. Using an innovative no-bake pressed brick technology, the structures are made onsite from adobe with walls thick enough to insulate from heat and cold. Farming techniques have been learned from tribal locals. All waste water is treated and all waste is recycled or incinerated. Govardhan serves as a health retreat and educational centre. Its website[8] describes various undertakings:

---

6 Vandana Shiva, *Oneness vs. the One Percent: Shattering Illusions, Seeding Freedom* (London: Chelsea Green, 2019).

7 Ibid.

8 www.ecovillage.org.in.

> Govardhan School of Sustainability (GSOS) is an education initiative based in Govardhan Ecovillage, an eco-community located around 90 kms from Mumbai. With its 250 residents, Govardhan Ecovillage is striving to set up a role model village, nested in an ecological infrastructure amidst a picturesque landscape of the Sahyadri mountains.
>
> The ecovillage is composed of farms, animal shelter, yoga school, ayurveda center, community area and geo-tourism site, all nested in the setting of an ashram. Now GEV has broadened its outreach by being a learning center oriented towards studies of ecology and transformation of self and society.

Visitors arrive from all over the world for Ayurvedic treatment, Yoga, and meditation.

Living in India, 2019

A first-time visitor to India quite often is taken aback by the sensory overload of animals wandering the streets, itinerant workers from the village living in tents along the highway, open fires, open sewers, seemingly endless piles of trash, and a cacophony of automotive, animal, and human sounds and smells. Depending upon the time of year and the place, one might find oneself in the most polluted air quality on the planet, particularly if one is in Delhi in the winter.

Living in Delhi each summer for nearly a decade and for the entire latter of half of 2019, I could not ignore palpable improvements since my first visit in 1981. The air quality, which seemingly hit an all-time low in 1997, has improved immensely since the CNG requirements were implemented. The municipal water supply now brings greater pressure to the tap and the availability of reverse osmosis activated granulated carbon filtered water has become pervasive. A nationwide government campaign called Swachh Bharat, roughly translated as Clean India, has dignified the work of street sweepers due to the positive nationwide press campaign that lauds tidiness as a patriotic duty. Recycling collection stations now appear throughout the city. Journalists have itemised the size and number of landfills within the capitol district: very small and very few. Slowly the pieces of the puzzle have begun to make sense for visitors and residents alike: Delhi, one of the oldest cities on the planet, was not built for the onslaught of modern consumer culture. Dealing with the detritus of plastic is quite different than disposing of banana leaves.

All through the early fall of 2019, four topics filled the news and newspapers: the 150th birth anniversary of Mahatma Gandhi, the implementation of a ban on single-use plastics, the reorganisation of Kashmir and Jammu, and the ban on refugees from Muslim nations. Clearly, for a Western liberal, the latter two pronouncements and the resulting social upheaval were disturbing. The cognitive dissonance of being culturally 'other' while living in India felt familiar; my progressive political views have generally been in the minority throughout my life. However, hearing and reading praise of Gandhi, and seeing the public resolve to back away from reliance on plastics was actually quite heartening. A stunningly direct article in the *Hindustan Times* (the newspaper co-founded by Gandhi that his son Devadas (1900–1957) edited from 1937 until his death) describes the perils of plastic, quoting studies that have received little mention in the Western media. Specifically, journalist Rhythma Kaul quotes Dr. N. Chandrasekaran, director of the Centre for Nanobiotechnology at the Vellore Institute of Technology in Tamil Nadu:

> Single-use plastics are largely the low-density variety, which can be quite harmful for human health.... [they are] light weight and get converted to micro- or nano-plastics which

> easily enter the body. Microplastics are between 0.05 nanometers (nm) and 5 nm in length while nanoplastics are 1,000 times smaller. [Nanoplastics] smaller than 50 nm pass through the intestinal wall, enter tissues and organs, affecting circulatory, respiratory, digestive, nervous, and endocrine systems.... [they] gradually get degraded inside the cell and converted into styrene, a possible carcinogen.[9]

Kaul notes that problems arising from nanoplastic intake might include 'obesity, abnormality in sex organs, early puberty, infertility, metabolic disorders, learning disabilities, impaired immune function, altered nervous system function, diabetes, even certain types of cancer'. Candrasekaran suggests that the 'solution lies in generating awareness about the harms of single-use plastic... at the grassroots level.' All over India, shopping bags generally are made of cloth and, despite inevitable protestations from the plastics lobby, the public seems squarely behind minimising the use of plastic.

After braving days in Delhi in the fall of 2019 when the particulate matter parts per million exceeded 700 (in Los Angeles persons are advised not go outdoors when levels hit 200, a once-in-a-decade occurrence), returning to the United States in 2020 brought many unanticipated events and challenges. The pandemic kept virtually everyone indoors, away from school, away from work, away from the highways. The Black Lives Matter movement accelerated due to the deaths of George Floyd, Breonna Taylor, and others. Fires raged from San Diego to Seattle, rendering dystopic skies, heavily polluted air, and the burning of millions of acres. The question of sustainability seems quaint and privileged in face of the loss

9 Rhythma Kaul, 'Growing Plastic Use Taking a Toll on Public Health: Experts', *Hindustan Times*, 7 October 2019.

of so many lives. The stark question of survival lingers: who is safe from disease? From environmental degradation? From social othering and denigration?

As we look toward the future of the planet, one possible beacon of light, at least in the perspective of a modern fiction writer, could possibly be India. Kim Stanley Robinson's 2021 novel *The Ministry for the Future* opens with a horrific description of a high temperature event in a town near Lucknow that kills as many as 20 million people in 2025. In response, India changed:

> A new party was voted in, a composite party composed of all kinds of Indians, every religion and caste, urban poor, rural poor, the educated, all banded together by the disaster and determined to make something change.... India's electrical power companies were nationalized where they weren't already, and a vast force was put to work shutting down coal-fired plants and building wind and solar plants, and free-river hydro, and non-battery electric storage. All kinds of things began to change.[10]

Immediately after the disaster, the Indian government, at the urging of the prime minister, seeded the atmosphere with sulfur dioxide, replicating and perhaps doubling the number of particles released during the Pinatuba volcanic explosion of 1991. For seven months Indian military aircraft released tons and tons of the stuff. This resulted in a temporary reduction in the earth's temperature.

Meanwhile an underground group known as Kali's Children initiated several radical actions to counter global warming.

---

10 Kim Stanley Robinson, *The Ministry for the Future* (New York: Orbit, 2020), 25.

These included poisoning of cows to stop beef production and shooting planes out of the sky to halt highly polluting air travel and the sinking of ships to end trans-oceanic trade. So much changed. So many aspects of modern life shifted to new technologies worldwide, including the development of vegan food sources, the use of dirigibles, and the flourishing of local manufacturing.

This book highlights key principles that distinguish the Indian worldview from its Western counterparts. The entire world is suffused with divinity. Breath energises all forms of life. All forms of life are interconnected. Each human carries depth memories of prior animal births, as taught by Puṇya to his distraught brother Pāvana. Animals demonstrate ethical agency. Humans have the capacity to attain heavenly states and even omniscience. All things are possible.

Furthermore, divergent things are possible simultaneously. Rather than cleaving to a binary approach to truth, Indian philosophy asserts that many things can be true at the same time. The inbreath can be linked to the sun. The outbreath can be linked to the moon and it can be linked to fire. The human being operates through four levels of awareness: waking, dreaming, meditative, and ineffable. One truth cannot suffice for all people. Writ large, Indian thought emphasises an unrelenting assent to multiple realities. This Jaina philosophy of multi-sidedness (*anekānta-vāda*) and its fourfold assessment of human awareness broadens the horizons of human possibility.

Anticipating Heisenberg's uncertainty principle, Husserl's articulation of noema, noetic, and noematic, and Heidegger's phenomenological perspectivalism, the world of the apparent has been an insufficient gateway to knowledge within India since the time of the Vedas. The origins of the world remain unknown; gods and goddesses were named after the emergence of the order of things. The waking state, the first level of human awareness, is only provisional, giving way each night to sleep and dream, the second state. As taught in the *Yoga-vāsiṣṭha,* dream realities anticipate waking realities and can actually alter the waking state. The third state of human awareness can be found in meditative repose. One takes refuge in a state of quiet, documented by modern science as the generation of alpha waves, proven to be restorative and salutogenetic, that is, health-generating. India developed an array of techniques to make this possible, include the practices of ritual (*pūjā*), recitation of *mantra,* and various forms of concentration (*dhāraṇā*) and meditation (*dhyāna*).

The Ministry for the Future celebrates the strengths of decentralisation that have defined the subcontinent of India for millennia. Though textbooks tend to speak in broad strokes about the imperial histories of India, in reality, no one central authority has ever truly ruled the land mass that extends more than 1000 miles east from the Khyber Pass to the mountains of Meghalaya, and 1000 miles south from the Himalayas to Kanya Kumari. The Buddhist emperor Aśoka never conquered the deep south. The Hindu Guptas and the Islamic Mughals formed alliances but never even aspired to hegemonic dominance with one-state rule. During the British East India Company's ascendence, it extracted taxes from only two-thirds of India's estimated 600 contiguous kingdoms. With the formation of the modern Indian state in 1947, five nations eventually arose on the subcontinent: Nepal and Bhutan (which had never been colonised), Pakistan, Bangladesh, and India. Within India more than 200 languages thrive, as well as countless political parties.

The novel describes the often-reviled chaos on the subcontinent as a strength:

> India is now leading the way on so many issues!...The true Indian way has always been syncretic, right from the begin-

> ning of our civilization.... [T]he upshot post-heatwave was a complete loss of faith in both Congress and BJP, such that the world's greatest democracy was left with no nationally dominant party.... [only] a broad coalition of forces... Much has been taken from Kerala.... Sikkim and Bengal have been developing an organic regenerative agriculture that, at the same time it provides more food than before, also sequesters more carbon in the soil, and this too is being taken up across the country.[11]

The words of Badim Bahadur, the deputy general of the Ministry for the Future, continue to revel in the emergence of the new alternatives posed by India:

> No one elsewhere has been used to thinking of India as anything other than a place of poverty, a victim of history and geography. But now they are looking at us with a little bit of confusion and wonder. What is this? A sixth of humanity on one big triangular patch of land, caught under the blazing sun, cut off by a mighty range of mountains: who are these people? A democracy, a polyglot coalition – wait, can it be? And what can it be? Do we make the Chinese, who so decisively stepped onto the world stage at the start of this century, look dictatorial, monolithic, brittle, afraid? Is India now the bold leader of the world? We think maybe so.[12]

This bold statement, though embedded in a futuristic novel, perhaps holds some hope that alternative realities will provide new restorative pathways.

In some ways, the positivity in regard to India's prospects are being borne out in reality. The book *This Changes*

11 Ibid., 124–125.

12 Ibid., 127.

Everything by Naomi Klein documents grass roots movements worldwide against coal-burning power plants. She dubs these forms of direct action as 'Blockadia' and presents this example from India:

> In India, Blockadia-style uprisings have been on full display in recent years, with people's movements against coal-fired power plants significantly slowing the rush to dirty energy in some regions. The southeastern state of Andra Pradesh has been the site of several iconic struggles, like the one in the village of Kakarapalli, surrounded by rice paddies and coconut groves, where local residents can be seen staging a semipermanent checkpoint under a banyan tree at the entrance to town. The encampment chokes off the only road leading to a half-built power plant where construction was halted amidst protests in 2011. In nearby Sompeta, another power plant proposal was stopped by a breakthrough alliance of urban middle-class professionals and subsistence farmers and fishers who united to protect the nearby wetlands.[13]

The Economist reports in its 2 October 2022 issue that India had already met its goal of 40 per cent renewable power generation slated for 2030 nearly a decade early. Change is possible.

Challenges into the Future: Will We All Become Ecosystem People?

Octavia Butler's *Parable of the Sower* describes a future wherein Lauren Olamina wanders from Pasadena to the Beach Cities of California's South Bay, dodging bullets and hunkering down in garages, without electricity, without a reliable food

---

13 Naomi Klein, *This Changes Everything: Capitalism vs. The Climate* (New York: Simon & Schuster, 2014), 350.

source before trudging north as if pursuing the Underground Railroad, following the Big Dipper to create a self-sufficient survivalist community in the far northern reaches of California. More than 60,000 people each night live in Los Angeles County without housing, many with fewer resources than the displaced Olamina family of Butler's novel. As I write this essay, the sky is red with smoke generated by fires that have claimed millions of acres up and down the western coast of America. Coronavirus has affected the lives of billions worldwide, and millions in the Americas. In Zoom class this week one student shared that her family has lost significant income. Her mother cleans houses and has become unwelcome in the homes of others due to Corona virus. Another student's uncle refuses all medical treatment because of his status as an undocumented worker and his consequent fear of being deported.

When we lived at Navdanya near Dehradun, we slept without heat in the cold Uttar Khand winter, rejoicing when the final night arrived and our hosts lit a bonfire that brought warmth and delight. Just beyond the boundaries of the farm, the local forest people lived in lean-tos and similarly gathered around the fire for warmth. During the day they ventured illegally into protected lands, lopping branches to feed their goats, using the dried branches for firewood. We interfaced with these families daily on our walks as they worked gathering fodder and firewood around the outskirts of the property.

Madhav Gadgil and Ramachandra Guha have identified three modalities of environmental emplacement in India: the urban omnivores, urban, educated, and well-housed; the ecosystem people, rural, largely uneducated, living in symbiosis with available resources; and ecological refugees who have fled to the cities to enter the cash economy. Throughout the globe we live at a crossroads, recognising that the urban omnivore lifestyle must change. Its extractive requirements cannot be maintained. The realities of climate change demand a restructuring of the global economy beginning with moving away from reliance on carbon energy, away from ever-increasing meat consumption, and away from the use and abuse of plastics. The omnivore must heed the pleas of the ecological refugees and learn lessons from the ecosystem people.

In my own life as an educator and as a practitioner of Yoga and meditation, I have worked with countless university students and students of Yoga to bring awareness to the delicate and precarious position of the human being. We hold far greater powers than could have been imagined 200 years ago. We can heat the sky, uproot the forest, and travel to the Moon and someday even to Mars. This power must be constrained and redirected. Rather than assenting to and blindly following the consumerism that has caused so much destruction, we must focus on turning inward, recovering intimacy with the senses, with things sensible, and with the Earth herself. We have no other choice.

Discussion Topic: Yoga Ecology

- Three very different communities have been profiled in this chapter: Eco Ashram, Navdanya, and Govardhan EcoVillage. Discuss the mission of each and how it may intersect with your own interests.

- Tell your own journey in relationship to awareness of ecological issues. Where might you be able to make a difference? Personal habits and choices? Advocating for systemic change?

- Authors Naomi Klein and Kim Stanley Robinson turn to India in their nonfiction and fiction writing for inspiration and hope. Do you share their enthusiasm? Why?

Further Reading

Naomi Klein. *This Changes Everything: Capitalism vs. The Climate*. New York: Simon & Schuster, 2014.

Swami Radhanath. *The Journey Home: Autobiography of an American Swami*. San Rafael, CA: Mandala, 2010.

Vandana Shiva. *Oneness vs. the One Percent: Shattering Illusions, Seeding Freedom*. London: Chelsea Green, 2019.

Glossary of Key Sanskrit Terms

agni: fire

ahaṃkāra: sense of self or ego

ahiṃsā: nonviolence

ākāśa: space

Āraṇyakas: philosophical books similar to the Upaniṣads

Artha-śāstra: collections of text that explain governance

aśva-medha: horse sacrifice

ātman: soul

Bhagavad Gītā: Conversation wherein Krishna instructs Arjuna about three primary forms of Yoga (*Karma, Jñāna, Bhakti*) along with meditation

brahman: universal divine presence

buddhi: repository of past karmas; often translated as intellect

dhāraṇā: concentration

dharma: righteousness, law, propriety, teachings

Dharma-śāstra: law texts governing daily life

guṇa: quality, feeling tone

jala: water

karma: action

mantra: recitation of sound in a meditative manner

Mahābhārata: one of India's great epics, telling of the conflict and eventual war between two sets of cousins in northern India. The oral version may date from as early as 3000 years ago. Written versions began to appear around 2500 years ago.

oṃ: sacred utterance that serves as a gateway to the ultimate

prakṛti: realm of activity

prāṇa: life energy

pratyāhāra: inwardness

prāṇāyāma: control of breath

pṛthivī: earth

pūjā: ritual

puruṣa: witness, consciousness

rajas: passion

samādhi: the eighth stage of Yoga, a state of meditative absorption

saṃsāra: repeated bondage and rebirth due to *karma*

saṃyama: application of the final three stages of Yoga: concentration, meditation, and absorption (*dhāraṇā, dhyāna, samādhi*)

sattva: lightness

śramaṇa: one who takes personal vows of renunciation rather than ritual as path to freedom

svarāj/swaraj: self-rule

tamas: heaviness

tapas: austerities such as fasting and silence that purify *karma*

tattva: factor of existence

Upaniṣads: philosophical and speculative texts attached to each of the four Vedas

varṇa: social group often maintained through marriage

vāyu: air

Vedānta: philosophy arising from the Upaniṣads that teaches the union between Self (*ātman*) and the ultimate reality (*brahman*); takes many forms

Vedas: primary revelatory comprising the Ṛg Veda (philosophy and veneration of multiple deities), Sāma (a collection based on the Ṛg Veda used in rituals), Yājur (ritual instructions), Atharva (the basis for Āyurveda medical practice)

yajña: sacrifice

Yoga-vāsiṣṭha: eleventh-century text arising from Kashmir that teaches a form of Vedānta influenced by Mahāyāna Buddhist Yogācāra philosophy and practice. It tells of the sage Vasiṣṭha's advice to the young prince Rāma.

zazen: the Japanese rendering, via Chinese, of the Sanskrit term *dhyāna* (meditation)

Bibliography

Abram, David. *The Spell of the Sensuous: Perception and Language in a More-Than-Human World*. New York: Pantheon Books, 1996.

Abram, David. *Becoming Animal: An Earthly Cosmology*. New York: Vintage Books, 2011.

Ackerman, Peter, and Jack DuVall. *A Force More Powerful: A Century of Nonviolent Conflict*. New York: Palgrave, 2000.

Anil Agarwal and Sunita Narain, 'Dying Wisdom: The Decline and Revival of Traditional Water Harvesting Systems in India', *Ecologist* 27, no. 3 (1997): 112–116.

Apffel-Marglin, Frederique. 'Sacred Groves: Regenerating the Body, the Land, the Community'. In *Global Ecology: A New Arena of Political Conflict*, edited by Wolfgang Sachs, 197–207. London: Zed Books, 1993.

Arnold, David, and Ramachandra Guha, eds. *Nature, Culture, Imperialism: Essays on the Environmental History of South Asia*. Delhi: Oxford University Press, 1995.

Arnold, Sir Edwin *The Book of Good Counsels: From the Sanskrit of the Hitopadeśa*. London: Smith, Elder & Co., 1861.

Balkaran, Raj. *The Stories behind the Poses: The Indian Mythology that Inspired 50 Yoga Poses*. London: Leaping Hare Press, 2022.

Banwari. *Pañcavaṭī: Indian Approach to Environment*, translated by Asha Vohra. Delhi: Shri Vinayaka Publications, 1992.

Biernacki, Loriliai, and Philip Clayton, eds. *Panentheism across the World's Religions*. New York: Oxford University Press, 2014.

Bishnoi.www.worldatlas.com/articles/india-s-bishnoi-community-have-fearlessly-protected-nature-for-over-500-years.html.

Bose, Abinash Chandra. *Hymns from the Vedas: Original Text and English Translation*. Bombay: Asia Publishing House, 1966.

Bowles, Adam, tr. *Mahābhārata Book Eight: Karṇa Volume One*. New York: New York University Press and JJC Foundation, 2006.

Braidotti, Rosa, Ewa Charkiewicz, Sabine Hausler, and Sakia Wiernga. *Women, the Environment and Sustainable Development: Towards a Theoretical Synthesis*. London: Zed Books, 1994.

Bunyard, Peter, and Edward Goldsmith, eds. *Gaia: The Thesis, the Mechanisms, and the Implications*. Cornwall: Wadebridge Ecological Centre, 1988.

Callicott, J. Baird. *Earth's Insights: A Survey of Ecological Ethics from the Mediterranean Basin to the Australian Outback*. Berkeley: University of California Press, 1994.

Callicott, J. Baird, and Roger T. Ames. *Nature in Asian Traditions of Thought*. Albany, NY: State University of New York Press, 1989.

Carson, Rachel. *Silent Spring*. New York: Fawcett Publications, 1962.

Chapple, Christopher Key. *Nonviolence to Animals, Earth, and Self in Asian Traditions*. Albany, NY: State University of New York Press, 1993.

Chapple, Christopher Key, ed. *Ecological Prospects: Scientific, Religious, and Aesthetic Perspectives*. Albany, NY: State University of New York Press, 1994.

Chapple, Christopher Key. 'Ecology in a Time of COVID'. *Tarka: Contemplative Studies and Practice* 3 (2020), 'On Ecology: Embodied Philosophy': 64–76.

Chapple, Christopher Key. *Karma and Creativity*. Albany, NY: State University of New York Press, 1986.

Christopher Key Chapple, ed. *Jainism and Ecology: Nonviolence in the Web of Life*. Cambridge, MA: Center for the Study of World Religions, Harvard University Press, 2002.

Christopher Key Chapple. 'Ahiṃsā in the Mahābhārata: A Story, A Philosophical Perspective, and an Admonishment'. *Journal of Vaishnava Studies* 4, no. 3 (1996).

Chapple, Christopher Key. 'India's Earth Consciousness'. In *The Soul of Nature: Celebrating the Spirit of the Earth*, edited by Michael Tobias and Georgianne Cowan, 145–151. New York: Plume, 1996.

Chapple, Christopher Key. 'Toward an Indigenous Indian Environmentalism'. In *Purifying the Earthly Body of God: Religion and Ecology in Hindu India*, edited by Lance E. Nelson, 13–38. Albany: State University of New York Press, 1998.

Chapple, Christopher Key. *Living Landscapes: Meditation on the Five Elements in Hindu, Buddhist, and Jain Yogas*. Albany, NY: State University of New York Press, 2020.

Chapple, Christopher Key, ed. *Yoga and Ecology: Dharma for the Earth*. Hampton, VA: Deepak Heritage Books, 2009.

Chapple, Christopher Key. *Yoga and the Luminous: Patañjali's Spiritual Path to Freedom*. Albany, NY: State University of New York Press, 2008.

Chapple, Christopher Key. 'Asceticism and the Environment: Jainism, Buddhism, and Yoga'. *Crosscurrents* 57, no. 4 (2008): 514–526.

Chapple, Christopher Key. 'Indic Traditions and Animals: Imitation, Reincarnation, and Compassion'. In *Call to Compassion: Religious Perspectives on Animal Advocacy*, edited by Lisa Kemmerer and Anthony J. Nocella II, 15–26. New York: Lantern Books, 2011.

Chapple, Christopher Key and Mary Evelyn Tucker, eds. *Hinduism and Ecology: The Intersection of Earth, Sky, and Water*. Cambridge, MA: Center for the Study of World Religions, Harvard University Press, 2000.

Chapple, Christopher Key and Yogi Anand Viraj (Eugene P. Kelly Jr.). *The Yoga Sūtras of Patañjali: An Analysis of the Sanskrit with English Translation*. Delhi: Satguru Publications, 1990.

Chapple Wright, Patricia. *High Moon over the Amazon: My Quest to Understand the Monkeys of the Night*. New York: Lantern Books, 2013.

Chapple Wright, Patricia. *For the Love of Lemurs: My Life in the Wilds of Madagascar*. New York: Lantern Books, 2014.

Cobb, John B. Jr. *Sustainability: Economics, Ecology, and Justice*. Maryknoll, NY: Orbis Books, 1992.

Cort, John E., tr. *Paṇḍitarāja Jagannātha: The Saving Waves of the Milk-White Gaṅgā*. Calcutta: Writers Workshop, 2007.

Department of Economics and Statistics, Government of Kerala. *Kerala Review 2003*.

Annie Dillard. *Pilgrim at Tinker Creek*. In *Three by Annie Dillard*. New York: HarperPerennial, 1990.

Dwivedi, O.P. and Christopher Key Chapple, trs. *In Praise of Mother Earth: The Pṛthivī Sūkta of the Atharva Veda*. Foreword by Karan Singh. Photographs by Robert Radin, Todd Mansoor, and Shailendra Dwivedi. Los Angeles: Marymount Institute Press, 2011.

Dwivedi, O.P. and B.N. Tiwari. *Environmental Crisis and Hindu Religion*. New Delhi: Gitanjali Publishing House, 1987.

Edgerton, Franklin, tr. *The Panchatantra Reconstructed: Volume 2. Introduction and Translation*. New Haven, CT: American Oriental Society, 1924.

Eliade, Mircea. *Shamanism: Archaic Techniques of Ecstasy.* Princeton: Princeton University Press, 1963.

Emett, Carolyn. 'The Tree Man'. *Resurgence: An International Forum for Ecological and Spiritual Thinking* 183 (July/August 1997).

Feldhaus, Anne. *Water and Womanhood: Religious Meanings of Rivers in Maharashtra*. New York: Oxford University Press, 1995.

Feuerstein, Georg. *Green Yoga*. Eastend, Saskatchewan: Traditional Yoga Studies, 2007.

Fisher, William F., ed. *Toward Sustainable Development: Struggling over India's Narmada River*. Armonk, NY: M.E. Sharpe, 1995.

Flinders, Carol Lee. *At the Root of This Longing: Reconciling a Spiritual Hunger and a Feminist Thirst*. San Francisco: Harper SanFrancisco, 1998.

Fox, George. *The Journal of George Fox*. Edited by Rufus M. Jones. New York: Capricorn Books, 1963.

Fox, Stephen. *The American Conservation Movement: John Muir and His Legacy*. Madison: University of Wisconsin Press, 1985.

Framarin, Christopher G. *Hinduism and Environmental Ethics: Law, Literature and Philosophy.* London: Routledge, 2014.

Frawley, David. *Yoga and the Sacred Fire: Self-Realization and Planetary Transformation.* Twin Lakes, WI: Lotus Press, 2004.

Gadgil, Madhav, and Ramachandra Guha. *This Fissured Land: An Ecological History of India*. Delhi: Oxford University Press, 1992.

Gandhi, Mahatma. *The Bhagavad Gita according to Gandhi: Text and Commentary. Translated from Gujarati*. Edited by John Stohmeier. Berkeley: North Atlantic Books, 2009.

Gandhi, Mohandas. *Hind Swaraj and Other Writings*. Edited by Anthony J. Parel. Cambridge: Cambridge University Press, 1997.

Gandhi, Rajmohan. *Mohandas: A True Story of a Man, His People, and an Empire*. New Delhi: Penguin Viking, 2006.

Gatta, John. *Making Nature Sacred: Literature, Religion, and Environment in America from the Puritans to the Present*. New York: Oxford University Press, 2004.

Godrej, Farah. *Freedom Inside: Yoga and Meditation in the Carceral State*. Oxford: Oxford University Press, 2023.

Guha, Ramachandra. 'Radical American Environmentalism: A Third World Critique'. *Environmental Ethics* 11, no. 1 (1989): 71–83.

Guha, Ramachandra. *How Much Should a Person Consume? Environmentalism in India and the United States*. Berkeley: University of California Press, 2006.

Haberman, David L. *River of Love in an Age of Pollution: The Yamuna River of Northern India*. Berkeley: University of California Press, 2006.

Hume, Robert Ernest. *The Thirteen Principal Upanishads: Translated from the Sanskrit*. London: Oxford University Press, 1921. Revised edition 1971.

Jack, Homer A. *The Gandhi Reader: A Source Book of His Life and Writings*. Madras: Samata Books, 1956, 1984.

Jain, Pankaj. *Dharma and Ecology of Hindu Communities: Sustenance and Sustainability*. Surrey, UK/Burlington, VT: Ashgate, 2011.

Jaini, Padmanabh S. 'Indian Perspectives on the Spirituality of Animals'. In *Collected Papers on Jaina Studies*, 253–266. Delhi: Motilal Banarsidass, 2000.

James, George Alfred. *Ecology Is Permanent Economy: The Activism and Environmental Philosophy of Sunderlal Bahuguna*. Albany, NY:SUNY Press, 2013.

Kaul, Rhythma. 'Growing Plastic Use Taking a Toll on Public Health: Experts', *Hindustan Times*, 7 October 2019.

Khanna, Madhu. 'The Ritual Capsule of Durgā Pūjā: An Ecological Perspective'. In *Hinduism and Ecology: The Intersection of Earth, Sky, and Water*, edited by Christopher Key Chapple, 469–498. Cambridge, MA: Harvard University Center for the Study of World Religions, 2000.

Kingsford, Anna. *The Perfect Way in Diet: A Treatise Advocating a Return to the Natural and Ancient Food of Our Race*. London: Kegan Paul, Trench, Trübner, & Co., 1892. http://archive.org/stream/perfectwayindie02king-goog#page/n139/mode/2up.

Kipling, John Lockwood. *Beast and Man in India: A Popular Sketch of Indian Animals in their Relations with the People*. London: MacMillan, 1904.

Klein, Naomi. *This Changes Everything: Capitalism vs. The Climate*. New York: Simon & Schuster, 2014.

Korom, Frank. *'On the Ethics and Aesthetics of Recycling in India'. In Purifying the Earthly Body of God: Religion and Ecology in Hindu India*, edited by Lance Nelson Albany, 197–224. Albany, NY: State University of New York Press, 1998.

Krishen, Pradip. *Trees of Delhi: A Field Guide*. Delhi: Dorling Kindersley, 2006.

Krishna, Nanditha. *Sacred Animals of India*. New Delhi: Penguin Books, 2010.

Krishnan, M. *The Handbook of India's Wildlife*. Madras: Travelaid, 1982.

Lancaster, Lewis. 'Buddhism and Ecology: Collective Cultural Perceptions'. In *Buddhism and Ecology: The Interconnection of Dharma and Deeds*, edited by Mary Evelyn Tucker and Duncan Ryuken Williams, 3–8. Cambridge, MA: Harvard University Center for the Study of World Religions, 1997.

Lay, Benjamin. *All Slave-Keepers that Keep the Innocent in Bondage*. New York: Arno Press and New York Times, [1746] 1969.

Lee, David. 'The Natural History of the Ramayana'. In *Hinduism and Ecology: The Intersection of Earth, Sky, and Water*, edited by Christopher Key Chapple and Mary Evelyn Tucker, 245–268. Cambridge, MA: Center for the Study of World Religions, Harvard University press, 2000.

Leibowitz, Ed. 'The Accidental Eco-Terrorist: How after a Night of Vandalizing SUVs a Gifted Caltech Student Became a Threat to Homeland Security'. *Los Angeles Times Magazine*, 1 May 2005.

Leopold, Aldo. *A Sand County Almanac*. London: Oxford University Press, 1949.

Lodrick, Deryk O. *Sacred Cows, Sacred Places: The Origin and Survival of Animal Homes in India*. Berkeley: University of California Press, 1981.

Martin, Rafe. *Endless Path: Awakening with the Buddhist Imagination: Jataka Tales, Zen Practice, and Daily Life*. Berkeley, CA: North Atlantic Books, 2010.

Mazel, David, ed. *A Century of Early Ecocriticism*. Athens, GA: University of Georgia Press, 2001.

McKibben, Bill. *The Flag, the Cross, and the Station Wagon: A Graying American Looks Back at His Suburban Boyhood and Wonders What the Hell Happened.* New York: Henry Holt, 2022.

Menon, Vivek. *Mammals of India.* New Delhi: Penguin Books, 2003.

Merton, Thomas, ed. *Gandhi on Non-Violence: A Selection from the Writings of Mahatma Gandhi. Edited and with an Introduction*. New York: New Directions, 1964.

Mickey, Sam. 'Contributions to Anthropocosmic Environmental Ethics'. *Worldviews: Global Religions, Culture, and Ecology* 11, no. 2 (2007).

Muktibodhananda Saraswati, Swami, tr. *Haṭha Yoga Pradīpikā: Light on Haṭha Yoga.* Munger, India: Bihar School of Yoga, 1985.

Murthy, B. Srinivasa, tr. *The Bhagavad Gita.* Long Beach: Long Beach Publications, 1985.

Nagarajan, Vijaya Rettakudi. 'The Earth as Goddess Bhu Devi: Toward a Theory of "Embedded Ecologies" in Folk Hinduism'. In *Purifying the Earthly Body of God: Religion and Ecology in Hindu India,* edited by Lance Nelson, 269–296. Albany: State University of New York Press, 1998.

Narayanan, Vasudha. 'One Tree Is Equal to Ten Sons: Hindu Responses to the Problems of Ecology, Population, and Consumption'. *Journal of the American Academy of Religion* 65, no. 2 (January 1997).

Nash, Roderick Frazier. *The Rights of Nature: A History of Environmental Ethics.* Madison: University of Wisconsin Press, 1989.

Nelson, Lance, ed. *Purifying the Earthly Body of God: Religion and Ecology in Hindu India*. Albany, NY: State University of New York Press, 1998.

Olivelle, Patrick, tr. *Pañcatantra: The Book of India's Folk Wisdom*. New York: Oxford University Press, 1997.

Olivelle, Patrick. *The Early Upaniṣads. Annotated Text and Translation*. New York: Oxford University Press, 1998.

Oliver, Mary. *New and Selected Poems*. Boston: Beacon Press, 1992.

O'Neill, Patrick. 'Quaker Hostage Killed in Iraq'. *Indy Week*, 15 March 2006. https://indyweek.com/news/quaker-hostage-killed-iraq.

Parik, Suryashankar. *Jāmbhojī kī Vāṇī, Jīvanī, Darśana, aur Hindi Artha Sahita Mūlavāṇī-pātha*. Bikaner: Vikāsa Prakāśana, 2001.

Pillai, Moozhikkulam Chandrasekharam. *Mannarassala: The Serpent Temple,* translated by Ayyappa Panikker. Harippad: Manasa Publication, 1991.

Preston, James J. *Cult of the Goddess: Social and Religious Change in a Hindu Temple*. Prospect Heights, IL: Waveland Press, 1985.

Prime, Ranchor. *Hinduism and Ecology: Seeds of Truth*. London: Cassell, 1992.

Radhakrishnan, Sarvepalli. *The Principal Upanishads*. London: Allen & Unwin, 1953

Radhanath, Swami. *The Journey Home: Autobiography of an American Swami*. San Rafael, CA: Mandala, 2010.

Raj, A.R. Victor. *The Hindu Connection: Roots of the New Age*. Saint Louis: Concordia Publishing House, 1995.

Rangarajan, Mahesh. *Fencing the Forest: Conservation and Ecological Change in India's Central Provinces 18601914*. Delhi: Oxford University Press, 1961.

Rediker, Marcus. 'The Cave-Dwelling Vegan Who Took on Quaker Slavery and Won'. *Smithsonian* 48, no. 5 (2017): 34–41.

Robinson, Kim Stanley. *The Ministry for the Future*. New York: Orbit, 2020.

Rudolph, Lloyd I. and Susanne Hoeber Rudolph. *Postmodern Gandhi and Other Essays: Gandhi in the World and at Home*. Chicago: University of Chicago Press, 2006.

Salt, Henry. *A Plea for Vegetarianism*. Manchester: The Vegetarian Society, 1886. https://archive.org/details/pleaforvegetaria1886salt/mode/2up.

Sampat, Payal. 'What Does India Want?' *World Watch* 11 (July/August 1998).

Satyamurti, Carole, tr. *Mahabharata: A Modern Retelling*. New York: W.W. Norton, 2015.

Satyananda Saraswati, Swami. *Asana Pranayama Mudra Bandha*. Munger, India: Bihar Yoga Bharati, 1966.

Sawant, Shivaji. *Mrityunjaya the Death Conqueror: The Story of Karna*. Translated by P. Lal and Nandini Nopanyi. Calcutta: Writers Workshop, 1989, Fifth edition 2014.

Sen, Geeti, ed. *Indigenous Vision: Peoples of India, Attitudes to the Environment*. New Delhi: Sage Publication, 1992.

Seshadri, B. *India's Wildlife and Wildlife Reserves*. New Delhi: Sterling, 1986.

Sethia, Tara. *Gandhi: Pioneer of Nonviolent Social Change*. Boston: Pearson, 2012.

Sheth, D.L. 'Politics of Social Transformation: Grassroots Movements in India'. In *The Constitutional Foundations of World Peace*, edited by Richard A. Falk, Robert C. Johansen, and Samuel S. Kim, 275–287. Albany, NY: State University of New York Press, 1993.

Shiva, Vandana. *Staying Alive: Women, Ecology, and Development*. London: Zed Books, 1988.

Shiva, Vandana, ed. *Close to Home: Women Reconnect Ecology, Health and Development Worldwide*. Philadelphia: New Society Publishers, 1994.

Shiva, Vandana. 'Women in the Forest'. In *Ethical Perspectives on Environmental Issues in India*, edited by George James, 73–114. New Delhi: A.P.H, 1999.

Shiva, Vandana. *Earth Democracy: Justice, Sustainability, and Peace*. Cambridge, MA: South End Press, 2005.

Shiva, Vandana. *Oneness vs. the One Percent: Shattering Illusions, Seeding Freedom*. London: Chelsea Green, 2019.

Singer, Peter. *Animal Liberation: A New Ethics for Our Treatment of Animals*. New York: Avon Books, 1975.

Skolimowski, Henryk. *Eco-philosophy: Designing New Tactics for Living*. Boston, MA: M. Boyars, 1981.

Skolimowski, Henryk. *A Sacred Place to Dwell: Living with Reverence upon the Earth*. Rockport, ME: Element Books, 1993.

Skolimowski, Henryk. *EcoYoga: Practice and Meditations for Walking in Beauty on the Earth*. London: Gaia Books, 1994.

Skolimowski, Henryk. *Dharma, Ecology, and Wisdom in the Third Millenium*. New Delhi: Concept Publishing, 1999.

Spanel, Ann. 'Interview with Vandana Shiva'. *Woman of Power* 9 (1988): 27–31.

Snyder, Gary. *A Place in Space: Ethics, Aesthetics, and Watersheds*. Washington, DC: Counterpoint, 1996.

Snyder, Gary. *The Practice of the Wild*. San Francisco: North Point Press, 1990.

Spanel, Ann. 'Interview with Vandana Shiva'. *Woman of Power* 9 (1988): 27–31.

Specter, Michael. 'Seeds of Doubt: An Activist's Controversial Crusade against Genetically Modified Crops'. *The New Yorker*, 18 August 2014.

Sri Aurobindo. *The Secret of the Veda*. Pondicherry: Sri Aurobindo Ashram, 1971.

Svātmārāma. *The Haṭha Yoga Pradīpikā*. Translated by Pancham Sinh. New Delhi: Munshiram Manoharlal, 1997.

Swami Venkatesananda. *The Concise Yoga Vasiṣṭha*. Albany, NY: State University of New York Press, 1985.

Swami Venkatesananda. *Vasiṣṭha's Yoga*. Albany, NY: State University of New York Press, 1993.

Taylor, McComas. *The Fall of the Indigo Jackal: The Discourse of Division and Pūrṇabhadra's Pañcatantra*. Albany, NY: State University of New York Press, 2007.

Thomashow, Mitchell. *Ecological Identity: Becoming a Reflective Environmentalist*. Cambridge, MA: MIT Press, 1995.

Thoreau, Henry David. *Walden and Other Writings*. Edited by Brooks Atkinson. New York: The Modern Library, 1937.

Tobias, Michael, and Georgianne Cowan, eds. *The Soul of Nature: Visions of a Living Earth*. New York: Continuum, 1994.

Vanucci, Marta. *Ecological Readings in the Veda*. New Delhi: D.K. Print World, 1994.

Vatsyayan, Kapila, ed. *Prakrti: The Integral Vision*. 5 vols. New Delhi: Indira Gandhi National Centre for the Arts, 1995.

Vishnudevananda, Swami. *The Complete Illustrated Book of Yoga*. New York: Bell Publishing Company, 1960.

Whitney, William Dwight. *Sanskrit Grammar*. Second Edition. Cambridge: Harvard University Press, 1889.

Whitney, William Dwight. *Atharva-Veda Saṃhitā*. Cambridge, Massachusetts: Harvard University, 1905.

Williams, Howard. *The Ethics of Diet: A Catena of Authorities Deprecatory of the Practice of Flesh-eating*. London: Pitman, 1883. www.ivu.org/history/williams/index.html.

Index

M

N

O

P

Q

R

S

U

V

W

Y

Z

MANDALA

An Imprint of MandalaEarth
PO Box 3088
San Rafael, CA 94912
www.MandalaEarth.com

Find us on Facebook:
www.facebook.com/MandalaEarth

Publisher Raoul Goff
Associate Publisher Phillip Jones
Publishing Director Katie Killebrew
Editorial Assistant Amanda Nelson
Creative Director Ashley Quackenbush
VP Manufacturing Alix Nicholaeff
Sr Production Manager Joshua Smith
Sr Production Manager, Subsidiary Rights Lina s Palma-Temena

Text © 2025 Christopher Key Chapple
Images © 2025 Mandala Publishing
All rights reserved. No part of this book may be reproduced in any form without written permission from the publisher.

Mandala Publishing would also like to thank Steve Turrington for copyediting this series.

ISBN: 979-8-88762-115-9
ISBN: 979-8-88762-143-2 (Export Edition)

Manufactured in India by Insight Editions
10 9 8 7 6 5 4 3 2 1

Library of Congress Cataloging-in-Publication Data

Names: Chapple, Christopher Key, 1954– author.
Title: Embodied ecology : yoga and the environment / Christopher Key Chapple.
Description: San Rafael : Mandala Publishing, [2025] | Series: The Oxford Centre for Hindu Studies Mandala Publishing series | Includes bibliographical references and index. | Summary: "This book explores how primary sources from the Hindu and Yoga traditions can inform contemporary conversations about the problems of environmental degradation both in India and from a global perspective. This author seeks to discern how Hindu and Yoga ideals can address the pressing problems of global consumerism, the proliferation of plastic waste, species extinctions, and global climate change"-- Provided by publisher.

Identifiers: LCCN 2024022187 | ISBN 9798887621159 (hardcover) | ISBN 9798887621166 (ebook)
Subjects: LCSH: Human ecology--Religious aspects--Hinduism. | Human ecology--India. | Environmental protection--Religious aspects--Hinduism. | Consumption (Economics)--Religious aspects--Hinduism. | Yoga.
Classification: LCC BL1215.N34 C35 2024 | DDC 294.5/177--dc23/eng/20240627
LC record available at https://lccn.loc.gov/2024022187

ROOTS of PEACE   REPLANTED PAPER

Mandala Publishing, in association with Roots of Peace, will plant two trees for each tree used in the manufacturing of this book. Roots of Peace is an internationally renowned humanitarian organization dedicated to eradicating land mines worldwide and converting war-torn lands into productive farms and wildlife habitats. Roots of Peace will plant two million fruit and nut trees in Afghanistan and provide farmers there with the skills and support necessary for sustainable land use.

FSC www.fsc.org MIX Paper | Supporting responsible forestry FSC® C016779